WOMEN IN JAZZ

CW01506930

Sammy Stein

8TH HOUSE PUBLISHING

8th House Publishing
Montreal, Canada

Copyright © 8th House Publishing 2018
First Edition

ISBN 978-1-926716-55-8

All rights reserved under International and Pan-American Copyright Conventions. No part of this book may be reproduced in any form or by any electronic or mechanical means, including information storage and retrieval systems, without permission in writing from the publisher, except by a reviewer, who may quote brief passages in a review.

Published worldwide by 8th House Publishing.
Front Cover Design by 8th House Publishing

Designed by 8th House Publishing.
www.8thHousePublishing.com

Set in Garamond, Delicious Heavy, Raleway and Caslon.

LIBRARY AND ARCHIVES CANADA CATALOGUING IN PUBLICATION

Title: Women in jazz : the women, the legends & their fight / Sammy Stein
Names: Stein, Sammy, 1962- author
Identifiers: Canadiana 20190147644 | ISBN 9781926716558 (softcover)
Subjects: LCSH: Women jazz musicians. | LCSH: Women jazz musicians—Interviews.
Classification: LCC ML3506 S82 2019 | DDC 781.65082—dc23

WOMEN in JAZZ

by

Sammy Stein

Author's Introduction

Women are hot right now. People are writing about them; they are the topic of radio shows, TV documentaries; and their presence in music is being taken seriously. In many areas (engineering, space exploration, politics, financial services, catering, teaching, science, fire fighting, the armed forces) the day has long come and gone where women's rights stopped being the biggest issue people had to deal with. The world moves on, society changes and we are developing inclusive ideas. Equality issues are turning into quality issues and slowly, things are changing. Gender is no longer binary in any case; what matters is what you bring to the business.

Then, there is jazz. Good old jazz with its wonderful music, its warmth, its community feeling, the generosity of the performers. Yet, women have told me that even in this day and age, there is still a sense of waiting for jazz to catch up with the rest of the world. Things are changing, just incredibly slowly. Many women feel they still have to prove themselves more than men and that the process repeats with them having to prove themselves not once but over and over again.

Jazz remains stubbornly misogynistic, stuck in some self-imposed time-warp that no amount of prodding, coercion or downright shouting about it seems to alter. It's as if jazz remembers where it came from—a world where women themselves and the world had different expectations of them—but it cannot yet clearly see where it is going on these issues.

Music expresses feelings with a profundity words cannot, each genre having its own dialect. Bestow upon a person the gift of being able to play an instrument and the wherewithal to do so without embarrassment or self-delusion, and you have a musician who can speak to the listener, making the voids of time, distance or ideology vanish in an instant. Jazz music is particularly successful in bridging these gulfs. It reflects society through rhythms and nuances from many cultures and speaks to the souls of listeners and players.

Behind some of the greatest jazz compositions, performances and recordings were immense struggles; some inspired by incredible suffering and seismic world events. John Coltrane, for example, wrote one of his great compositions, *Alabama* in response to terrible events in that resulted in the deaths of four black children. As society changes, jazz reflects this change like a mirror. There is jazz for the misplaced, the angry, the happy, for lovers, the frustrated, the bereft, devastated, bereaved, creative, lonely and those celebrating the joy of life. Jazz embraces an ever-increasing number of mini-genres with unifying characteristics, their origins diverse yet the connections solid. Jazz has witnessed far reaching changes over the past decades and giant steps have been taken from within the industry itself to address issues like racism, prejudice and injustice.

Of all music genres, those who play jazz are probably in the best position to understand prejudice. Many musicians in the past were on the receiving end of racial abuse and segregation from the time 'jass' became known as 'jazz' (because the men who sold records and magazines wanted a catchier name). Great musicians like Louis Armstrong, Duke Ellington, Miles Davis and John Coltrane were subjected to injustices based on their colour and many had to endure the humiliation of having to use different entrances, lodgings, rest rooms and dining facilities than those of their white counterparts.

This was unfortunate. Yet there was another group of musicians who faced the same prejudices too; all of the above plus one more—that of gender. These were and are, the women of jazz. This book explores the journeys of women and their changing roles; their expectations and whether these have changed. It also gives more than a passing mention to women who have worked behind the scenes, laid the foundations for future change and influenced jazz music in profound ways.

Following the publication of, 'All That's Jazz' in 2017, and a successful mini-festival in London, I was asked to write several radio series for Jazz Bites—a US jazz radio station. One which saw listening ratings sky-rocket was titled, 'Women in Jazz' where we celebrated women through the decades to the present day. Feedback was so strong it seemed natural to find out why these shows evoked such interest.

With the support of my publishers, 8th House Publishing, as well as that of the many women who gave their time, this book looks at how, in the early years of jazz, women were received and the changes they precipitated, even if interminably slowly at first. It investigates how social changes, rights' movements and a war worked together to accelerate these changes, and the impact this had and how women initiated and embraced these changes.

Jazz has survived a period of history covering some of the most radical changes in society, not least the sensibilities surrounding gender. How far attitudes have changed was part of the curiosity which inspired the writing of this book. There is neither judgement nor agenda and no desire to deliver a political message, though the reader may come across some here—the women who raised these issues in the course of interviews and their voices should never be silenced. The words quoted are delivered with no alteration or edits. People gave their time and trust. They understood that the aim was to present the facts and tell things as they are.

Here, the women in jazz have space to talk about their journeys. They knowingly share their thoughts with us. We hope you find what they have to say interesting, insightful and thoughtful. We hope their words bring you closer to the heart of what jazz music is; the different kinds of jazz and the beauty of the music. More than all this, we hope you enjoy reading.

So, come to the table. We are all gathered here. Women who made past journeys, those still travelling and those whose journeys are just beginning. We are together and talking. We are singers, musicians, agents, educators, promoters, radio show hosts, PR people, composers and more. Our topic is women in jazz and how those gathered around the table feel about it. Are there any problems on being a woman in jazz? How do men react? Do women feel jazz has moved on or is it still anachronistic in its attitudes towards women? Is there misogyny still? Do any of the women have stories of success to share or stories where they have been made to feel gender is an issue? How do we view women of the past? How would they advise a newcomer to jazz?

The discussion is, at its heart, simply about the glorious, wonderful, women of jazz. It celebrates their presence, hears their voices, wonders at their prowess and revels in their being. It is an ongoing discussion and a lively one.

I spoke with, interviewed and wrote to many women involved with jazz in many ways. They responded, offering their ideas, thoughts and profound insights into how women feel in the jazz industry today. We had that discussion and want to share it with you. There are stories, adventures, suggestions, advice for newcomers, and explorations on what the future may hold. The established performers share years of experience whilst those newer to jazz reflect observations and changes they have seen.

I have been stunned by the generosity of those who allowed me to ask questions and then answered them profoundly and honestly. I am amazed at the positivity with which women have responded and the energy and thought they have put into their answers. To each woman I would like to express my thanks, not just for the words and your time but for the insights and understanding you have given me.

WOMEN IN JAZZ

Contents

New Orleans—Past & Present

JAZZ MUSIC originated in New Orleans, Louisiana. It was born out of oppression and an intermingling of cultures with strong rhythmic and musical backgrounds. Knowing it would be impossible to write a book on jazz without understanding New Orleans and its history, I went to the city to see if jazz was still there and feel the atmosphere for myself. I was given a tour by New Orleans resident, jazz vocalist Carmela Rappazzo, and experienced the music in big and small venues.

I am happy to report that jazz is very much alive. New people are coming into it, bringing their unique voices to the music. New Orleans continues to feed parts of the jazz industry as it always has and there is a real sense that all cultures find a place here and a community spirit which is deep and abiding.

New Orleans—NOLA—is a city of less than half a million people, sixty miles inland on the Mississippi river, whose mighty waters empty into the Gulf of Mexico, panning out into a protective area of mud flats in such a manner there is no tidal reach in the Mississippi. Here the hottest months coincide with the greatest amount of rain so it can be humid, sticky and close. The city has witnessed terrible consequences of natural disasters, as well as suffering caused when people of one ethnicity were traded and considered possessions of others rather than fellow humans with equal rights.

In the 300 years since 'La Nouvelle Orleans' was established by French colonists, many cultures have stamped their indelible mark on the city including African, Dutch, English, German, Irish, Italian, Spanish,

Sicilian and more. It was and is a cultural cauldron. The different influences are apparent in its architecture, food, art and of course, music.

Historically, New Orleans was a major port and key trading point for sugar, cotton, agricultural produce and slaves. Today it continues to draw people from all over the world as well as from other regions of the United States. NOLA has always been a melting pot for humanity.

Wealthy business families also had an insatiable appetite for enslaved labour. Slaves were brought in, mainly from Africa, and traded. Under Spanish rule, a law called *coartacion* was introduced in New Orleans, which proved important in the development of music. *Coartacion* was a way in which slaves could make a down-payment and negotiate a price for their future freedom. Matters degenerated however as various laws were later introduced to stop freed slaves remaining in the state and prevent some from ever being freed; but *coartacion* was key to a slightly more humane slavery than that experienced in the rest of the US. It should be noted that New Orleans and the surrounding counties maintained different laws than the rest of the country for governing the treatment of slaves.

When I was in the city, I overheard a tour guide explaining the 'benefits' of the *coartacion* laws to a group of wide-eyed tourists in Congo Square. She explained, "Slaves had to have three sets of clothes including Sunday Best. Also, on Sundays, they could take time to rest and it was at these times in places like right here in Congo Square, that slaves would gather and socialize. They often played music."

Though the tour guide made it sound like being a slave in New Orleans was a stroke of luck and neglected to mention the degradation, humiliation and suffering, she was right on one point. They were, (until 1817 when the mayor issued a law limiting the gatherings of slaves in public places), allowed to gather and cultural exchanges happened, not just between different slave groups but between slaves and New Orleans residents who would come to hear the music, see the dances and contribute their own instruments and ways of playing.

Congo Square Memorial Plaque. Inscription Reads:

Congo Square is in the "vicinity" of a spot which Houman Indians used before the arrival of the French for celebrating their annual corn harverst and was considered sacred ground. The gathering of enslaved Afrtican vendors in Congo Sqaure originated as early as the late 1740's during Lousiana's French colonial period and continued during the Spanish colonial era as one of the city's public markets. By 1803, Congo Square had become famous for the gathering of enslaved Africans who drummed, danced, sang and traded on Sunday afternoons. By 1819, these gatherings numbered as many 500 to 600 people. Among the most famous dancers were the Bamboula, the Calinda and the Congo. These African cultural expresssions gradually developed into Mardi Gras Indian tranditions, the Second line and eventually New Orleans jazz and rhythm and blues.

It was possibly the only time where the free and enslaved gathered with a common interest. Slaves from different cultures shared rhythms, dances and music, much of it African in origin. They used home-made versions of traditional instruments like bamboulas, banzaz, quill pipes and reed instruments and added instruments from the land in which they now found themselves—pipes, trumpets, horns and stringed instruments which many of them learned to play. A slave who played an instrument well could earn a little money by playing at cultural events. With Western influences added including church songs and folk music, the music developed its own tongue—combining them with ragtime, blues and deeply spiritual African and Eastern music and the Cake Walk—a high, strutting step with syncopated accompaniment popular with slaves in the fields during the 1880s. New music evolved in Congo Square. Marches and brass instruments became entwined in the mix and 'jass' music was born—not in an instant, but over time and a lot of suffering between Sundays.

Buddy Bolden, a cornet player, led one of the first jass bands, though he and others wrangled for the title of being first 'jass band' leader. Bolden blended gospel, blues, ragtime and improvisation in a unique style—noisy, brash and different from anything heard before. He made the cornet central to this new form of music and used different rhythm patterns like 'the big four'—a marching, brassy beat which allowed for improvisation. He also used syncopated rhythms, creating a distinctive sound. No recordings are known to have survived but band leaders like Joe 'King' Oliver and Bunk Johnson were inspired by Bolden to form their own bands and record.

The groups played ragtime, melodies, marches, quadrilles (a song form based on a European square dance), and blues. It was not sophisticated, but it was new and different. The first band to make recordings which survived were the Original Dixieland Jazz Band—the term 'Dixieland' referring to both jazz music played by white musicians of the early New Orleans school and later to traditional New Orleans jazz in general. Recorded jazz was rare—partly due to the fact that the entire band would have to gather around a horn-like machine which recorded their sound as they played, transferring it on to the wax recording master discs. Recording sessions were cramped and unwieldy with instruments, not something conducive to improvisational or inspired playing. Jass became 'jazz' once the people who sold records wanted a catchier name. The music flourished, especially in Storyville (the red-light district of New Orleans). Influential musicians at the time included Bolden, Oliver,

Louis Armstrong, Sidney Bechet, Barney Bigard and Kid Ory.

Jazz evoked a social response even back then. It was radical and very different from music 'cultured' Americans were used to. Its popularity outside New Orleans grew slowly at first. However, the extensive reach of the Mississippi riverboats was to prove crucial in its rise. Many riverboats employed jazz bands. They provided entertainment and the music was danceable. The riverboats plied the vast Mississippi network of interconnecting tributaries and canals and huge distances were covered. Where the boats docked, concerts were put on and locals could attend. Cincinnati, St Louis, New York and Philadelphia were all linked by the riverboats, so jazz was heard far and wide. This not only helped to develop audiences and appreciation for the music quickly, but several famous jazz musicians were initially influenced by what they heard from the river boat bands. Soon jazz bands were springing up everywhere.

Cities themselves had different cultural influences. The jazz in Philadelphia and New York developed its own characteristics and distinct accents. Most of the musicians on the boats came out of New Orleans and some were Creole so had mixed heritage, which meant the otherwise strict colour bars became blurred. Musicians could mingle and be part of a band which was neither in one camp nor the other. Italian musicians proved key in breaking colour bars. Where did they sit in terms of colour? Who knew or cared? In the riverboat bands, people of mixed race found employment and more importantly, income.

Some of the band leaders encouraged a mix of races in their bands—or rather, they used the best musicians and did not really bother if they were black, brown, white or somewhere in between. These included Kid Ory, King Oliver and Bolden himself. One of Kid Ory's later bands set up in Los Angeles, where prejudice was rife. They were given the nickname *Kid Ory's Brown-Skinned Babies*. Throughout 1922-1923 the band played in California and released the first recordings made by an African-American band, including Ory's *Creole Trombone* and *Society Blues*.

There were also those, including some powerful people, who disregarded colour bars when it came to music. Italian-Chicagoan bandleader Joe Marsala and others recruited black musicians to play in their bands, flying in the face of prejudice in favour of good music. There were white musicians who played alongside black and mixed-race musicians like Bix Beiderbecke. There were people who encouraged cross-Atlantic cooperation, with Europe and the UK, helping spread jazz and challenging discrimination. These included producer and promoter John Hammond who, through his work with *Melody Maker* and *Columbia*, and his employment of both white and coloured musicians for his radio series, encouraged the sharing of jazz music to a far wider audience. As a young man, Hammond was encouraged to listen to classical music, but became transfixed by the music he heard coming from 'below stairs' in his home and sought it out in Harlem. He came to love jazz and later disregarded colour bars. He is known to have walked out of a radio station because the venue required the black musicians that he invited on as guests to use a side entrance. He wrote in his memoirs, "I heard no colour line in the music". However, many heard that colour line right up until fairly recently. Even in the 1950s people like Ken Colyer who came to New Orleans and sat in with coloured musicians, ran the real risk of arrest and physical danger in doing so because people wanted to prevent integration. On the other hand, many of the musicians felt jazz music belonged to those who had undergone the pangs of its birth, and that it had been taken over by the white recording bosses and magazine sellers. They were right. The early recordings of jazz music were nearly all by bands comprised of white musicians. The commercial overlords in the 1950s who recorded and sold jazz records were white men with money. There was irony in the fact that the stars of the music were often black performers and while venues would sell out on the back of their names, the performers themselves could not use the club facilities or even have their own family come to the show.

By the end of the 1950s jazz had become so popular that American politicians began to see it as a tool for spreading American culture.

Because of the popularity of the music, it was adopted as 'America's national music' and money was found to send musicians out on grand tours with their bands. In the 1950s and 1960s the State Department sent jazz musicians—including Dizzy Gillespie, Duke Ellington and Louis Armstrong—on tours abroad as 'good-will ambassadors'. Jazz was presented as American culture to show the rest of the world. There was also hope that these artists would refute accusations of racism in America. The musicians were lauded and treated well. In reality, black people in many states were discriminated against in appalling ways. Yet, musicians, being creative, spoke out, not always directly but often in their music. One such musician was Louis Armstrong.

Armstrong toured the Eastern Bloc in 1965 with the Cold War in full swing. He played cities, including East Berlin, to enchanted audiences. He fell short of openly criticizing his government on the tour, but in Berlin he included a slowed-down version of his number, *(What Did I Do to Be So) Black and Blue?* This song had not been in his set lists for several years. Now he slowed it right down so the lyrics rang out loud and clear. They included the lines,

> *I'm white inside,*
> *But that don't help my case,*
> *Cause I can't hide*
> *What is on my face.*
> *I'm so forlorn.*
> *Life's just a thorn,*
> *My heart is torn.*
> *Why was I born?*
> *...My only sin*
> *Is in my skin,*
> *What did I do*
> *To be so black and blue?*

Armstrong, in his quiet, determined way, had made his point.

Jazz may have been born of people who were oppressed and downtrodden, yet also blessed with an unsurpassed and unsubduable passion for music.

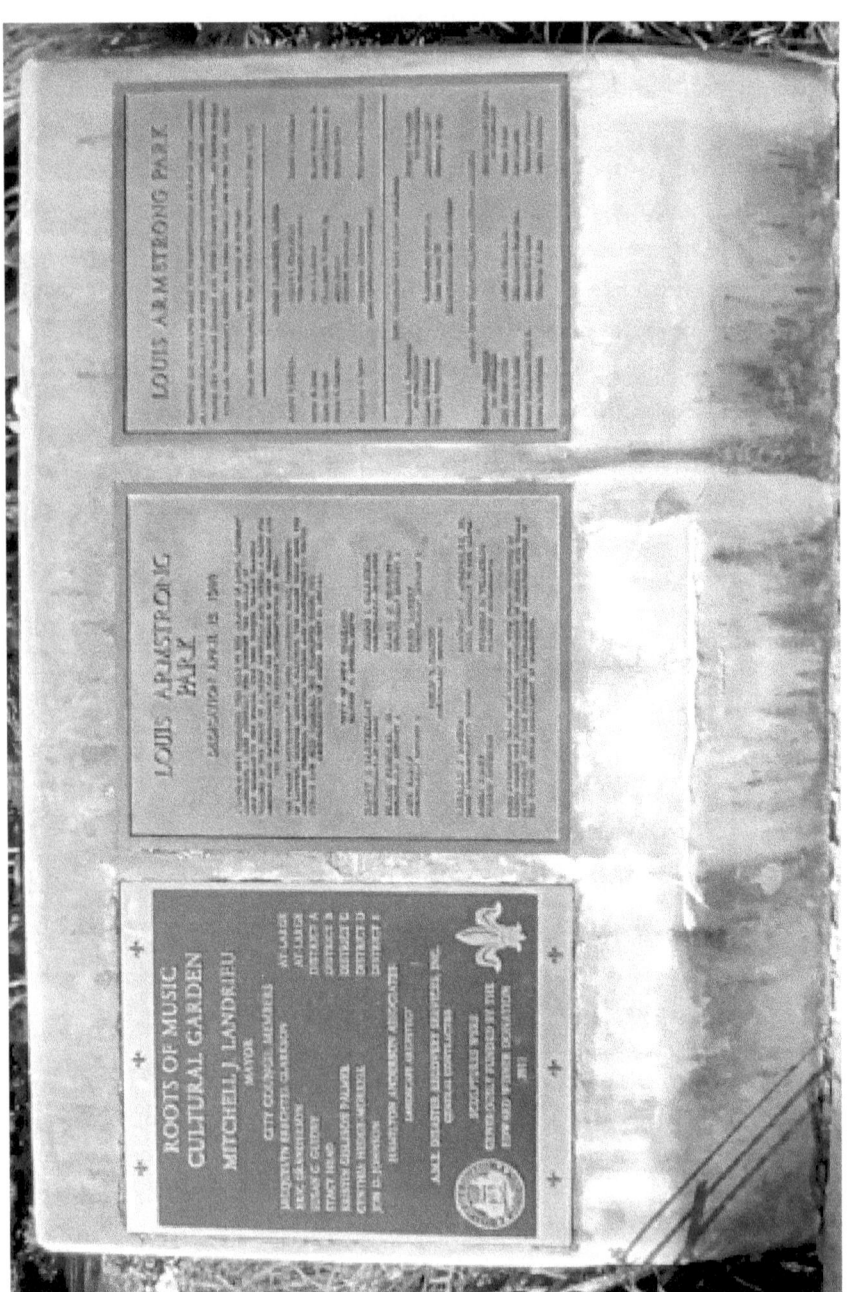

Plaque commemorating Louis Armstrong at Louis Armstrong Park, New Orleans

They were united by a need to express themselves in a world where they were seldom listened to. By the 1950s, in the face of prejudice and white musicians taking over, those who had created jazz found themselves in danger of being pushed into a background role, especially when it came to live performances. It is hard to imagine how difficult it was for musicians when prejudice was legislated and condoned.

However, nothing had quite prepared audiences for the popularity of the Big Bands. The inventiveness of some of the early jazz musicians and their coupling with some very entrepreneurial venue managers led to jazz becoming a huge commercial success in a relatively short time. Musicians from gospel, blues, theatre bands and house bands in restaurants now began to play jazz music, much to the enjoyment of patrons.

The improvement of recording techniques and commercialization of record sales meant musicians could be heard not just in America, but also before a world-wide audience. Record companies became wealthy with profits made from jazz music, especially in the late 1950s. They also became 'gate-keepers', supporting and developing their own 'label' musicians, releasing only selected recordings to the hungry public. An ex-manager of Sony revealed that musicians were groomed for public exposure, guided on how to dress, act and even what to say to magazines and fans. A few did well.

For others however, this was too controlling and they felt the improvisation—so much a part of jazz—was being lost and tailored to suit a different audience than it was originally intended for. They developed other forms of playing, steeped in improvisational techniques. Musicians like Ornette Coleman, Charlie Parker, John Coltrane, Pharaoh Sanders and many more went along a freer path, attracting a different audience and filling a niche.

After WWII, and in greater numbers in the late 1960s, European free players exploded onto the jazz scene offering an anarchic response to what was happening in the world and beautifully exploring new ways of playing. Peter Brotzmann, one of the key European free players, once explained to me that young European players were reacting partly to the race riots and atrocities happening in the States, partly to rebel and partly because the music had grown and expanded from its American origins. New instruments came into jazz from all over the world as musicians travelled more and networked. In Brazil, street parties and festivals incorporated jazz into their traditional rhythms and Frevo jazz became a distinct form of jazz in some areas. The music lent itself to being blended with local rhythms and tunes across the globe. Even today, influences from other cultures continue to shape different genres, from the Far East to Scandinavia. Wherever jazz is found, it seems the most flexible genre and quickly adopts characteristics of that region. Japanese jazz sounds quite different from American jazz for example, yet both kinds are played in both countries.

European jazz musicians created their own interpretations of the music, infusing cultural references from a wholly different origin. In the UK, jazz set out along its separate path, largely helped by a Musicians' Union dispute in the 1950s which barred US musicians playing in the UK and vice versa for several years. Isolated, the Brits created their own very distinctive jazz culture. There were many schools of jazz in the UK with those preferring either the traditional jazz of New Orleans, swing and dance music, over a freer, modern style or a blend of popular, sentimental music—'smooth' jazz. By the time the Musicians' Union ban was lifted in the late 1950s by luminaries and innovative entrepreneurs like Ronnie Scott, Ken Colyer and others, jazz in the UK had become a far freer music and one which still has a very distinctive 'British' style. Many centers in Europe and the UK are where jazz musicians come together to develop and exchange musical ideas, with London in particular being a hub for free jazz. The music is gaining popularity again, and not in a small way, due to the huge numbers of young people coming into the music. The creative process continues, with the Internet providing easy access to a huge number of influences.

The jazz which originated in New Orleans is referred to as traditional jazz, with funereal, marching rhythms, particularly heard at Mardi

Gras. Today, things have changed a little and streets like Bourbon Street swing to the rhythms of hip hop, garage, soul and funk. However, walk just a couple of blocks to Frenchman Street in the Faubourg Marigny and one can't move without hearing jazz. It flows out of the cafés, doorways, large restaurants, pubs, bars. It spills over into the surrounding streets. Different kinds of jazz, different instruments, street musicians and singers on corners, this part of the city lives and breathes jazz. Across New Orleans, jazz remains popular with patrons and attracts a different crowd for every performance. There are jazz clubs in hotels, large concert halls and in small bars. It is easy to go from gig to gig from late morning to the early hours. Almost every hour sees a new performance underway. And if you want traditional New Orleans jazz, you can find it easily. You can even take a 'jazz trip' on a river boat—*The Nachez*—but you can also find a treasure trove of different jazz music.

Attractions like the *New Orleans Jazz Museum* and various galleries chart the progress, photographically or in paintings, of particular movements or musicians. Venues like *Snug Harbour* and *Preservation Hall* are packed each evening with audiences wanting to see and hear traditional jazz being played. Many venues have two or even three sets per night with Preservation Hall sometimes having four or five to accommodate the enthusiastic punters. In many pubs and small clubs, there are tiny stages with instruments laid out. Patrons can pick them up, play and see who joins in.

Yet, in the vibrant modern day city of New Orleans, there are poignant reminders of a city built on the slave trade. Many big houses in the very posh Garden District have a little house attached to the back. These small homes housed slaves and some are said to have been built with connecting tunnels so the master of the big house could visit the women slaves at will during that time.

Jazz is not just history in New Orleans, however. It is very much alive and part of the present. The breadth of music and types of jazz found there today is incredible. Armstrong was considered the first improviser and his influence is everywhere, from Armstrong Park and Congo Square to various plaques and notations around the town; but there are many good young musicians still making their mark in NOLA. They play not just in clubs and jazz venues, but also in the street.

Alicia Renee AKA Blue Eyes. Photograph by Summer 'Nicole' Emerson Williams

Walking along Frenchman Street, I heard the most wonderful vocalist one evening. I followed the sound of her voice and came across Alicia Renee *aka* 'Blue Eyes' singing on a street corner. Alicia has sung at *The Jazz Café* in London, *La Scene* in Paris, the *North Sea Jazz Festival* and with Quincy Jones, BB King, Stevie Nicks and others. Alicia told me she lives in town and "just felt like doing it". I also heard the *Slow Rollas*—a brass combo who play loud and very fast—on the street. There were brass bands practicing outside offices, duos playing in several bars and cafés and sometimes someone would just be sitting on a bench playing jazz on an instrument. Jazz is everywhere.

Early on, other genres like *Rhythm and Blues* found a center in New Orleans as well as jazz. Jelly Roll Morton, Professor Longhair and Fats Domino were excellent players of New Orleans' Rhythm and

Blues piano. *The Neville Brothers*—Aaron, Art, Charles, and Cyril—introduced a New Orleans brand of funk music as leaders of bands like *the Meters and the Wild Tchoupitoula*s in the 1970s, 80s and 90s. But it was, and still is, jazz which dominates.

Delfeayo with his Big Band at *Snug Harbour*. Photo by Sammy Stein

Music—jazz in particular—has made New Orleans a vibrant cultural hub and attracted a whole new wave of jazz musicians to make New Orleans their base. Vocalist Carmela Rappazzo moved from New York to be in New Orleans, the legendary Marsalis family, which includes trumpeter Wynton, saxophonist Branford, trombonist Delfeayo and their father, pianist Ellis help bring attention to jazz and New Orleans as they play regularly. I saw Delfeayo with his Big Band at *Snug Harbour* when I was there. He played two sets in one evening. The city also hosts the annual *New Orleans Jazz and Heritage Festival*, one of the largest jazz and blues festivals in the country.

So, just to be sure, what is jazz?

A trademark of jazz is syncopation, with emphasis placed on the weaker or 'off' beat. Simple as it seems, give this concept to a creative musician and variations happen—swing, acid jazz, folk jazz, rock jazz, house jazz and free jazz. Against the steady measure of the beat or pulse (most likely provided by the rhythm section or the left hand of the pianist), the melody instruments emphasize the off beats of a 2 or 4 count measure (though this can also be 5/8, 7/8 or other rhythms). Changes may be predicted by bringing in chords a tad early or sometimes, one musician simply switches key and the rest follow—it depends.

The melody lines can be short, driving riffs of a few bars or long, curving lines as a solo. 'Blue' notes—those notes between the tones— are used in jazz music to impart a melancholic (blue) feel or create added interest. '*Glissando*' covers notes both blue and true by sliding up or down between them. This works well for brass or woodwind players but is difficult for pianists who use short, inserted notes called 'grace' notes. Because it is difficult to transcribe with all the grace or blue notes, a jazz score might simply have numbers for some lines, indicating which interval in the scale they should be on at that point (and this may be approximate). With free jazz, often there is no score, the music being created at the time with a collective idea of the way it will run or develop and the root chords around which everyone will improvise. So, within jazz there is controlled, scored music and completely unscored free playing though the essences of syncopation and harmonics remain.

The rhythms of jazz are distinct. Many originate from the marching band music which gave its rhythms to New Orleans jazz. Each drummer has one drum in a marching jazz band, so one drummer would play on the down beat (first line) and another would play on the up or off beat (second line). The invention of the bass tom pedal, meaning a player could keep the beat going whilst playing other drums was innovative and led to drum kits which made the inclusion of other drums, grace notes and a whole lot of different additions possible. The rhythms became more complex with the drummers doing a lot more than just maintaining the tempo.

Any musical genre can be syncopated, turning it into a 'jazzed version', but at the heart of jazz is improvisation. A player takes a musical idea, a set of chords, a progression or key and improvises around it, returns to it, basing themselves there but soaring away, working up and down to it, generally experimenting and deciding, often on a whim, or reaction to the moment, where the music will take them, yet rooted by the idea. For an accomplished player it is a very satisfactory way to play and great musicians speak directly to the audience through improvisation.

Another important aspect of jazz music is personalization. A piece is played differently by every musician and often every time it is played— even by that same musician. It is difficult for jazz composers to write jazz music and dictate precisely how it should be played because of this emphasis on improvisation. A composer can provide a framework with instructions, but it is necessarily limited and musicians will interpret it differently. This is personalization. For example, how can you direct every slide, tremor, glissando, type of attack (rough, smooth, heavy, light)? It is impossible. Each musician picking up the same musical template will interpret it as they feel it. The emotive way a player delivers music often has as much to do with whether an audience engages with them as whether they play the right notes. This concept is expressed by saxophonist and composer Trish Clowes when she says,

> *It's worth noting that one's personality affects how you improvise. Jazz is a social music (as famously observed by Miles Davis), and more often than not, how we play (or talk) is a reflection of who we are as a person. This is a key consideration in trying to understand on-stage dynamics. I stress here that this is not a comment on people's instrumental abilities, more a comment on how someone chooses to play—because in jazz, we have that choice.*

Since its birth, jazz has undergone many transformations, never losing a genre but rather adding more. Composers such as Ellington created orchestral arrangements of jazz pieces and thanks to leaders like Paul Whiteman, jazz began to be played by orchestras as well as smaller ensembles. Gershwin's *Rhapsody in Blue, Blue Monday* (a jazz opera) and *Porgy and Bess* are well known jazz-classical compositions and this music format linked classical form to jazz interpretation. In the 1960s Gunther Schuller coined the term '3rd Stream' to mean music like that of Gershwin, Debussy and others which was half-written (and what was written, adhered to) and half-improvised.

Claude Debussy is often cited as an influence for jazz musicians. Yet he wrote just one extended piece for saxophone and orchestra, which he never finished because he didn't like the saxophone. It was commissioned by arts patron Elisa Hall who played the saxophone and was trying to increase the repertoire for the instrument. Apparently when Debussy saw Elisa play the instrument, dressed in a pink dress, he disliked it even more. His *Rhapsody for Orchestra and Saxophone*, was eventually given orchestration after his death by Jean-Roger Ducasse. His place in history as a major jazz influencer becomes understandable when one learns of his methodology. In his *Rhapsody for Orchestra and Saxophone*, he explores the range and sound of the instrument (which was new to him). He used whole tone scales and minor key harmonies. In other works, such as his *Nuages,* he developed several techniques later adopted by jazz composers. In modern times, composers like Mats Gustafsson have written orchestral pieces for saxophone and orchestra.

Today, talking to musicians about 'what is jazz', they add that it has changed and some jazz today is almost unrecognizable as having originated from traditional jazz, though the syncopation and improvisation is still there. There may be two, three or more meters competing with each other and there is more spirituality in modern and free jazz. The emphasis is on communication and listening to changes from other musicians. There is a move away from analysis which used to fill columns of the heavy-weight magazines and made many feel jazz was elitist. Terminology, niches, elitism, these things are not really part of jazz now. Rather, jazz has changed to be a more liberal genre. There are many young players and these are bringing changes to the music—either enjoying jazz in its purer forms or combining it with other music like house, garage and hip-hop.

Overwhelmingly in recent days, jazz has a positivity about it; an energy which has come from nowhere. For a few short, awful years, jazz felt like it had lost its muse. Now, the muse has arisen, is powerful, energy-fired and delivering music the like of which the world has never heard. Key to that change have been many women.

Jazz has a world-wide audience, it is the most expressive genre, the one which reflects what we do, how we live and what people want to say. In many ways jazz is all that we are and want to be. Jazz is us.

Women

WOMEN HAVE BROKEN GROUND in many fields. We have lots of 'firsts' to hold up as examples of women who smashed the proverbial glass ceiling. Margaret Thatcher, Amelia Earheart, Emily Pankhurst, Sandra Day O'Connor—the first woman appointed to serve on the US Supreme Court—the list is extensive. There are others including Condoleezza Rice, Oprah Winfrey, Teresa May, Angela Merkel, Marin Alsop (first female conductor of *Last Night of The Proms*). The list of powerful and famous women goes on. Many areas once traditionally male are now populated by an increasing number of women from astronauts, to engineers and scientists. Once those first female pioneers open the door, other women follow. Now, no-one is surprised to find the head of *Virgin Money* is a woman, as is the Chancellor of Germany and the prime minister of the UK. Women can be judges, MPs, members of congress, chief executives, academics, classical composers, engineers, lorry drivers, medical professionals. In an increasing number of industries women and men now face each other on an equal footing in most areas. It is success all round and huge pats on the backs are deserved by all those who fought misogyny, oppression and discrimination on the grounds of gender—and then there is jazz.

Jazz is a still a man's world. There are more male 'everythings' in jazz. From PR people, to agents, radio hosts, writers, producers and of course, musicians.

Interviewing and working with many musicians and people in different areas of jazz means enjoying the diverse, creative music of an equally diverse body of people. However, noticeably, there aren't many women.

I don't mean there are none. There have always been women in jazz and there are women in jazz today, yet their numbers remain minuscule compared to men in all areas. Change feels incredibly slow and it begs the question why? Why are there so few women at gigs? Why are there not more women musicians? Why is nearly every record producer, PR person, agent, critic and musician a man? Is jazz still playing catch-up to other genres which have included more women?

There are amazing women in jazz—both in its past, its present, and those just emerging as incredible talents within the genre. Many musicians, of course, play more than one genre but many specialize in jazz, playing across the world, regularly filling both intimate and large concert venues. There are just so few women compared to men.

Misogyny is not illegal, though many view it as a form of abuse. Many women have experienced degrees of harassment in the work place and in Europe and North America considerable steps have been made, both in laws and changes in attitudes regarding the treatment of women. There is still a way to go in terms of pay gaps and professional advancement. Gender equality remains a goal rather than a reality in some areas. In many professions, men still get paid more than women and once you get above Musician Union rates in the music world, this is still the case.

It must be remembered that there are many who fully support gender equality, not just in music but in every aspect of society; and that this contingency includes many men. Many people simply see talent, rather than gender. Despite this, the jury is out on whether changes in jazz are happening and whether they are happening fast enough. Jazz was born in a male-dominated environment. It was led by men at the beginning and perhaps insufficient time has passed for change to have established itself deeply enough. In so many other genres of music, there is growing equality. Yet jazz remains male-dominated and the speed of change is slow. We should celebrate the advances we've made, but jazz feels like it is dragging its heels.

Without women many male players would never have been able to get their music to an audience, let alone keep touring, recording and communicating with people of influence. Women have been vital for the success of jazz since its birth. Besides composing, performing and producing, they have also nursed, nurtured, supported, been butts of jokes, subject of songs and muses to great jazz performers. They have been mothers—people like Robert Glasper's mother who directed the choir in a Baptist church and provided him with the musical environment that nurtured his jazz music; and Billie Holiday's mother who encouraged her when Billie decided to become a jazz singer. Women have also been among the great performers of the past and are certainly among those of the present. Yet ask a jazz lover to name musicians and they will reel off a list of male performers and perhaps a few female singers. Few will know or mention female musicians—even though many of them made a real difference. A look at the line ups of many festivals reveals few women solo artists or leaders. In one famous publication of great jazz interviews out of over one hundred twenty interviews, under ten percent were with women. From performers to PR, radio shows, writers, film makers, record label managers, almost no women are as powerful as men. So why not more of them?

Talking to people in the jazz industry, it is clear this is an important topic—not only for women but some men also. It is surprising how many men want women to be represented more in jazz and are slightly at a loss to explain why they are not. There is a definite age division here with older ones explaining they believe the attitudes to women in jazz persist because some musicians think of women as wives, mothers and supporters and jazz as a male industry.

In contrast, younger people seem genuinely unable to explain the dearth of females in jazz. They have been brought up to consider everyone equal regardless of gender, colour or culture and for the most part, their world is one of equality. Yet in jazz they find themselves stuck in a world full of by-gone values. Jazz feels like a dinosaur clumsily floundering in the wrong era. These younger jazz people are trying to explain why gender inequality is still so pervasive in a creative medium, where gender should be the last thing people are concerned with.

There is a mix of reactions when the views of women across jazz today are heard. Some have had sexist comments and remarks directed at them, some have had incidents where their gender has been an issue and others have had no problems at all. Some have taken the issue to heart and fought for women's rights and others have not given sexism much thought. What is apparent though is that there are more women coming into the business, whether as musicians or managers, record label bosses, promoters, radio hosts and other associated roles. Whether jazz offers them equality is still a matter of debate, but change *is* happening. It is just a question of how quickly.

Surprisingly, there have been lots of studies into this area. Interesting reading can be found by looking at papers carried out as part of research studies as well as magazine articles. Just a few are:

Biddy Healey's *Be a Good Girl and Play Like a Man* (2016)—this makes particularly interesting and detailed reading.

Steinberg's 2001 *"Take A Solo" An Analysis of Gender Participation and Interaction at School Jazz Festivals.*

K. McKeage's *Gender and Participation in High School and College Instrumental Jazz Ensembles* (2004)

Dr Arial Alexander's guest editorial in *JazzEd Magazine*, Sept 2011 titled *Where Are The Girls?*

Marie Millard's *Five Things To Teach Your Female Students About Jazz* article in *Brass Chicks* (2018).

There are many more articles and papers but these above give a great overview. The views of each writer vary slightly and the demographics used in each study group affect the result, but in general the conclusions are that:

- The number of women in jazz ensembles remains significantly lower than that of men. Moreover, the drop-out rate when they do join is far higher for women than for men.

- Women are still encouraged by parents and teachers to choose instruments which are seen as 'feminine'. Piano is commonly taught to women. This may have developed because women who came through the gospel route to jazz learned to play piano in church, so it was an acceptable instrument. A consequence of this bias is a decreased chance of playing jazz as they will have not have studied an instrument typically sought after in a jazz ensemble (not that some let that stop them).

- There is no discernible difference in the ability of women and men when it comes to improvising, but young women perceive their ability to be less than that of men. This may lead to them to under-perform.

- Jazz music is perceived by students as having a masculine stereotype, mainly due to historical trends and the associations these create.

- Women feel more secure in a traditional ensemble (chamber orchestra, full orchestra etc.) than in a jazz group.

- Women feel less able to connect playing jazz with career aspirations.

- Women get less solos in jazz bands than men. In other genres solos are more evenly distributed. Jazz seems to have its own foibles in terms of gender balance.

- Networking often occurs during the down-time before or after a performance and women can feel socially excluded from these sessions.

- The lack of role models has a significant impact. It means there is less expectation from women because they see very few successful women on which to model themselves. In other careers where there are women role models, more women follow. In jazz there are few female role models for women. If you look at the number of women represented on college and university music faculties it is below fifteen percent.

- Not having many women as role models makes it harder for young females in jazz. Men are far more likely to mentor men, so it is hard for female musicians to find female mentors because they simply do not exist or aren't available.

Saxophone player and band leader Kim Cypher backs up some of the findings when she says,

> *Throughout secondary school I had many opportunities to be involved in musical activities and although my musical talent was encouraged, my desire to follow a musical career path was not. In fact, it is fair to say it was discouraged (not by my family, but by the education system). I can see that it is not a particularly secure career path to take and so I understand why this was the case. So, I was channelled along a more academic route and this resulted in a protracted journey which ultimately led me back to following my musical dreams but at a much later stage in life.*

Further discussions with women lead to more observations. Some say that when in full creative flow, blowing on a horn is not 'attractive' and this can put some women off blowing hard or stretching out in jazz (or maybe in any genre). Some women feel that if they lead a band they are seen as 'bossy' and don't like that connotation. Some women still find it hard to take the lead role—surprising when we have made massive strides in equality.

And there is the dreaded 'tokenism'. Some women feel they are allowed to be present simply because they are female rather than chosen for their talent. This may be difficult to prove or disprove, but can lead to doubts in a musician's mind.

Many female jazz composers or musicians find other women frequently ask them for advice. Maria Schneider is a jazz composer, a renowned

Kim Cypher, 'Love Kim x' UK album tour launch with Pee Wee Ellis & Chris Cobbson - Photo By Ron Milsom

musician and role model for others. Trumpet player Ingrid Jensen says in Radhika Philips' book *Being Here; Conversations on Creating Music* (2013, Radhio.org):

> *Maria has been a real mentor you know. She is an amazing woman. What she's done with her life is really extraordinary.*

In jazz there are strong, fully switched-on creative women who care not a hoot for those who would keep them from their place as leaders and performers. They know they are good; they know how they play and are concerned far more with performing than any issues which those close to them or which the wider audience might want to put on their art. Music is their chosen career and what drives them, nothing else.

There are also male jazz musicians and teachers who encourage women. Saxophone player, band leader and composer Jane Ira Bloom is quoted in Radhika Philip's book mentioned above as saying,

When I was in 9th grade I began to study with a master saxophone teacher, Joe Viola. He was head of the woodwind department at Berklee College of Music. If you talk to saxophone players, they often talk about these special teachers. He was one of them........he was giving me all the tools I needed and an understanding of the saxophone so I could express myself on the instrument....

Kim Cypher recalls,

I had the most incredible music teacher called Mr Harrison who allowed me freedom to grow as a musician and nurtured my talent.

For Maria Schneider, it was Bob Brookmeyer. He made her first opportunities to compose for the Mel Lewis Orchestra a reality.

Think about it. When we are born there is a roughly fifty percent chance we will be female. In jazz music, there is roughly a twenty percent chance a musician will be female and even less of a chance they will be a jazz writer, record label boss or radio host.

Research done by the National Bureau of Economic Research in Cambridge, MA revealed a fascinating fact. They showed that in blind auditions (ones where the selection panel cannot see the players), women are more likely to be selected than men. Also, having a screen to hide them, multiplied the chances of a woman winning overall if the auditions were done by a means of successive elimination rounds. In classical music, this change in audition methods has increased the presence of women in orchestras from around ten percent in 1970 to over thirty percent today. Would results be the same if this 'blind audition' method were used for jazz bands? Given that only three of a recent twenty-strong music school's jazz band who toured Europe were women; two members of Harvard's jazz Monday Band in 2017 were female; and that in 2013, only two of the musicians in the *National Association of Music Education* All National jazz band (US) were women, it would be an interesting thing to try. A recent discussion with musicians at a gig in London garnered support for such an idea.

When seeking reasons for the shortage of women in jazz, the search becomes simple if we look at the history and culture of that place and time. Jazz grew out of a predominantly male subculture in the early 20th century—a time when women had few privileges and reputation was everything. Women were less likely to visit the clubs, bottle-clubs, speakeasies and other night-time hang outs where jazz was played and even less likely to play jazz—music which became enmeshed with the hazy world of hard drugs and alcohol. Racism and sexism were the norm at the time jazz first became popular and it is not difficult to see how this behaviour became entrenched. Record labels put out jazz music on 'race labels'—so called because they were sold and bought largely in areas where black people lived and worked, while the artists recorded for the labels were also black. Women at the time were objectified, seen as ornamental; and this was re-enforced on screen as well as on stage, with the only female musicians allowed to perform being for the most part young, pretty, wearing revealing dresses, high shoes and lots of make-up. Instead of the trumpet, trombone or saxophone ('masculine' instruments) they played 'feminine' instruments like the piano, violin, flute or harp, or they sang. Meanwhile, excepting a few, none of the major jazz bands included any of the 'feminine' instruments in their line-ups.

A couple of decades after it emerged, the commercial viability of jazz was realized and the music was lifted from the seedy, illicit places of its birth and into more uptown clubs where it became cerebral, 'intellectual' and accepted into the mainstream. The music was analyzed and became elitist, with men being by far the biggest population both in audiences and on stage. So, men got a good head start on women when it came to jazz music—maybe it is time to for women to catch-up.

Jazz is only just over one hundred years old, which in terms of music genres is young. The first jazz recording was not made until the early 1920s. Women who are now considered early pioneers of jazz like Cleo Laine and Clora Bryant are still around today. But the roles of women in society and the attitudes towards them were very different in jazz's early years. The gender difference was established early on and stuck. There remains a stubborn refusal to accept women as serious jazz musicians and this attitude feels like it comes from the past where, for example, in 1938, *Downbeat* published an article where the author stated that jazz was, 'a hard, masculine music with a whip to it' and that women, 'liked violins, but jazz deals with drums and trumpets'.

Cleo Laine photographed by David Sinclair

What we, writing or reading from our enlightened position in the 21st century must remember is that our attitudes are a world away from those which existed when jazz first emerged. Jazz has had its fair share of debates, fallouts and arguments, even violent clashes between supporters of modern and traditional jazz (Beaulieu, UK 1960s). Opposition to racial integration became an issue itself and meant the role of women and their absence seemed to have been forgotten until someone bothered to point it out. This 'pointing out' is still on-going. In 2017, a rash of articles appeared. One in the *Financial Times* was titled *Jazz Gets A Blast of Female Energy* which opened with, 'The genre still suffers from a severe gender imbalance but change is afoot'. *The*

New York Times published a piece titled *For Women In Jazz: A Year of Recognition and Reckoning* which discussed several female musicians who are becoming more prominent. So, it seems people want to highlight the issue and in some ways things are getting better. Later on in this book, women musicians and many in other roles tell of their current journey in jazz.

Research for this book revealed incredible and interesting stories. It is impossible to include all the women who have made a difference in the world of jazz. They have always been there, unnoticed. The piano was the inroad for many as it was considered a 'suitable' instrument for women to play and a female pianist was accepted almost anywhere, even playing with a big band. Out of gospel music came female vocalists with huge voices and an incredible range—women like Mahalia Jackson. They sang with soulful emotion which transferred easily to jazz arrangements. Female vocalists set the standard for jazz singers. Many combined piano playing and singing. Sweet Emma Barrett, Jeanette Kimball, Mary Lou Williams and Sarah Vaughan were just a few successful women jazz pianists and singers. Mary Lou's playing style and arrangements influenced bebop artists including Dizzy Gillespie and Thelonious Monk. From early on in jazz, women were few in number, but huge in effect. Behind the scenes women were also providing something for the musicians to parade for, as well as running fan clubs and looking after the musicians on tour. A woman even helped Louis Armstrong decide on a solo career. Lil Hardin played piano with King Oliver's Band. Louis joined in 1922. He and Lil had a romance, eventually marrying and it was she who encouraged him to try a solo career.

Many early female jazz performers worked with male composers and musicians. Soon, compositions were being written for female singers. Such songs provided opportunities for women like Billie Holliday, Nina Simone and more to find their place in the jazz world, many becoming composers themselves.

Whilst some writers and musicians found women an oddity, many were not averse to women playing alongside men and respected them as performers. Armstrong was one of them. Valaida Snow from Chattanooga, Texas, was part of a show business family. She learned to play several instruments and specialized in the trumpet as well as dancing and singing. She became so popular, she was nicknamed 'Little Louis' after Louis Armstrong. Critics were saying she simply mimicked Armstrong. Apparently, Armstrong himself, after seeing her perform at the *Sunset Café*, Chicago in 1928 remained clapping long after everyone else had stopped and commented, 'Boy, I never saw anything that great,' showing she had his full support. He later is said to have called Valaida the world's second-best jazz trumpet player after himself. She went on to become world-famous and toured the world.

Women leading smaller jazz groups gradually became more common, especially when the effects of the Great Depression in the 1930s in America meant women lost opportunities, so more men could find employment. In response, women formed their own jazz groups. Some of the women who led small combos were Barbara Carroll, Hazel Scott, Nellie Lutcher, Hadda Brooks, and Marian McPartland. However, some men remained resolutely against women in jazz. In 1938, *Downbeat* published another article entitled, *Why Women Musicians Are Inferior*. In it, the author argued that women were 'emotionally unstable' and 'could never be consistent performers on a musical instrument', and other stupidly blind-sided comments. The conclusion was that women would never blow on brass or reeds for fear of looking unattractive and had neither the time, patience, ambition nor economic motivation to 'woodshed' (practicing techniques until you get it right). The writer also pointed out that women only had a few years' experience in jazz whereas men had far more history, and that piano and strings were more suited to women. According to him, if more girl drummers had been mothers (with cradle-rocking experience) they might be able 'to get on the beat'.

The fact this article is only cited more recently as being highly sexist and is more controversial now than when first published demonstrates the prevailing attitude of the time. Some psychologists in the past even thought that women who wanted to succeed in a masculine world (like jazz music) showed symptoms of dreaded 'masculinity complexes'.

In 1938, journalists were allowed to write comments like:

> *'Why is it that outside of a few sepia females, the woman musician was never born capable of 'sending' anyone farther than the nearest exit? It would seem that even though women are the weaker sex, they would still be able to bring more out of a defenceless horn than something that sounds like a cry for help'*

This is the opening quote from the Downbeat article cited above. Even when renowned female musicians responded, the publishers resisted, entrenching themselves in the pervading sexism. Peggy Gilbert, a music educator and saxophone player, responded to the article, pointing out that men were hired for their talents, but women still had to rely on their looks to a large extent. There were double standards and it was not unknown for women to be asked to raise their skirts at auditions for band members to prove they had good legs. She asked the question, *How Can you Smile with a Horn in your Mouth?* The magazine did publish her response, but gave it the demeaning headline of, *How Can You Blow a Horn with a Brassiere?* Their response backfired. It raised awareness of the misogyny which prevailed at the time and gave Peggy national fame as an advocate for women musicians, which garnered a lot of support for her cause.

Although women had taken on more important roles in America since the nineteenth amendment in the 1920s and gained more independence after the First World War, it took another war for women to become really accepted as the talented musicians they were. During the later years of World War II, when many male jazz musicians had been drafted into the military, all-women jazz bands became increasingly popular and were seen as supportive of the wartime community, holding the fort musically while the men were away fighting. These bands were racially segregated at first, mainly due to divisions in their audiences—

white Americans were mostly listening to *Ina Rae Hutton and her Melodears*, while African-Americans were enjoying *The Darlings of Rhythm* (a swing band) and *The Prairie View Co-Eds*. *The International Sweethearts of Rhythm* played for the segregated black troops in Europe. The band was one of the first to hire non-Afro-Americans for their line-up, thereby smashing the colour barrier which had previously been in place. Other all-female bands include Ada Leonard's *All-American Girls*. Notably, white bands did not hire non-white musicians.

As well as all-female bands, female musicians began to fill gaps left by drafted male musicians in big bands. The drafts meant large numbers of men left at once, leaving bands bereft of musicians. Woody Herman hired trumpet player Billie Rogers; Gerald Wilson hired trombonist Melba Liston; and Lionel Hampton hired saxophonist Elsie Smith, providing these extraordinary female musicians opportunities which, had the men not gone away, they probably never would have had. After the war, most women lost their places to returning GI musicians. A few stayed as soloists, leaders and recording artists and faced harsh criticism and sexual harassment from their bandmates now that the men had returned. But had anything changed really? However, doors had been pushed and just a little later in the 1950s, as sophisticated modern jazz flourished, a few female instrumentalists were enjoying success, especially as pianists and trio leaders, sometimes gaining long residencies in prestigious venues. Marian McPartland and the pioneer jazz pianist Barbara Carroll led trios in New York for several decades. Pianist and singer Blossom Dearie gained wide-reaching recognition. In the UK, singers Annie Ross (celebrated for her tongue-twisting lyrics) and Beryl Bryden found fame. Opportunities remained few however.

In spite of a few notable successes, the limited role of women in jazz is highlighted in a photograph titled *A Great Day in Harlem*. Taken in 1958 by freelance photographer for *Esquire* magazine Art Kane, this photograph featured the era's greatest jazz musicians collected in Harlem. Of the fifty-seven musicians featured in the photo, only three were women and all three pianists or singers—Marian McPartland, Mary Lou Williams and Maxine Sullivan.

Marian McPartland photographed by Gerard Rouy

A major change came about in the late 1950s when TV provided more opportunities for women. TV bands during the late 1950s and 1960s hired women musicians including Ina Ray Hutton and Ada Leonard. TV audiences warmed to seeing women in bands. There were social changes taking place and TV was at the forefront of reflecting this back at audiences. Though controlled largely by conservative men, TV network companies had little choice but to include women musicians when the public demanded it.

Women also became celebrated musicians in their own right. These included vocalists like Ella Fitzgerald, and musical luminaries such as pianist, harpist and composer Alice Coltrane and pianist, organist and composer Amina Claudine Myers.

By the late 1960s, the women's liberation movement was shining the spotlight on women and their rights. They were carving deep inroads into what had been male-dominated areas—including jazz. No longer content to be present as tokens or novelty acts, scattered frugally around festivals, women demanded to be taken seriously. A decade later, after a slow beginning, matters were kick-started by some major events. The first *Women's Jazz Festival* was held in Kansas City in 1978, followed swiftly by the first annual *New York Women's Jazz Festival*. The Kansas festival was started by Carol Comer and Diane Gregg, who decided to organize a women's festival after seeing the *Wichita Jazz Festival* which had included Buddy Rich, Clark Terry, The Louie Belson Big Band Explosion, Joe Williams and many more, but very few women. The women knew the industry had many great women musicians in it and decided there and then to organize a women's festival in Kansas City.

The New York Times reported on March 16th, 1978:

> *The festival will be a two-day program of clinics, concerts and jam sessions that will include the Mary Lou Williams trio, Marian McPartland's duo, the big band led jointly by Toshiko Akiyoshi and her husband, Lew Tabackin, and two singers, Betty Carter and Marilyn Maye. There will also be a Women's Jazz Festival All-Star group, led by Miss McPartland, that will include Janice Robinson, trombonist; Mary Fettig Park, saxophonist; Mary Osborne, guitarist; Lynn 'Milano', bassist, and Dottie Dodgion, drummer. For Miss Comer and Miss Gregg, the idea of a women's jazz festival was a natural progression of their backgrounds and interests. Miss Comer has been a prominent jazz singer in Kansas City for the last 20 years. Miss Gregg produced jazz programs on KCUR-FM, a Public Radio station, and, in January 1977, she started a weekly program, 'Women in Jazz,' which so far has featured recordings by more than 60 women jazz musicians.*

The festival is still an annual event and there are now many Women's Jazz Festivals around the world including Sydney, Palm Springs and Knoxville.

Yet fast forward to today more than forty years later and however you look at it, the number of women in jazz is still small. Why is that? We can argue the points, think of many reasons why it might be so, but what do women think? Are we missing the point? Could it be women are simply not drawn to jazz music? It is possible. I was driven to find out.

Amy Winehouse photographed by David Sinclair

Do women maybe do themselves a disservice by flirting and trying to remain 'pretty', falling into all the clichés provided by films, adverts and fashion magazines? Does this serve to emphasize their perceived 'faults and weaknesses' to men? Does it help that women players will tell you they model themselves on Ayler, Rollins, Armstrong—all men?

There are women who have brought jazz into the world of pop music in different ways, from Alison Moyet, Lady Gaga (a woman steeped in the jazz of NYC who has collaborated with Tony Bennett and others) and Amy Winehouse, who brought jazz techniques to singing in such beautiful ways and enchanted the world with her voice and stage presence. It seems impossible to be writing about her in the past tense, but Amy had one of the best jazz voices heard for a long time—and people loved it. Amy's influence extended to young jazz singers such as vocalist Indira May who says,

As a young teenager, I got into Amy Winehouse and listened to 'Frank' all the time and that's when I realized that jazz had the potential to be current. Amy reflected what women have always felt and brought it into the present. So I think she was very important to a lot of young women because she was one of the first people to do it in the modern day so truthfully and honestly. She mixed being an outspoken woman with jazz and being expressive. In Gloucestershire (Indira's home) *at that time, there was a massive divide between what boys could do and say and what girls could do and say. I remember swearing at school and one of my teachers saying, 'Oh, don't stoop down to the boys' level,' and kind of feeling like they almost got away with it – being able to express themselves as a teenager. And the girls were always being told to be 'ladylike'. If me and my friend, Hattie, were pissing about, or burping, teachers and adults, would always tell us to be 'ladies'. But Amy wasn't some little mousey character, with a 'perfect' appearance. She was a Jewish girl; she had big facial features. She wore what she wanted; she had tattoos; and she was unapologetic, which I liked.*

Indira May photographed by Penny Nakin

From what musicians, writers, radio show hosts, agents, venue managers and many others tell me, the industry is edging towards change though pockets of resistance persist. There seems to be this real conundrum where women think things are changing while nearly all can give examples of encounters with people who prove that in some areas jazz still needs to correct itself and modernize its attitudes. Race, it seems, is no longer an issue and differences are celebrated as new and different music forms, instruments and musicians are brought into jazz. Women are still on the edge, however. We find them on the threshold of acceptance, but not quite fully there. Though a vital and active part of the music now and of the future also, they remain small in numbers.

One older male musician recently said,

> *Well, they (women) came, they stayed and now we wouldn't be without 'em—women I mean!*

Another said (and see if you can work this one out),

> *I'm glad they (women) are in the music, not that they were ever far from it but yeah, we laughed at them because we felt a bit weird. Now though, the 'guy' reviewing the gig is just as likely to be a woman, and the 'guy' who books me is just as likely to be a woman too! Heck, even the 'guy' who drives me from the airport might just be a woman—sheesh!*

The great reeds player, Peter Brotzmann contributed to my last book and when I told him I was writing a new book—this time on women in jazz he grinned and said,

> *Good, I am glad I can't be in this time as I am definitely not a woman, but it is a good idea all the same.*

I think so too—it is time for women to be heard.

Women of the Past—Major Influencers

WOMEN WERE PART OF BIG BANDS, orchestras and theatre pit bands way before the turn of the last century. They were breaking ground. The first saxophone solo given by a black American in an orchestra was by Elsie Hoffman in 1889 when she played with the *Will Marion Cook Orchestra* in Washington D.C. Though it was not jazz they played (Cook was a student of Dvorak and a specialist in classical music with folk elements), Elsie set a precedent for black female soloists—and she played the saxophone. These seemingly small steps were critical. When jazz became popular, the presence of the few women were bright beacons of light and provided role models and mentors for those following them into the largely misogynist world of jazz. They were inspirational for women whose aspirations went beyond being a decorous addition to a section in a big band. In the meantime, opportunities for early female jazz musicians to record were few and far between. Dolly Hutchinson (an African-American trumpet player) became the first trumpet player to record a jazz record as part of Albert Wynne's *Gut Bucket Five* in 1926. It was not an overwhelming success and she did not record again until 1941 as part of the *Stuff Smith Sextet*.

The 1920s to 1940s saw female jazz bands playing in theatre houses and as part of performing family groups. In Chicago, the *Ingenues* were multi-instrumentalists who played everything from violins, to trombones and accordions; and toured widely. There were other female groups including *The Schuster Sisters Saxophone Quartet, The*

International Sweethearts of Rhythm led by Anna Mae Winburn, *Ivy Benson's Rhythm Girls, The Harlem Playgirls, Lil Hardin's All-Girl Band* and more. Female bands are still popular and today include the Sydney-based *Young Women's Jazz Orchestra, Sherrie Maricle* and *The Diva Jazz Orchestra,* Scheila Gonzalez's group *'Dekajazz'* and the London-based *Quintette.*

There are many important, influential women throughout the history of jazz. Many forged paths for others to follow, proving that to be female did not mean contenting oneself with mere supporting roles. It took strength and will for these women to pursue careers in jazz and play the music they adored. It also took time and a good deal of in-your-face bravado. Along the way, they provided the entertainment world some wonderful colour and different musical directions. They opened doors for others to enter, bringing with them new ways of experiencing music and a whole world of idiosyncrasies which blessed and adorned the music in more or less equal measure. There is only room here for a very few of them.

Bessie Smith by Carl Van Vechten, 1936-02-03

Bessie Smith 1894—1937

Known as 'The Empress of the Blues' Bessie Smith was larger than life and equipped with a powerfully resonant *alto* voice. A blues singer, she influenced many jazz and gospel vocalists as well, including Billie Holiday and Mahalia Jackson. Bessie's voice had a quality that was emotive, yet possessed an undertow of vulnerability. She expanded her held notes in particular, creating a swelling from deep within. Her expressive phrasing influenced jazz singers and instrumentalists alike. Her recordings with Louis Armstrong on trumpet and Fred Longshaw on harmonium in 1925 titled *St Louis Blues* were a highlight of early jazz-blues interpretations, fusing blues with the emergent jazz music beautifully. The achingly emotive expression of her melody is echoed by the trumpet, providing Armstrong a perfect opportunity to showcase his techniques as he echoed and matched her blues inflections—techniques which Armstrong later reversed, using his own voice to imitate instrumental characteristics. He later began to use his gravelly voice like an instrument and became good at 'scatting' as the technique became known.

Bessie began her career as a minstrel and vaudeville singer. She joined a travelling troupe and modelled her early style on singer Ma Rainey, with whom she worked during 1912. That same year, she danced in the chorus line of an Irvin C. Miller show. In 1913, she played in Atlanta's *81 Theatre* and her fame began growing. She had a 'huge' voice, no other word for it; and too big for some. Three record labels turned her down in 1920. She tried for the Black Swan, but they felt she was too rough for their label. Then came Columbia and over a period of around ten years, Bessie Smith recorded approximately 180 songs. The songs encompassed religious, spiritual and blues music with Bessie's voice and delivery imparting them life and deep emotion. The word 'majestic' crops up often when reading about Bessie Smith and it fits her perfectly. Her records sold in huge quantities given they were limited to Columbia's 'Race Records' series which they launched in 1923. She recorded prolifically for the label including the songs, *Poor Man's Blues* and *One and Two Blues*. These 'race records' were 78 *rpms* recorded from the 1920s to the 1940s by Columbia and other labels including Victor Talking Machine Company, Paramount and Emerson. They were marketed initially at African-Americans and were recordings of African-American music including jazz, blues, gospel and some comedy. They provided the largest opportunities for recording in the US at a time when only a handful of African Americans were marketed to the general population. 'Race Music' was an acceptable moniker at the time and designated music with origins in African-American culture. Meanwhile, 'Race Records' provided a recording base for the emerging music genres and white Americans began buying the records also. What set Bessie Smith apart in her presentation and her respect for the music was her use of top quality musicians like Coleman Hawkins, Louis Armstrong to record with her. Another idiosyncrasy—she rarely used drums in her arrangements.

Thanks to musicians like Bessie, influential people like John Hammond, later correspondent, reporter, radio host and record label boss, would go to Harlem and buy recordings as a child and come to love the music, and help in its development. Later when Hammond became a producer for *Okeh* records, he asked Bessie to record for them and produced her alongside a more modern accompaniment with a view of transitioning to swing. Unfortunately, Bessie suffered several tragedies in the 1930s including the loss of her husband and son. Though they maintained their high quality, the number of her recordings dwindled

Interestingly, Bessie Smith, though immensely popular, was largely ignored by the general press until her death in 1937 when some uncomfortable issues were raised. She was touring with a revue when on September 26th her car was involved in an accident. Associated Press released a brief account claiming she had been killed when her car overturned. They also said she had come to fame when she sang in a Beale Street show house and attracted the attention of Eastern theatrical agents which was inaccurate. Other press releases were also misleading—one reporter picking the random figure of 1026 to be the number of recordings she made for Columbia; others claiming she had spent vast amounts of money and saved Columbia Records from collapse and that Gershwin had asked her opinion on the score of *Porgy and Bess*. All this was not proven or probably untrue and it was clear the media actually knew very little about her. John Hammond, as a reporter for *Downbeat*, raised some disturbing issues when he put forward the question of whether Bessie Smith had in fact bled to death while awaiting medical aid and proffered the possibility that she had been a victim of institutional racism and died because of it.

According to Hammond, who apparently got the information from members of Chick Webb's orchestra who arrived on the scene shortly after the crash, Bessie had suffered severe injuries to an arm after the car she had been travelling in, hit a truck. She was attended to after some time by a doctor and then taken by this doctor in another car to a white Memphis hospital. As fate would have it, this car was involved in a second, minor accident on the way to hospital, which delayed her treatment. When she finally arrived at the hospital, she was refused treatment apparently because of her colour. An assessment of these events leads us to believe that she may have died from blood loss while waiting for medical treatment. The car the doctor hit on the way to the hospital, was occupied by a white couple who, according to some witnesses, received prompt medical attention, which supports this conclusion. In his article, Hammond asked Memphis citizens to corroborate or deny the story, given it could have been magnified in the telling. He offered no further proof. Stories persisted and in jazz circles and rumours of racism grew.

Years later, Hammond admitted his story was based largely on hearsay and that he had not checked facts. If Bessie had indeed been refused treatment due to her colour, it would have fueled the antagonism between those who supported segregation and those fighting against it. A second article appeared claiming Bessie had been taken straight to the black hospital in Clarksdale where she died of blood loss. There was no mention of her being refused medical treatment at the white hospital. Her driver, Richard Morgan was in the car with Bessie and survived; but neither he nor the highway patrol men who attended were questioned at the time. As time went on, people began adding to the tale. This includes the doctor who arrived on the scene and attended to Bessie. He said that after his car was hit by another car carrying a white couple, two ambulances were called. One ambulance driver took Bessie to the black hospital and the second took the other couple to the white hospital. Bessie had never been to a white hospital to be refused treatment. Whatever actually happened (and bear in mind the doctor did not was not at the hospital with Bessie as the accident foiled his plan to drive her there), the lack of clarity surrounding Bessie's treatment, brought to surface issues which many had wanted discussed and which Hammond thought important to address.

Whatever controversy her death may have caused and issues it raised, Bessie is seen as an important and influential figure by singers even today. At the time, she was one of the highest paid black entertainers of the time, selling records in formidable quantities.

For all her talent, Bessie Smith was buried in an unmarked grave. It was not until 1970, when a woman from Philadelphia got the support of Juanita Green and Janis Joplin and together, that the three women split the cost of a headstone to finally honour Bessie. Forty-three years after her death, the inscription on her headstone reads, 'The greatest blues singer in the world will never stop singing.'

Billie Holiday 1915-1959

Billie Holiday at the Downbeat club, New York City. circa February 1947 by William P. Gottlieb

Billie Holiday (Eleanora Fagan) had a voice unlike any other. She poured emotions into her songs which the listener could not help but feel viscerally. With Billie you shared the pain, the joy and longing she put into her music. She brought a wholly novel way of phrasing, sliding up and down to notes which seamlessly lent itself to jazz singing—and just about any other kind of singing. Her delivery was unique and unsurpassed. A complex and emotional character—she spent time in jail and had a turbulent life—she could capture the heart when she sang. Her very complexity added to the emotive content of her singing and she had a way of making a single held note almost tell a story on its own.

Billie's mother Sarah, after being evicted from her home in Baltimore for being pregnant and unmarried, went to Philadelphia to live with an aunt. Billie grew up largely in the care of her mother's half-sister's mother-in-law. Besides working as a maid, Billie's mother periodically took work on the railway network, meaning she travelled and was away from home. Billie soon got into trouble due to her mother's long absences and began to truant, earning small change by scrubbing the doorsteps of white people's homes. Her lack of attendance at school resulted in her being sent to the Good Shepherd reform school for nine months in 1925.

A religious woman, Billie's mother took her to mass on Sundays where perhaps Billie was influenced by the soulful melodies she heard in church.

Tragically, aged just eleven years, Billie was the victim of attempted rape. To add cruelty to tragedy, when the case was brought to court, far from being the innocent victim, it was alleged that Billie of eleven years had incited the perpetrator, a neighbour. As punishment the judge sent Billie, the true victim, back to reform school. Billie never returned to ordinary school after her release, but found a job as errand girl at a local brothel where she dispensed towels and soaps for clients. By 1928, her mother had moved to Harlem, New York. Billie joined her in 1929 and together they lived in an apartment on 139th Street. Billie was only fourteen when both she and her mother became prostitutes. The house where they worked was raided and Sarah and Billie were sent to prison, Sarah for three months, Billie for five. Upon her release Billie found a job singing in a pub and the attention she received made her realize her talents lay outside the brothel. She had been hearing music by Bessie Smith and Louis Armstrong and was influenced by these two in her style, the latter having a 'dirty' style of vocalization. Armstrong's tone was rough, his voice impure, but heavily laced with character. Billie's mother became too ill to work and she did not want to be a maid, so Billie was faced with a tough decision if she was not to turn back to the life of prostitution.

Fate took a hand when things came to a head. The rent was overdue and Billie and her mother were faced with imminent eviction. She had to act quickly. Her father, Clarence, had fathered Billie when just sixteen and moved away shortly after her birth to try his luck as a jazz musician. He played guitar and banjo and had made a name for himself playing with leaders like Benny Carter and Don Redmond. Billie learned he was playing with Fletcher Henderson's band at the *Roseland Ballroom* in New York. His lung problems—the result of damage he received after being exposed to mustard gas in WWI—had yet to manifest and he was enjoying the life of a musician and the attention of women. Billie, still a minor but already looking mature, began showing up at the Roseland and asking him for money. He resisted at first but Billie, knowing he did not want his women friends to realize he was old enough to have fathered a woman who looked older than the teenager she was, began pleading loudly and calling him 'Daddy'. This did the trick and money changed hands.

The little money her father gave them wasn't enough however. Eviction soon stared mother and daughter in the face once more. Billie took herself to 133rd Street, which at the time was full of restaurants and cafés. She went into one, after many others, called *Pod's and Jerry's*. Telling the manager she was a dancer, he let her try out and asked the pianist to play. Billie danced the two steps she knew and was so bad she was told to stop. As she was preparing to leave, the pianist asked her, 'Can you sing?' Billie told him she had been singing all her life and asked if could he play *Trav'lin All Alone*? It turned out he could and as Billie sang, the café crowd grew hushed. Billie was hired immediately as one of the café's singers. At the time, it was customary to place money on the floor or on the tables if you enjoyed the act. Singers could come and collect as they sang or take floor money when they finished. Billie collected over thirty dollars from the floor and tables. She split the money with the piano player and for eighteen dollars a week, she joined other singers at the café who sang to clients, going table to table and collecting tips as well as a decent wage. Billie was soon winning the most in tips leading the staff to nickname her 'Duchess'. People realized she was destined for greatness already. She took a professional singing name, formed from the name of an actress she admired and the surname of her father (Halliday) and became Billie Halliday. She later changed her stage surname to Holiday which was her father's stage name. She began to perform at clubs like the *Brooklyn Elk* and the *Bright Spot*. By 1932, she had replaced the vocalist at *Covan's Club* where she was spotted by producer John Hammond. He recorded two songs with her on vocals and 'King of Swing' Benny Goodman on clarinet, which sold well. Hammond was impressed by the lyricism she brought to songs and her skills as an improviser. Billie wasn't paid royalties for these first recordings but with Hammond's support, she won a professional recording contract with *Brunswick* in 1935. She also recorded some pop songs with pianist Teddy Wilson, a musician she would have a long association with. By 1936, Holiday was gaining a reputation as an artist without equal in her field, able to evoke and charge her performance with a vibrancy and emotion never heard before. She also formed an association with Lester Young, a tenor saxophone player who she had known since he boarded at their apartment in 1934. She nicknamed him 'Prez' and he called her 'Lady Day'.

In 1937, Billie joined Count Basie's band. Though she could not record with them for contractual reasons, they did tour and everywhere they went, Billie saw the divided country that was her home. In southern and western USA, she was treated as a second-class citizen. She was not permitted to enter venues by the front door where she herself was starring; and black members of the audience were assigned seats in the balconies. This must have seemed all the more ironic to her given the fact that there had been no colour barriers to clients when she had worked as a prostitute. Meanwhile, what Basie did for Holiday was allow her to choose her own songs and create her own arrangements—a freedom few vocalists at the time enjoyed. Ella Fitzgerald, who sang with the

Chick Webb band was also popular at the time and she and Holiday became friends. At a 'battle of the bands' at the Savoy, *Holiday and the Basie Orchestra* won the vote of the critics and Webb's band with Fitzgerald won the audience's vote. Holiday, however was not easy to work with and apparently got herself fired for being unprofessional and difficult. What Holiday brought to her music was all the experiences she had so far—the rejection, the rape, the blame, the discrimination. Singing was the place to let it all out and share the pain—and she did.

Holiday was then hired by Artie Shaw and became the first black singer to work and tour with a white orchestra. At the time, this was largely unheard of and at some venues in the deep South she was subjected to verbal abuse and requests that she stand separately from other vocalists appearing with the orchestra. Shaw refused this and Holiday's reaction was to give back in kind with verbal abuse of her own, leading to her being escorted from the stage on occasion. Not only was she a black woman singing with a predominantly white orchestra, but she refused to take abuse quietly. Shaw hired a second singer (who was white) and eventually Holiday left, but not before her vocal prowess had been recognized by radio stations and recording companies. Holiday was now a star, though she was still asked to use service elevators and facilities separate to those of the white members of the band.

A place where black and white people mixed together without barriers was Harlem in New York City. Here was where Billie found her musical home, a place to which she returned again and again.

In 1939, *Café Society* in Greenwich Village, NY was the first interracial jazz club. It was known as 'The Wrong Place for the Right People', a motto given to it by founder Barney Josephson, who wanted a club where all races worked together behind the footlights and sat together out front. Barney heard a song based on a poem by Lewis Allan (actually named Abel Meeropol) which graphically conjured up images of the lynching and burning of black people in the deep south. Holiday heard it and this poem, *Strange Fruit* reminded her, apparently of the death of her father who, having developed chronic lung problems due to his earlier exposure to mustard gas in WWI, was refused treatment initially because of his colour. Meeropol had put the song to music and, with his wife and singer Laura Duncan, performed it as a protest song. Holiday was initially unsure about performing the song as it was evidently going to be controversial; but when she sang it, adding texture and layers of emotion natural in her voice, the effect was instant. This song, above any other, became synonymous with Holiday. Her delivery made a simple melody intense and emotional. She worked the lyrics to huge effects, particularly her 'bitter' which she gave added emphasis and meaning to. The song was set in the key of B flat minor, which adds a haunting, slightly other-worldly quality. It also ends on an F with Holiday singing 'crop', the final letter almost spat out, leaving a sense of the unfinished—an effect used dramatically in Holiday's performances when the lights would go out, then come back on to reveal just a spotlight where the singer had vanished.

Holiday's version of the song was brave, dangerous and controversial. It was written about deep-seated issues and even Holiday was fearful of the backlash that might come from recording it. However, she knew when she sang it that people stopped stock still. They listened; they stared; there was silence followed by thunderous applause. Holiday's version of the song became so strongly associated with her that no one has come close to putting their own stamp on it since, though many have tried. The lyrics spoke of injustice, atrocities committed upon human beings. They were shocking. Few had dared voice the sentiments of the song. But someone dared—Holiday dared.

> *Southern trees bear strange fruit*
> *Blood on the leaves and blood at the root*
> *Black bodies swinging in the southern breeze*
> *Strange fruit hanging from the poplar trees...*
> *For the sun to rot, for the trees to drop -*
> *Here is a strange and bitter crop*

That a black woman sang it caused criticism from some quarters and admiration from others. It was banned by many US radio stations and the BBC in London. Holiday sang with such emotion that people began to see the original performance as a watershed for the civil rights movement. To record it, she had to go to a small label, *Commodore*. *Columbia*, her label at the time, would not touch it. Billie Holiday was using her rising profile to speak out.

Now a star, Billie left the residency at *Café Society*. She demanded more money from her manager and her mother, now the parent of a successful singer, borrowed and lost a lot of it—something Billie knew little of until she herself needed money and her mother could not give her any. She and Billie fell out and Holiday, moved deeply by the betrayal, wrote *God Bless The Child* with pianist Arthur Herzog, the biggest hit of her career.

She recorded with *Capitol* in 1942 under the name 'Lady Day' to avoid contractual conflicts with *Columbia* and in 1944, moved to Decca. She recorded another of her huge hits *Lover Man* during this time. Several more hits followed, including *Don't Explain* which she wrote after catching her husband having an affair.

In 1946, she began filming for her first and only major film 'New Orleans' opposite Louis Armstrong and Herman Wood. Again, racism raised its ugly head and several scenes featuring her and Armstrong were cut because the film company did not want people to think black people had invented jazz music. She recorded some of the songs for the film including *Goodbye to Storyville* (Storyville being the red light district of New Orleans). Holiday was apparently shocked at the amount of filming they did and the subsequent cuts. Her role in the end seemed only a minor one. However, pleasing the critics was not the studio's only worry. Holiday's addiction to drugs was also becoming a problem on set.

Over the course of her career, Billie had transformed herself from call girl turning tricks into an icon. She recorded both jazz and pop music and took her unique sense of style and lyric interpretation to a wide audience. She took a lot on the chin on her way up, from the segregation issues which flew in the face of her being the star performer to having to wear black make up by some venues because audiences, who were mostly white, expected jazz performers to have dark skin. She recorded with Columbia and Decca and by 1943 she was one of the 'Big Three' (the others being Art Tatum and Coleman Hawkins) who drew large crowds on *The Street*—the name by which 52nd Street was known to musicians who worked on the thriving jazz scene there. 52nd Street became the heart of the bebop scene.

Privately, however, Billie battled an addiction to heroin. It had been made illegal in 1914 and Holiday found herself targeted by the narcotics police. She was arrested for possession and served a year in prison from 1947-1948. She played to a sold-out Carnegie Hall upon her release. She sang twenty-one numbers and took six encores despite having fainted just before the concert and having sustained a head wound from the fall. Her drug problems continued and she also had legal problems dogging her. She had made some foolish business decisions which meant she received very little in the way of royalties from her recordings pre-Decca days even though those records were still selling.

By 1947 she had lost her cabaret card which meant she was effectively blacklisted by many venues. She could no longer legally work where alcohol was sold. These venues paid higher fees. Those without alcohol licenses could offer lower fees because they knew the artists had fewer places to choose from to play. All the same, Billie played the *Ebony Club* illegally and no conviction followed. She repeated her Carnegie Hall appearance in 1956, but it was a different concert this time—one peppered with Gilbert Millstein reading from her autobiography. It had a disconnected feel and she punctuated her songs with narrative about her life. She was in danger of becoming the focus of everyone who had been victimized as her act and emotional state became entwined. She was addicted; her reputation was suffering and she had damaging relationships. Eventually her problems began to affect the thing she valued above all else—her voice. She once told a *Downbeat* magazine interviewer that no one had made as many mistakes as she had. She was arrested again in 1949. In the same year she recorded her second-best seller, *Crazy, He Calls Me*. However, her airplay began to fall off and bookings became more difficult. Her colour, addiction and unreliability began to take their toll.

In 1954, Billie Holiday toured Europe with Buddy DeFranco, Sonny Clark, Red Mitchell and several other acts in the Jazz Club USA tour, initiated by Nils Hellstrom. She switched to the *Verve* label—the same label as Ella Fitzgerald—and made several popular recordings with the label though her voice had already begun to lose its vibrancy, if not its edge. Even though her health was failing and her body frail by the late 1950s, she transformed when she sang, still flooding her songs with emotion. She made her final recordings for MGM records and returned to Europe one last time in early 1959.

In May 1959, she was taken to hospital with cirrhosis. There she was again arrested for drug use and cuffed to her hospital bed just days before she died. She was only forty-four years old. She died with just a few hundred dollars to her name, even though she had transformed the fortunes of several record labels and earned a lot of money over her life time. She left over 300 songs that influenced American culture. *Strange Fruit* became the sound track for the civil rights movement and her example of a woman using her power to protest opened the doors to others who followed.

Today Billie Holiday is widely recognized as one of the greatest jazz singers of all time and cited as an influence on many vocalists including Amy Winehouse and Frank Sinatra. *Esquire Magazine* gave her several awards while she was alive and four *Grammy Awards* were awarded after her death, as well as posthumous inductions into the *Grammy Hall of Fame*, the *Ertegun Jazz Hall of Fame*, the *Rock and Roll Hall of Fame* and the *ASCAP Jazz Wall of Fame*. A true legend, she has become even more enigmatic in death, with several films and documentaries attempting to chart her unconventional and disparate life. In spite of being influenced by several other singers, she distilled piquant elements into her own unique delivery. With an innate ability for interpretation, she not only sang a song, she *was* the song, her style a blend of vulnerability, innocence, sexuality and heart-wrenching pathos. Billie Holiday had a life which was chaotic, dramatic and challenging yet she left memories of a voice and lyrical interpretations without equal.

The International Sweethearts of Rhythm

Not one woman, but a whole band of women—*The International Sweethearts of Rhythm* were massively successful in the 1940s and broke more glass ceilings than most. Mixed race, mixed sexual orientations, all female, young and amazing musicians—and not all painted dollies either.

They began in 1938 in Piney Woods Country Life School in Jackson, Mississippi where Laurence C. Jones was principal. Piney Woods was a school for black children, mainly orphans, and there were thousands of them. Mr. Jones made sure all the children learned a trade and secured funding from local businesses. He wanted to find ways of raising more money, always in short supply, to support the children. One of the key areas in the school was music. The school had marching bands and several other musical groups. It was the swing era and many big bands like those of Ellington, Arty Shaw, Benny Goodman and Glenn Miller were hugely popular. All girl bands began to sprout up to like that of *Ina Ray Hutton and Her Melodears, The Ingenues, Ivy Benson and Her All Girl Orchestra* (UK). Mr Jones thought this was a splendid idea after hearing Ina Ray and her band in Chicago and created *The Piney Woods All Girl Jazz Band* to raise funds for the school. Early members of the band included Helen Jones on trombone and Pauline Braddy on drums. Initially they played at local events only. Soon, they became well-known and their reputation spread. Mr. Jones sometimes recruited talent while the band was on tour. He spotted Grace and Judy Bayron on saxophone in Harlem on such an occasion, whom he invited to Piney School where they learned and played. The girls, though young, proved a hit and made funds for the school. They were looked after and, because it proved impossible to book hotels for a mixed-race group, the tour bus was modified to hold bunk beds.

However, touring proved a hard and strict life with very little downtime. The girls found it tough. Their polished, professional look on stage belied the tiring, long and lonely trips between shows. There were sixteen girls—and they were girls—at around fifteen or sixteen years of age, from various backgrounds and ethnicities working hard as fundraisers for two years. Then, promoter Daniel M. Gary from Washington D.C. began to act as booking agent for the band and got them bookings across the US.

With their success came difficulties. The girls began to question Mr. Jones on financial and other matters. He in turn felt he was losing control and demanded they return to Piney Woods or they would not get their high school diplomas. They refused and Mr. Jones had their chaperone arrested, accusing her of instigating the theft of the bus, clothes and instruments the girls had been given by the school. Dan Gary sorted everything out and the school's possessions were returned while the girls continued touring under Mr Gary's direction—with new equipment.

A huge attraction and an integral part of the *Sweethearts* was Ernestine 'Tiny' Davis on trumpet and vocals. 'Tiny' was well rounded and billed as '245 pounds of solid jive and rhythm'. She had a comedic presence on stage and her timing was perfect. A star of the band, her playing style was strong and lyrical. The group opened and closed the shows at the *Apollo Theatre* in Harlem and often pulled in more audience than the stars. The band was different—it was integrated, with members coming from various ethnic backgrounds.

Membership in the band was fluid and several members came and went over the years, due to marriages, personal events and one or two of them not wishing to travel with the band when they turned professional. The stalwarts included Helen Jones and Ina Belle Byrd on trombone, Willie Mae Lee Wong on baritone sax, Pauline Braddy on drums, Edna Williams and 'Tiny' Davis on trumpets and vocals, and Johnnie Mae Rice on piano. Anna Mae Winburn was brought in as conductor and vocalist. She had previously led an all-male band called *The Cotton Club Boys*, but resigned from there and led *The International Sweethearts*. Anna Mae was extraordinarily beautiful and dressed in chic, fashionable gowns while her band wore black skirts and jackets with white blouses and a flower in their hair. It was a tight, smooth operation and organized with a keen eye on presentation by their manager Rae Lee Jones.

Several people who joined the band went on to successful careers thanks in part to their experience and stint in the band. These include vocalist Evelyn McGee, and saxophone player Rosalind Cron to name just a couple.

The theaters the band played in catered mostly to black audiences. Few white people ever saw *The International Sweethearts* play. When they went overseas to entertain the American troops during the war, they played to segregated black soldiers. Soon however, a smattering of white faces eager to see the band began appearing in the audiences. Such was their reputation. One such face was that of the ever-supportive producer John Hammond. He thought highly of the band, as did pianist and band leader Earl Hines. Some people felt they could never be as good as a male band and even their own director, Maurice King commented, "You could put those girls behind a curtain and people would be convinced it was men playing," perhaps revealing more of the attitudes of the time than he realized.

A ten-bedroom house was bought and the girls were given a base in Arlington, Virginia where they could rehearse comfortably. They believed they were headed for the big time. Anna Mae's beauty and presence became part of the reason for the band's continued rise. The band played all over the US and were hugely popular. From the initial fifteen dollars a week the band was making, the girls were now earning as much as fifteen dollars a day *each* by the end of the 1940s—heady days indeed.

With bookings now in major theaters, they had to expand their repertoire and Eddie Durham—an arranger and composer—was hired to do just that. He wrote parts for the band members who loved improvising, allowing them to reach further as well as developing the skills of several band members.

Playing on the audience's belief that girls could never play as well as men, Durham used to pretend he was playing guitar when the curtain opened and then stopped to let people see that it was actually the girls doing the playing. Through his careful arrangements, which leveraged the strengths of each musician, while hiding some of their technical limitations, the girls grew stronger musically and bookings were regular and often to packed halls.

Some things never change however; and no matter how successful they were, the girls often had to eat in poorly run restaurants, sometimes even having their food handed to them through a back window. Even the white members of the band suffered if they stayed at the same hotels as the other members of the band. On stage, harassment came from two sides, first because they were a mixed-race band and then because they were all female. In some places, the white and mixed-race members used dark make up and wigs and their chaperone used false documents to state the girls were Negro. Police used to harass and intimidate the band in some venues. Once when Anna Mae tripped and fell by the stage. An audience member rose to help while a policeman stepped in and stopped him.

The band hired Jesse Stone as manager and with the hire, came changes in personnel. Stone brought on Marjorie Pettiford and Amy Garrison on saxophones, Lucille Dixon on bass and Johnnie Mae Stansbury on trumpet. These high calibre musicians helped take the band to new musical heights. Stone also used some of the band members to create a singing group which proved a hit with audiences.

Their success grew and band members realized they were not getting paid what they were worth. Egged on by Stone they began arguing with Mrs. Rae Jones their chaperone. They should be earning more and accused her of taking advantage of them. Rae Jones had become trustee when the girls left Piney Woods and it was her name on the deeds of the large house they had bought in Arlington. Jesse Stone left at the end of his two-year contract, refusing, ostensibly, to sit and watch while the girls were exploited. Some of the band members left also, several to join Eddie Durham's own outfit in 1943—his *All-Star Girl Orchestra*.

Incidentally, Eddie Durham's *All-Star Girl Orchestra* had stellar players including Lela Julius and Sammy Lee Jett on trombone, Flo Jones and Edna Williams on trumpet and Alma Cortez, Ellarize Thompson and Margaret Buckstrum on saxophones. They performed during the 1940s, but were disbanded when the war ended because organizers now wanted to give men the work. Durham however returned to New York and trained the singer Jean Parks to take over fronting the *All*

Stars and the band became re-banded as *Jean Parks All Girl Band.* They did theatre tours with Ella Fitzgerald, Moms Mably and Butterbeans and Susie until Jean Parks fell ill and the band disbanded.

By 1944, there were more all-girl bands and orchestras and the *Sweethearts* were becoming less enthusiastic about the life they were leading. Roz Cron joined the band, leaving Ada Leonard's band to do so. Shortly afterwards Maurice King joined them as manager. He proved to be tough and a stickler for rehearsing and getting everything perfect. They now had competition and needed to be even better. He wrote numbers for the band and their musical game rose another notch.

Although there had been all female groups before, the *International Sweethearts of Rhythm* were the first female band to compete on level field with bands led by Count Basie, Fletcher Henderson and others. King proved inspirational and an expert teacher. The band included several excellent solo players like Vi Burnside on tenor sax, Ray Carter on trumpet and still the stellar drummer, Pauline Braddy, whose collaboration with bass player Margaret 'Trump' Gibson meant the *Sweethearts* had a solid and reliable rhythm section.

They went to Europe to entertain GIs in 1945 and audiences relished their free and happy take on music. The band made radio recordings while in Europe, which were enjoyed both by the troops and those back in the US. Maurice King was now chaperone for the trip and he found it difficult to control the young women, who regularly took off into the night clubs after curfew. The band members were given the choice of having King act as their finance manager as well. Those that opted for King found they had money in the bank when they returned to America.

Then Leonard Feather came into the band's sphere. He was a recording producer and had long supported all-girl bands. He got the girls to record for RCA Victor and Guild Records. They also appeared in a short film called, *That Man of Mine* and several other films.

From then on, the band became more fluid. Musicians came and went;

some of the originals got married and others returned home. Billboard magazine reviewed them, and though they received ever higher praise, they were no longer the original band of girls who had left Piney Wood all those years ago. In 1948 Helen Jones, the adopted daughter of Mr Jones who had begun the band's journey and the only member who had left her money to be looked after by Rae Jones, found it had vanished, spent by Rae Jones on a house for her parents and the rest frittered away. In spite of this supreme mismanagement, Helen was pragmatic, stating simply that lessons were learned. The band stopped playing after Rae Jones died in 1948.

Interestingly, the *Sweethearts'* music became popular again in the 1960s and 1970s when historians of jazz decided to write more about them. Although the band disbanded, they did not all stop playing jazz and in 1980, nine original members reunited to play at the *Kansas City Women's Jazz Festival*, including pianist Johnnie Rice, saxophone player Willie Mae Wong Scott and trumpet player Clora Bryant—who had enjoyed her own superb career. This reunion was instigated by pianist Marian McPartland. *The International Sweethearts of Rhythm* were important and their public performances critical. Through them, audiences got used to seeing women playing instruments incredibly well. They got used to seeing women out-compete men. They saw mixed-race bands performing together as equals and that gender was no restraint to achieving international fame. *The Sweethearts* proved all that.

Hazel Scott 1920-1981

Hazel Scott was a Trinidadian-born musician who came to the U.S.A. at age four with her mother and grandmother. American life was hard and upon arrival Hazel, suffered bullying and violence, including one incident where she was pushed into a deep trench and another where the family home was broken into, money demanded and Hazel beaten up. Her mother, Alma worked initially as a maid but soon decided to return to the music she had been part of in Trinidad—jazz.

Alma taught herself the saxophone, and eventually joined Lil Hardin Armstrong's orchestra in the early 1930s. Alma's association with the band made the Scott household a mecca for musicians and both Alma and Hazel benefited from the guidance and tutelage of jazz greats Art Tatum, Lester Young and Fats Waller, all of whom she considered to be like family. As a young child, it was completely normal for Hazel to be lounging with Fats Waller while he showed her syncopation on the piano, listen to Lester Young or chat with Billie Holiday who, just five years her senior, came to be like an older sister. Hazel fondly remembers a piece of advice Billie gave her after Hazel got upset once. 'Never let them see you cry,' she said.

Hazel was something of a child prodigy. She learned music very easily and had a wonderful ear. Still a child, she began playing piano at dance classes and churches. Then at just eight years old, an event happened which helped shape Hazel's future. She was playing Rachmaninoff's *Prelude in C Sharp Major* substituting the 9ths for 6ths. Listening was the founder of the *Juilliard School* in New York, Walter Damrisch. He was outraged at the substitution

Hazel Scott. 14 March 1956, by James Kriegsmann

initially, but then realized the child was transposing the intervals because her hands were too small to make the 9ths. No one had taught her how to substitute successful interchanges. He realized she was a genius and immediately offered her a special scholarship at Juilliard. Too young for a standard scholarship (which one had to be sixteen to be awarded) her special scholarship meant she was to be taught personally by the school's assistant dean, Oscar Wagner, a well-known jazz teacher and academic. By thirteen, she had joined her mother's jazz band, *Alma*

Long Scott's American Creolians and was given a spot playing piano at the *Roseland Ballroom*, playing after the *Count Basie Orchestra* finished. She instigated her own boogie-woogie style and proved a popular and engaging pianist.

While her scholarship to the Juilliard educated Hazel in techniques, much of her musical education came from the jazz musicians who visited her home. By the time she was sixteen, she had performed on the radio and was the featured vocalist and pianist in many jazz bands.

At that time (1936) most jazz clubs were segregated. Even the *Cotton Club* where Duke Ellington and Cab Calloway headlined was segregated and it was still rare for blacks and whites to share the stage. There were exceptions, notably *Café Society* in Sheridan Square, New York. Billie Holiday, a headline act at the club, got Scott her first steady engagement at the age of nineteen. After Holiday left, Scott became the club's headline act. Her great piano playing, along with her sultry voice, made her a popular and enduring entertainer. She was also beautiful.

The club became very popular, so much so that a second *Café Society* opened in an uptown neighborhood where Scott became a regular performer. The wife of the then president, Eleanor Roosevelt was so moved by Scott's performance when she visited the club that she asked to meet Hazel after the show. Scott was still only twenty-two.

Adam Clayton Powell, the city's first African American congress candidate also took special notice of her during a performance. He begged an introduction and romance blossomed. Adam was in fact married to singer Isabel Washington and he and Scott made few attempts to hide their affair. In 1945, eleven days after divorcing Isabel, Powell married Scott. Married, Hazel dipped out of the limelight to concentrate on being the wife of a politician and mother to their son. She did, however play concert halls and toured when her husband was away on political business and remained popular. She was offered a fifteen minute regular TV slot—*The Hazel Scott Show* on DuMont

Television Network. She was the first black woman to have her own show. It featured acts from all musical genres including, of course Scott herself and jazz music. Scott had transcended the young, uber-talented beauty to become a mature, highly-respected jazz musician of stature.

Then everything changed for Hazel Scott when her name appeared on a list of 151 people in the TV and Radio industries who were suspected of being communist sympathizers in the McCarthy era in 1947. The list—called 'The Red Channels: The Report of Communist Influence on Radio and Television' was unofficial and drawn up by *Counterattack*, a right-wing journal. It named actors, broadcasters, writers and musicians who, according to its sources, held communist sympathies and were manipulating the entertainment industry towards communist objectives. Some of those named were already being denied employment because of their political beliefs, history, or association with suspected subversives and the publication effectively placed the rest of them on the industry blacklist. Unofficial but extremely influential, it resulted in Scott appearing before the House on Un-American Activities Committee. Many were called to appear before the committee, refusal or dismissal of the call being seen as an admission of guilt.

That she was on the list perhaps came as no surprise. Scott had long developed a keen sense of justice and supported causes for racial equality. She had refused to play halls where they segregated the audience. 'Why would people come to see me, a black woman play and then not want to sit next to someone just like me?' she is remembered saying. There is a story of her being escorted from a town in Texas when she refused to play after arriving at the hall to find the audience segregated. She was offered film roles, but because she refused to wear a maid's costume or take parts which portrayed black people in an inferior role, her film career was short-lived. In her final film, she insisted the cast be given more appropriate clothes to replace the dirty aprons they were issued for a scene in which the women were seeing their men off to war. Her argument that people would not wear dirty aprons initially went ignored by direction so the cast—mostly black actors—went on strike for three days with Hazel refusing to budge on the issue. Eventually the film makers—*Columbia*—gave in. Her film career would be limited from then on with only tiny roles being offered. To add to her list of communist crimes Scott, of course, had played regularly at *Café Society*—a place where it was long suspected communist sympathizers met. She had also recently won a lawsuit against the owners of a restaurant who had refused to serve Scott and her friend because they were black. Scott won her case, empowering other African-Americans to challenge racial discrimination and inspiring civil rights organizations to continue pushing for equality in public places. It wasn't Scott's victory alone, but a victory for civil rights as well.

Just one year later after publication of the *Red Channels* that same victorious woman stood in front of the House on Un-American Activities Committee hoping to clear her name. Scott was neither a communist nor a member of the communist party and she appeared before the committee voluntarily, against her husband's wishes, as she felt it was important to redress the damage caused by the Red Channels. She believed the publication was partly responsible for the flood of paranoia sweeping across the United States and felt a responsibility to try and stem this, as well as achieve her own exoneration. She testified before the committee, warning them of the profiteers in patriotism and the danger of allowing people to be pointed out as communists simply for having particular views. She pointed out that artists were part of an important group of people and there was a danger that they would be become people who felt wronged and whose creative value was destroyed. She not only vindicated herself, but requested the committee put measures in place to protect people against false accusations. Her actions were applauded by the entertainment community, but her career was doomed. After just a few months her show was cancelled and concert bookings fell away. Her marriage fell apart next and Scott, like so many others during that period, left America.

She went to Paris, and there she found other American entertainers who had left America also. Scott's apartment became a focal meeting point for American entertainers now living there including Lester Young, Mary Lou Williams, Dizzy Gillespie, and Max Roach as well as musicians from the Ellington and Basie bands. On a brief return to America she recorded with Charles Mingus and Max Roach, *Relaxed Piano Moods* (Debut 1955), now regarded as one of jazz's most important recordings and recently inducted into National Public Radio's *Basic Jazz Record Library*. She remarried in 1961.

Ten years after leaving America, Scott returned to find a hugely changed entertainment industry. Rock and roll, rhythm and blues and other new music had replaced jazz in many venues. She continued to perform to a loyal fan base and to explore new ways of playing. She was also signed for some television work, but her career was nothing like it had been before. Hazel Scott died in 1981, leaving a legacy of important changes in both the music and the lives of many people, and a TV show that provides hope for Afro-American entertainers and women. She fought for civil rights and was never persuaded to keep quiet for the sake of maintaining the status quo, even when it meant jeopardizing her own career. A true hero, she was brave enough to use her position as a lauded entertainer to stand up for the rights of those who had less power.

Maxine Sullivan 1911-1987

Maxine Sullivan was a woman with huge talent and a smooth, sensual voice imbued with a richness of tone which few could emulate. Her uncle led a local band called the *Red Hot Peppers* in her home town of Homestead, and Maxine worked radio shows and local concerts with him, singing and playing piano. She became a singer at the local speakeasy, nicknamed the *Benjamin Harrison Literary Club*. One evening, Gladys Mosier, a member of *Ina Rae Hutton's Big Band* dropped in and saw Maxine perform. Entranced by this young woman's smooth, beautiful voice, she arranged a recording session at the *Onyx Club* in New York and introduced Maxine to the pianist Claude Thornhill. Maxine soon found herself hired by the *Onyx* and recording with *Thornhill and his All*

Star Band from 1937-41. Still Marietta Williams, she became the band's star and only then began going by the name of Maxine Sullivan. At the *Onyx*, she met and formed a partnership with John Kirby, a bass player of some renown who had recorded with Teddy Wilson, Lionel Hampton and Fletcher Henderson. The partnership turned into a romance and Kirby became Maxine's second husband. In August 1937, he and Maxine recorded, with Thornhill on piano. In 1939, she was in a film, *Swingin' the Dream*—a swing version of *Midsummer Night's Dream*—cast in the role of Titiana,

Maxine Sullivan. April 19, 1938

Queen of the Fairies. She also sung on the title track of the 1939 film *St Louis Blues* and her recording of the Scottish folk song *Loch Lomond* captivated hearts. Not a new song, it had been recorded before and also performed live in 1938 by the *Benny Goodman Band* at Carnegie Hall; but Maxine was ideal for the song with her pitch-perfect delivery and the crisp sweetness with which her voice was blessed. Recorded in 1940 and released by John Kirby and his orchestra, Maxine's voice proved absolutely suited to the jazz/swing version of the Scottish folk song and it sealed her stardom. The track's success also type-cast Maxine as a 'swing' vocalist, so much so it meant she rarely recorded other styles, even though she had a broad range. Proof of this can be found on her later LP titled *Maxine Sullivan, 1950s* where she was described on the cover as *Swingin' Miss Loch Lomond*. Maxine's voice created a sense of intimacy with its soft, persuasive tones and hits followed including *Blue Skies, St Louis Blues, Nice Work If You Can Get It, Meet Me Where They Play The Blues* (with Jack Teagarden), *Skylark* and *Annie Laurie*. She stole the show at a Gershwin memorial concert in 1938 with *Summertime* sung in her own inimitable manner, assuring her place as one of jazz's great vocalists. She landed a film part opposite Louis Armstrong in *Going Places* and by 1940, Maxine had appeared on the cover of *Life Magazine* and was known as 'The Pint Sized Songstress'.

In 1940-1941 Maxine Sullivan and John Kirby became the first black hosts of a weekly radio series, *Flow Gently Sweet Rhythm* establishing a landmark for black, female presenters of musical entertainment. In 1941, she toured with the *Betty Carter Orchestra*. She then took a few years off music before returning with long running residencies at clubs including *Le Ruban Bleu, Village Vanguard* and *Penthouse*. Later in the 1940s Maxine, then divorced from John, recorded with Teddy Wilson, Benny Caret and other big bands. The next few years were quieter with just a couple of recordings with Bob Haggart and Ellis Larkins (songs very different from *Loch Lomond* in an effort to break her stereotypical casting). She toured the UK in 1948 and had a spell on the CBS television show called *Uptown Jubilee.* Then in the 1950s, Maxine came back big time recording tracks with Dick Hyman, Buster Bailey and other musicians. She took to the stage again in a 1953 production called *Take A Giant Step* and in 1954, toured the UK again. In 1956, she recorded *A Tribute to Andy Razaf* for Perio Records which featured raunchy, blue-based songs quite different from the sweet, smooth style that people associated her with. Songs included Fats Waller tunes, *Stompin' at The Savoy* and *Ain't Misbehavin* and featured a sextet which included some of John Kirby's musicians—Charlie Shavers on trumpet and Buster Bailey on clarinet.

Maxine also re-acquainted herself with the valve trombone, flugelhorn and pocket trumpet. Clifford Jordon, her husband at the time (she had four) bought her a valve trombone because Maxine had decided to play something big and brassy, but also wanted something small. The flugelhorn and pocket trumpet were ideal. She had learned them all when she played in her uncle's band and after some re-acquainting, she played these at several festivals before turning to nursing as her chosen profession in 1958.

She married stride pianist Cliff Jackson (who had played with Chick Webb) her fourth husband in 1966 and returned to music, playing several festivals. She performed occasionally until 1968, playing with the likes of Bob Wilder, Scott Hamilton, Doc Cheatham and performing with Dick Gibson's *The World's Greatest Jazz Band*. In 1970 a recording with Earl Hines entitled *Live at The Overseas Press Club* was released on *Chiaroscuro Records*. She performed in France and Sweden many times between 1975 and 1984. Her last recorded concert was *The Fujitsu-Concord Jazz Festival* held in Tokyo in September of 1986, aged seventy-five and just eight months before she died. Her final recording was the same as her first—*Loch Lomond*. She received three *Grammy* and one *Tony* award nominations and in 1998, was posthumously inducted into the *Big Band* and *Jazz Halls of Fame*.

Maxine is considered one of the best jazz vocalists and inspiration to many women. She played several instruments, none of them 'feminine' apart from the piano. She proved women could be successful presenters on radio and performed into her seventies.

Sarah Vaughan 1924—1990

Sarah Vaughan, along with Ella Fitzgerald, dominated mainstream jazz in the 1940s and 1950s. Born to a religious family, she grew up in Newark where her parents were active in the local Baptist church. Sarah had piano lessons from age seven, sang in the church choir and loved listening to records and piano. Her inspirations were popular singer and actress Rosemary Clooney and singer Marian Anderson— who was an important civil rights figure in the 1930s and the first black woman to sing at the Metropolitan Opera. Sarah went to Newark Arts School, but left to concentrate on her music, which she was already performing in clubs. The story goes that her friend, Dora Robinson, entered a competition as a singer at the *Apollo Theatre* amateur night. Sarah accompanied her on piano. The prize was a week's booking at the theatre. Dora came second but Sarah went back as a singer and tried herself and won. She performed for an hour to an enchanted audience. In November 1942, at just 18 years old, she had a week's work opening for Ella Fitzgerald.

Sarah Vaughan. Photography by Gerard Rouy.

During this time, Billy Eckstine heard her and told fellow bandleader Earl Hines about Sarah's voice. Earl gave her a place in his band as second pianist and singer in 1943, replacing his first singer with Sarah shortly afterwards. She was just nineteen. Eckstine and Hines formed a friendship and became like fathers to the young singer. Sarah was encouraged by other band members and proved herself a talented pianist. She eventually left the *Earl Hines Band* to play piano in *Billy Eckstine's Band*. Marvin 'Doc' Holladay—clarinet and saxophone player who played with Ellington, Basie, Cannon Ball Adderly and Billy Eckstine told me recently from his home in Ecuador, that it was Billy Eckstine who realized his pianist was being wasted where she was because, while she was a decent pianist, her voice was truly amazing. Eckstine decided to hire another piano player for his band so she and he could sing together. They went on to become world famous as a duo, recording numerous songs and performing together. Sarah was increasingly influenced by the musicians in Eckstine's band—musicians like Dizzy Gillespie and Charlie Parker—and wanted to capture the horns' sounds in her singing. Her *contralto* voice with a range of more than three octaves was incredible and she could scat like a demon. When the big band performed, she and Dizzy would dance.

Sarah won a recording contract with *Continental*, then *Musicraft* and decided after a short time, to work as a solo artist. Still largely unknown by the general public, she won a recording contract with *Columbia*.

Dave Garroway, anchor for NBC and a television personality sang her praises and helped bring her to the attention of the public. Her unofficial fan club, already some several hundred strong, expanded exponentially as her fame grew and she became a star.

She realized the value placed on looking good and transformed herself, with the aid of good clothing and exquisite make up, into a stunning vision in *haute couture*. The slightly gawky singer she was in her youth when she played with the big bands had come a long way. Her voice was superb and she gained the affectionate nickname 'Sassy' for her temperament while the media dubbed her 'The Divine One' because of her vocal range and control.

She married her manager George Treadwell in 1947 and this partnership saw Sarah's career take off, largely due to Treadwell's managerial skills combined with her prodigious talent. Sarah also had the loyalty of people such as John Garry and Modina Davis who managed her affairs, leaving Sarah with just one responsibility—to sing.

By 1957, she was signed to *Mercury-EmArcy* and recorded pop music for *Mercury* and jazz for *EmArcy*, allowing her to straddle both camps. Sarah never stopped listening to other performers and loved musicians including The Modern Jazz Quartet, Mahalia Jackson, Ella Fitzgerald and Billie Holiday.

Sarah Vaughan was never completely satisfied with what she had achieved, especially in terms of her spirituality. She believed one of the keys to singing was to put one's soul into it. She never forgot her childhood singing with the Baptist church choir and even late in her life, she returned to join the choir from time to time. She gained a huge and loyal following. Her church choir background and soul influences resulted in her singing being infused with emotion and soul. As she matured, she began to influence other jazz singers and developed her unique style. As a jazz singer, with a foot in the world of popular music, she remains a singer many modern vocalists admire. Today, she is remembered as one of the key jazz vocalists, delivering soulful, powerful vocal lines and as a musician who concentrated on the musical delivery. Sarah Vaughan has proved an inspiration to many who followed in her footsteps and paved their own paths.

Ella Fitzgerald 1917—1996

Ella Fitzgerald—or simply 'Ella' has been called the 'Queen of Jazz'. It is a title well-earned. She was a huge character and took part in many projects, from orchestras and massive shows, to theatre projects. Her overriding gift though,

Ella Fitzgerald. Photography by Gerard Rouy

was unquestionably her voice. For many, Ella sums up all that is jazz. In her trademark songs like *Little Girl Blue,* Ella demonstrates her gift for storytelling in songs, along with her wonderful vocal athleticism and prefect tonality—an imprint on every song she sang.

Ella was born in Newport News, Virginia in 1917. She did not know her father and grew up with her mother and step-father in Yonkers, New York. She loved dancing and bunking off school to watch singer Dolly Dawn with the *George Hall Orchestra*. She danced on street corners for tips. Her favourite singer was Conee Boswell, who she listened to on the radio. She regularly skipped school and had various jobs including, lookout for a bordello and runner for a Mafia operation. After being placed in the *Colored Orphan Asylum* in the Bronx, she was moved to the *New York Training School for Girls*, a reform school in Hudson, before running away and living around 7th Avenue where dancers, novelty acts and jugglers hung out. She earned tips and got by as best she could, but the stage beckoned.

Initially Ella wanted to become a dancer. She and her friend Charles Gulliver would go to the *Savoy Ballroom* in Harlem to pick up the latest steps. They used to get dance jobs around Yonkers in small clubs. However, when the *Apollo Theatre* held a talent competition, billed as 'Amateur Night', Ella decided to sing and won. In the audience happened to be musician and band leader Benny Carter, who introduced her to John Hammond. Carter's band at the time was house band for an NBC radio series and he bought charts from Fletcher Henderson, a well-known arranger and band leader. Together he and John Hammond took Ella to see Fletcher who was singularly unimpressed.

Luckily, CBS came to hear of her and signed her to do *Street Singer*, a stage show with singer and actor Arthur Tracy. These appearances were often precursors to appearing on the popular Andy Williams Show so it felt like a massive opportunity for Ella. Unfortunately, Ella's mother died just before the show and Ella was now an orphan and a minor with no adult to take responsibility for signing a contract on her behalf. She returned to the amateur circuit and performed at the *Lafayette Theatre* in Harlem. Her confidence knocked, she was booed off stage because her performance lacked polish. This experience had an abiding impact on Ella and stayed with her even when she became a star. It provided the spark which fueled periods of self-doubt. It would never happen again.

In spite of these set-backs, she was offered a contract for a week's work at the *Harlem Opera House* for fifty dollars, following Tiny Bradshaw's band. When his band had finished, the audience began to drift off while Tiny introduced Ella as, 'the girl who's been winning all the competitions'. Ella began to sing and the remaining audience sat back down, rooted to their seats.

Chick Webb was a hunchbacked drummer who led his own band and also played at the *Opera House*. People suggested he give Ella a try. He refused, his reason being that he did not want another singer in his band—he already had a male singer, Charlie Linton. Besides, Ella seemed unkempt and not very glamorous. The theatre staff were not to be denied though. They hid Ella in Chick's dressing room and made him listen. He hired her on the spot to play in Yale the following day. Staff at the theatre clubbed together to buy Ella a suitable gown for the performance and the concert went so well that the following week, Ella was singing with the band as they opened at the *Savoy Ballroom* on 140ᵗʰ and Lenox—this time for a week's contract. Chick Webb was only twenty-seven, but became Ella's guardian and a staunch supporter of the younger singer. She was just seventeen, but quickly became a much-loved performer under Chick's mentorship. Initially Chick employed Ella to sing on rhythmic numbers, whilst ballads were assigned to Linton. Soon, it became Ella the audience wanted. Chick was not the best business man and the pay was not the best, but he did secure three slots a week on the all-important radio (Radio WJZ). The show featured Webb and Ella with Charles Linton on vocals. It gained them huge exposure and Webb's reputation soared along with Ella's. In 1937's *Downbeat* and *Melody Maker* polls, Ella beat Billie Holiday and Mildred Bailey to the number one slot. All this within a year of the awful experience of being booed off the stage at the *Lafayette Theatre*. In 1938, Ella recorded *A Tisket a Tasket*—a version of a nursery rhyme—and it was well received. Chick Webb died in 1939 and Ella took over leadership of his band, re-naming it *Ella and Her Famous Orchestra*.

Ella found great pleasure in her singing and delighted when audiences reacted to her. When the orchestra played Los Angeles in 1940, some of her musicians were earning a bit of extra money playing at jazz sessions organized by a young Norman Granz (one year Ella's senior) at a local jazz club. Granz happily used her musicians, but not Ella herself as he did not like her style. A few years later, Ella attended a concert to see bass player Ray Brown. She was spotted in the audience and a song was requested. Granz initially refused to let her sing, but the audience insisted so Ella came on. Both the audience and Norman Granz were blown away. Granz offered her a contract on the spot. They formed a professional relationship which endured for many years. In 1945, after recording *Flying Home*, a number which pushed Ella's vocal range and included ground breaking experimentation, Ella teamed up with *Decca's* Louis Jordan. In 1946, she cut two tracks with Louis Armstrong, *You Won't Be Satisfied* and *The Frim Fram Sauce* and this proved a natural pairing which was really well received. The bebop post-war era suited Ella and from 1947 to 1952, she sang in many venues along 52nd Street, New York. She knew instinctively when to go from the bottom of her register to the top and on a 1947 tour with Dizzy Gillespie, he encouraged her to use her wordless vocal improvisation known as scat singing. Ella excelled at it and it became a trademark.

Granz and Ella made recordings with *Jazz at the Philharmonic*—a touring jazz show which fostered the talents of jazz musicians. Granz had to cut Ella's parts on those recordings however, because she was still under contract to *Decca*. In 1955, he successfully negotiated her release and put her on his own record label, *Verve*.

Granz and Ella's working partnership was not entirely smooth and they often fought, mainly over choice of materials; but it worked well for many years and Ella's career sky rocketed. She loved Europe and played to appreciative audiences in Paris, Dublin and Hamburg, and began to sense in the American audience a growing criticism and that music was going nowhere there.

One of the keys to her success was her unrivalled skill at scat singing—a kind of singing where the voice is used as an instrument, imitating the bop style of improvisation (a style of jazz, heavy on featured solo work). She had long considered Duke Ellington a genius and when he heard her at Birdland in 1949, he invited her to record with him and his orchestra, which she did.

In 1960, *Ella in Berlin* was recorded. Ella really opened up on this album and explored vocal avenues. The album was inducted into the *Grammy Hall of Fame* in 1999 in recognition of its historical significance. Her *Songbook* recordings made from 1956-1964 remain among the best-selling jazz albums.

Though a powerful and influential woman, Ella also faced discrimination and in Dallas, Texas her entire band was arrested by police who barged backstage. She was strong and became known as the first lady of song and it is easy to hear why when one listens to a recording of her singing. It is not often a performer gains such a reputation that they become known simply by one name, but 'Ella' for many sums up all that is good about jazz. Simply one of the greatest jazz voices ever, she sent many a soul into temporary ecstasy.

Betty Carter 1929-1998

Betty Carter at the Pori Jazz Festival in Finland, July 1978. Photographer: Kotivalo

Betty Carter was a role model, a pioneer in many ways and an inspiration, not only for her music but because she was a jazz musician who actively encouraged young people. Her voice was one which could bring colour to music. She never sang a song the same way, but each time added variations, sweet strokes or brash undertones, which gave the song a different colour, a change of texture, molding it to suit the time and mood.

During the 1940s, Betty was singing modern jazz in and around Detroit where she grew up. She studied piano at the Detroit Conservatory, but it was clear she was never going to be a great piano player. So she sang. Her breathy undertones might not please every singing critic, but she was a success. She won her first singing competition and signed to a talent agency who got her work with Dizzy Gillespie, Charlie Parker and Miles Davis to name just a few. At the time, Detroit had the liveliest jazz scene outside of New York and New Orleans. Gillespie's and Davis's support gave her determination to succeed with her scat style of singing, with which she peppered her performances. She was lucky to join Lionel Hampton's band where she found support for her fledgling talent and a source of inspiration. Behind Lionel and his band was his wife, Gladys who was the business manager. She mentored the young Betty Carter. Gladys also founded and managed a record label, *Glad Hamp Records* which recorded many artists including singers Anna Belle Caesar and Roberta Sherwood backed by the Lionel Hampton bands. Gladys taught Betty how to travel with men, how to be disciplined and how to be patient when waiting on buses for hours. Betty is quoted as saying, "I learned a lot from Gladys and Hamp both, not always realizing what I was getting."

Interestingly enough, Lionel Hampton is said to have fired Betty seven times because he disapproved of her singing style. She would improvise, something Lionel hated, but which he eventually made a big part of '*Betty Be-Bop's*' routine—and then she came to dislike it. In spite of the ups and downs, he usually took her back and they were friends for over twenty-five years. Betty attended Lionel's 90th birthday celebration at *Blue Note* and friends noted that whenever there was an important event in Lionel's life, Betty was always by his side.

Early in her singing career, Betty received encouragement from Miles Davis as we noted, and Ray Charles and toured with both of them. Then in the late 1950s, Betty went to New York, recorded with *Epic Records* and played the *Apollo* in Harlem which sealed her popularity as a performer. ABC records decided a duo album with Ray Charles might be popular with the public and together they recorded an album titled, *Ray Charles and Betty Carter*. Memorable numbers like Frank Loesser's *Baby, It's Cold Outside*, Oscar and Hammerstein's *People Will Say We*re In Love' and Cole Porter's *Ev'ry Time We Say Goodbye* proved memorable numbers and the single release of *Baby It's Cold Outside* topped the R'n'B charts. The album was her breakthrough recording and she went on to record for different labels and tour with the likes of Sonny Rollins.

Her career faltered for a while in the late 1960s and early 1970s because of the rise of pop music and rock and roll. Jazz became a harder sell to young audiences; but by the mid-1970s there was a resurgence and people began to appreciate the treasure that was Betty Carter.

She established her own label, *Bet-Car* in 1970 when record deals fell away. She also established her own production and management company (Bet-Car management) and released albums including *The Audience with Betty Carter, Betty Carter* and *The Betty Carter Album*. She began to draw her musicians and backing singers from the International Association of Jazz Educators conventions and Berklee. She visited colleges, lecturing on jazz history, inspiring and injecting energy into their studies and used young musicians in her bands as well. Many young musicians wanted to play with, and for, this inspiring woman. Soon she had a varying assortment of developing young musicians behind her and began working in earnest again. Her career took off once more and she toured Europe, South America and the US, appearing on the first *Saturday Night Live*, in 1976. She performed at *Newport Jazz Festival* in 1977 and 1978 and became known as much for her business acumen as her musical talent. Michael Bourne said in a *Downbeat* interview,

> *She's worked most often since the '70s with young musicians, usually newcomers to the scene. She's become the virtual godmother to a generation of musicians, especially young rhythm sections—encouraging them, fighting for them, fighting with them. It doesn't matter who they've played with before or what and where they've studied, when they join Betty's band that's when the real schooling begins.*

Betty would allow young musicians new to the jazz performing scene to explore, challenge themselves and learn, learn, learn. She would visit colleges like Berklee and see who she felt was good and check out young players she was told about. If they were really good and Betty felt they had something, she gave them a chance. Betty had an ear for potential. Often the musicians she chose were not getting everything right at the time, but she heard something in them which could be developed. Pianists Benny Green, Stephen Scott, bass players Curtis Lundy, Ira Coleman and Eric Revis and drummers Kenny Washington, Lewis

Nash, Winard Harper and Gregory Hutchinson all benefitted from Betty's inspiration and there were many more.

Betty signed to *Verve Records* in 1988 and they re-released some of her previous albums as well as allowing her artistic control over her new recordings. Her first *Verve* release in 1989 was titled *Look What I Got* and indeed, it got her a *Grammy*. Other albums on *Verve* included *The Be-Bop Girl* (1988), *Droppin' Things* (1990), *I'm Yours, You're Mine* (1996) and *Betty Carter's Finest Hour* (2003). She also recorded for other labels like *Jazz Door, Global Rhythm Press* and *Warner.*

Betty would take standards and play with the rhythm, often changing tempo and generally making the musicians performing with her work their socks off. She also got them to follow her and learn and do exactly as she needed. She had incredible musical imagination and young minds she found, were very open to influence, which had a two-fold benefit—for her, she could take them along with her on explorations of musical diversity and for them, it was a baptism of fire. They had to learn fast and hone their craft quickly to keep up.

Many young musicians benefitted from Betty's direction and in 1989 she recorded *Tight* with the young Branford Marsalis on saxophone, where she set up a duet with sax and her voice as an instrument.

A regular favorite in readers' polls and critics reviews, Betty Carter was renowned for her tenacity, energy and integrity. She enjoyed success later in her career, touring with other jazz greats including Dave Holland and Jack DeJohnette, with whom she had worked before; and recording in London and the US. She was known also for her respect for her audience. She gave a lot, but also appreciated that people had to turn out to concerts for her to continue working—they did, she did and her ability to scat is legendary still.

In 1993, Betty Carter established the *Jazz Ahead Program* which takes twenty young musicians a year and gives them the chance to work with great musicians on composition and performance. When Betty was alive, they worked shoulder to shoulder with her. Today, the program lives on, being held in the *Kennedy Center for Performing Arts* in Washington. It ends with a series of concerts, providing more experience to young musicians. In 1994, she sang at *The White House, Carnegie Hall* and the *Istanbul Jazz Festival* where her performance was said to be definitive.

Betty Carter took scat singing to a different level. She used her voice as an instrument and was a born improviser from head to toe. Her voice possessed a breathiness and she had her own style and expression and was very much an individual. She was first a musician, second a singer, and could weave wonderfully beautiful musical pictures. Sometimes her scat delivery had a ferocity behind it; at others it was gentle and entrancing. One of her gifts was arranging pieces for small ensemble performances. She was different and a completely engaging musician who continued to inspire until her death in 1998. Betty Carter is a role model for any aspiring jazz musician, especially women.

Melba Liston 1926 -1999

Melba Liston was born into a musical family in Kansas and loved listening to her grandfather play guitar. A salesman visited her school when she was seven years old and showed the children a trombone. She later saw one in a shop window and described the feeling as, "I thought how beautiful it looked and I had to have one." She asked if she could have one and, unusually for the early 1930s, Melba's family encouraged her to play the instrument she wanted to. The brassy, sassy, trombone became hers. She moved to Los Angeles in 1937 where she met Eric Dolphy and Dexter Gordon in

Melba Liston. Photography by Gerard Rouy

school. She was taught by Alma Hightower, a teacher and advocate for black culture. At sixteen, she joined the Musicians Union and decided to become a professional. In 1942, she got a job in a pit band at the old *Lincoln Theatre* in Los Angeles. A time for some hard lessons. It was almost unheard of for a woman—a soloist at that—to progress this far in the jazz world and she was bullied by both anti-women and anti-youth musicians. However, she also met and was inspired by the *International Sweethearts of Rhythm* Big Band.

She moved to Gerald Wilson's band in 1943, persevered and became one of the most popular trombone players in the US. In 1947, she recorded with erstwhile school mate Dexter Gordon—who dedicated his track *Mischievous Lady* to her—and was mentored in her early career by Mary Lou Williams. Her major break came when Dizzy Gillespie invited her to the East Coast to arrange pieces for his band. She had found the jazz world to be tough for a woman, especially in getting her arrangements heard and played, so this was a momentous opportunity. Apparently, band members drew a sharp intake of breath when Melba showed up with an arrangement for the band and drew another one when they tried to play her complex charts. John Coltrane was one of the musicians and Melba gained inspiration from him as well. She was accepted into the band, (though apparently, she also cut hair and did the sewing when they went on tour). In 1949, Melba toured with Billie Holiday, finding herself again playing with Gerald Wilson. Billie became a good friend even if the tour had its difficulties. The further South the tour got, the fewer people came to see them. Eventually, the money ran out and the band had to send for more before they could return home. Finding the touring and difficulties disheartening, Melba returned to LA and became a secretary for the Board of Education. She also took extra work in films with minor roles in *The Prodigal* (where she wandered around holding a harp) and *The Ten Commandments* in 1955.

Her passion for music remained undiminished though and she returned to play in Dizzy Gillespie's band again—and recorded what is probably her best known recording as a soloist on Gillespie's track

Cool Breeze from the album *Dizzy Gillespie at Newport* recorded at the *Newport Jazz Festival* in 1957. Melba accompanied Gillespie's band when they were commissioned for the State Department tours, performing shows in the Middle East, Latin America and Europe. In 1958, she recorded her album *Melba Liston and her 'Bones'* for Metro Jazz. The album included many great (male) trombone players of the time such as Bennie Green, Frank Rehak, Al Grey, Jimmy Cleveland, Benny Powell and the baritone sax player, Marty Flax; but it was led by Melba. That same year, Melba also formed an all-women quintet, toured Europe and took part in the theatre show *Free and Easy*, where she met and worked with the show's musical director Quincy Jones.

In the late 1950s, Melba arranged an entire album of music for the up-and-coming singer Gloria Lynne. Lynne's first album had done well, and she was allowed to choose her own arranger for her next project; she chose Melba. Quincy Jones helped on the album when Liston was ill and spoke highly of her work. She went to Europe with his big band and not only played trombone, but also contributed arrangements and original compositions to Jones' orchestra.

Melba worked often with trumpeter Clark Terry, co-leading his big band over the next few years. She also played for Charlie Mingus, appearing at his infamous New York Town Hall concert of 1962. Infamous because Mingus attempted to perform his two-hour long *Epitaph* without success and to mixed reviews. It did however, give Melba contact with some of the greatest jazz musicians ever to walk this planet: Zoot Sims, Pepper Adams, Jimmy Cleveland, vibraphonist Milt Hinton and many more. She also began her long association with Randy Weston.

It was when she took a role as arranger and conductor for *Riverside Records*, that Melba's most successful musical partnership began. There she met another musician working for the label—Randy Weston. Weston asked her to add weight to his compositions because she knew how to expand musical ideas. They worked well together. The partnership proved long-lasting and resulted in a prolific composition rate. Liston and Weston collaborated on music for ten albums including *Uhuru Afrika* (Roulette 1960) and *Highlife* (Colpix 1963)—an album which sees Weston explore the music of Africa. South Africa banned *Uhuru Afrika* in 1964, probably due to the lyrics, which were written by activist Langston Hughes.

Many tunes from the period Melba worked with Weston became standards, including *Stella By Starlight* and *My Reverie*. Melba also worked with Marvin Gaye, Billy Eckstine, Milt Jackson and The Supremes transcending genres and linking jazz rhythms with Afro-pop and Motown sounds. She spent most of the 60s working in New York freelancing as an arranger and playing on studio sessions while maintaining her post as house arranger and conductor for *Riverside*.

Melba dropped out of the jazz scene in the late 1960s. She moved to Jamaica in 1973, where she lived for six years, teaching at the University of the West Indies and as director of the department of Afro-American Pop and Jazz at the Jamaica Institute of Music in Kingston, helping young Jamaican musicians to learn about different music. On her return to the U.S., she formed an all-girl septet called *Melba Liston and Company* which included Erica Lindsay, Fostina Dixon, drummer Dottie Dolgion and several others. They headlined the *Kansas City Women's Jazz Festival* in 1979. Although she dropped the all-girl line up, the band survived until 1983. She enjoyed a new-found popularity and was due to perform at the *Camden Jazz Festival* in London in 1986, but was prevented from appearing by the first of what was to become a series of strokes that ultimately left her wheelchair-bound.

She continued to work as composer and arranger into the early 1990s until ill-health finally caught up with her. She died in 1999 leaving a legacy as a trail blazer and as a role model for those to come. She decided and was determined to be a professional arranger, composer and instrumentalist when the path for a woman in the jazz world was incredibly difficult. Melba was unusual in that she endured abuse from men she worked with who found it difficult to work with women as equals. She talked about the fact she was part of a culture that tolerated if not condoned sexual assault. Women were overlooked, ignored. One of the important things Melba Liston did for women who followed is she made it possible and acceptable to discuss issues which were being swept under the rug until then. She once said in an interview for the *Independent* that she had suffered the perils of being the only woman in travelling big bands.

> *Rapes and everything. I've been going through that stuff for all my life. 'Yeah, well, you know, it's a broad and she's by herself.' I'd just go to the doctor and tell him, and that was that. But the older I got, the less it happened. I don't know how old I was, but it stopped all together.*

Her career lasted for almost forty years, spanning huge changes from the 1940s to the 1980s. Melba Liston was strong and supremely talented, particularly as an arranger. She made herself invaluable to fellow musicians and leaders in more ways than one. Her talent, willingness to speak out and tenacity are an example for many who follow.

Nina Simone. Photography by Gerard Rouy.

Nina Simone 1933-2003

Nina Simone had a voice which once heard, was never forgotten. She had the ability to turn her voice into an instrument. Her voice—sweet, raunchy and always emotive—had a massive impact on listeners and her pitch was beautiful—squeezing up to a note if she hit it slightly below and somehow it felt all right. Her interpretations of Gershwin's music are renowned and her poignant expression pulls at the heart. She was a solid supporter of civil rights and was particularly affected by the death of Martin Luther King. A singer who straddled the two worlds of jazz and popular music with ease, she said in an interview with *Downbeat's* Michael Zwerin in 1968, "because of the better quality in pop music I find the gap between my audience and what I'm trying to say is closing".

Nina was influenced by some of her favourite artists including McCoy Tyner and Oscar Peterson. She considered music an art with its own rules, one rule being that you should pay more attention to the music than anything else in the world if you are going to be true to yourself.

She also felt that jazz was in many ways given a less than perfect opportunity to be heard at its best due to the limitations of some of the venues. She insisted on having decent microphones, a tuned piano and an amplified bass so that all of the music could be heard.

In the same *Downbeat* interview, she is quoted as saying,

> *You can see colours in music. Anything! Anything human can be felt through music, which means there is no limit to the creating that can be done with music. You can take the same phrase from any song and set it up so many different ways – it's infinite!*

Nina Simone was a true storyteller. She was also fiercely supportive of liberation and artists using their status to empower others. Some of her supporters spoke of her as the 'High Priestess of Soul' because of her ability to weave such a spell through her songs that it was akin to being hypnotized. The listener was drawn into the narrative, feeling at one with the vital spirit which was Nina Simone.

Before she became Nina Simone, she was Eunice Kathleen Waymon in her hometown of Tryon, North Carolina. Her mother was a Methodist minister and her father a handyman. Nina was their sixth child. Nina showed her musicianship early on when she began to play the piano by ear at only three years old. A little later, she began to play in her mother's church, able to play nearly anything by ear. She took classical piano lessons and came to love the work of Bach, Beethoven, Chopin and Schubert. She gave her first public performance of classical music in a library at the age of twelve, and also had her first experience of the injustice meted out to black people when her parents were asked to sit at the back of the venue. Nina refused to play until they were moved to better seats. After graduating from high school, her community raised money to fund a scholarship to *Juilliard* in New York. She later applied for a scholarship to the *Curtis Institute of Music* in Philadelphia where her family had relocated, but her application was refused. She believed this was because of her colour, and the experience contributed to her enthusiasm for civil rights activities later in life. Even though she took piano lessons from one of the professors at Curtis, the sense of rejection stayed with her throughout her life. She never forgot it.

After getting turned down at the *Curtis Institute*, Eunice needed to earn money. She began working as a photographer's assistant and giving music lessons. Neither of these jobs made much money, so she auditioned as a pianist/singer at the *Midtown Bar and Grill* in Atlantic City. She got the job but was told she would have to accompany herself. She sang Cole Porter, Gershwin and other popular composers' tunes and infused in them jazz, blues and hints of classical, making them very much her own style. Her amazing sultry voice suited her playing perfectly and she was invited to play at many clubs along the East Coast. Eunice changed her performing name to Nina Simone to hide the fact she was working in bars from her mother—who she knew would disapprove. Nina meant 'girl' in Spanish and Simone was after an actress she admired. Earning around ninety dollars a week meant Eunice could give her parents money too. Her parents viewed jazz as 'the devil's music'. When she was working in Atlantic City a fan gave her a copy of Gershwin's *Porgy* from *Porgy and Bess*. He told Nina he liked Billie Holiday—Nina once said in an interview with BBC's *Hard Talk* she couldn't stand her. She practiced the song and sang it in a bar. An agent heard her, took her to NY and put it on a record.

Nina as she now was, submitted songs to record labels and at twenty-four won a contract with *Bethlehem Records,* an imprint of *King Records.*

She was allowed to select her own songs and she chose jazz numbers. She got a job recording a song over a video for Play-Doh to be advertised in the UK—the song was *My Baby Just Cares For Me*, a song which became incredibly popular and cemented her arrival as a new jazz star. Later, this song would be used by Chanel to advertise its perfume and became a massive hit. Nina Simone changed overnight from cult to legend.

By 1957, she was playing *Carnegie Hall* and was very successful. Yet still that grumble from her past rose its head and she wrote to her parents, "this is where you wanted me to play but I should have been playing Bach." She loved the audience and performing, but deep down inside she still wanted to play classical music.

In 1959, Nina moved to *Colpix Records* and released her first LP for the label titled, *The Amazing Nina Simone*. Importantly, she had complete artistic control of her song arrangements, something rarely afforded to artists by labels. She played the Town Hall in Manhattan and, realizing her magic worked best in live performances, *Colpix* recorded a live concert in September 1959. One of the songs, *You Can Have Him* was a highlight of the evening and began with a brilliant arpeggio on the piano which would become her signature for decades.

This live performance was so incredible that forty-five years later, with her only daughter Lisa Simone Kelly on vocals, some of the same musicians would do a tribute concert to a sold-out audience.

Simone performed at the growing *Newport Jazz Festival* in 1960 where she teamed up with bass player Chris White, drummer Bobby Hamilton and guitar player Al Shackman, who would remain a long-term collaborator. In 1960, *Colpix* released her version of the Betty Smith soul classic *Nobody Knows You When You're Down and Out* which was her second single success and in 1961 another single, recorded live at Newport in 1960, was released, *Trouble in Mind*. Nina recorded nine albums with *Colpix* including many stand-out recordings like *Cotton Eyed Joe*, *The Other Women* and *Black is the Colour of My True Love's Hair*. In her narrative singing, Nina created vivid images, entwining the lyrics with emotive and evocative phrasing. She also recorded a civil rights song called *Brown Baby* which was included on *At the Village Gate*, her fifth album for *Colpix*. Her recordings and performances included spirituals and children's songs, which gave critics palpitations as they could not put their finger on her style though they pleased a wide range of people. Her style had classical and jazz influences, but she occasionally delved into blues and folk.

Her main appeal remained the New York night club audience. When she signed with the *Phillips* label in 1963, it was obvious her goals had shifted to reach an even wider global audience. In 1964, her first LP for *Phillips*, *In Concert* made clear her stand on freedom and justice. She became a symbol and leader of the civil rights movement in America. Her self-composed release, *Mississippi Goddam* was written in response to the murders of Medgar Evans, a civil rights activist, and four black children in the 16th Street Baptist church in Birmingham, Alabama. That it was banned across the South, left Nina undaunted in her commitment to liberty. *Four Women* and her version of *Strange Fruit* cemented her place as a spokeswoman for civil rights. It was risky and few artists dared to take a stance like this, but Nina proved herself a stolid and unyielding advocate. Initially, Nina herself had seen little point in trying to combine music and politics, but with *Mississippi Goddam* which she said, 'just burst out of me', she realized there was a point to make, and that she could make it. She spoke at civil rights movement rallies and supported violent, rather than pacifist actions to force a change in politics.

Nina Simone brought many personalities to her music. Onstage, it was said you got the complete Nina Simone. She would bring her current mood, her sense of outrage, her peace and she would make audiences wait until she felt ready to play, citing her piano teacher's advice which went something like, 'Don't you dare touch that piano until you are ready to play'. From the soulful, emotional woman singing *Don't Let Me Be Misunderstood* to the sultry seductress singing *I Put a Spell On You* and the tender lover of *Black Is the Colour of My True Love's Hair*, she could bring any number of different characters to a song or unleash herself on numbers like *See Line Woman* or create a sense of brooding restraint on her version of *Strange Fruit*.

In 1967, she moved to *RCA* records and released *Do I Move You?* which was cheeky, provocative and the overtly sexual, *I Want A Little Sugar In My Bowl* and *Backlash Blues*, all of which were included on the album, *Nina Sings The Blues*.

Nina wrote two songs featured in the musical *Hair* and recorded covers including George Harrison's *Here Comes the Sun* and Dylan's *Just Like A Woman*, each given the 'Simone treatment', creating something different and special. She wrote *Young, Gifted and Black* in memory of her friend, civil rights speaker and author Lorraine Hansberry.

Nina left *RCA* in the early 1970s and moved around, spending time in Liberia, Barbados, England, Belgium, France, Switzerland and The Netherlands. She felt at home in Liberia. She lived in a lovely house, spent a lot of time on the beach and had house maids. Liberia at the time often became a refuge for black people from the US. She left the US and would not return because of "Racism. Pure and simple," she said. She wasn't the only one. After seven years she made a brief return and found she was treated well, but underlying and insidious racism would not let her live happily in America. She described racism as 'being in the very fabric of America'. In 1978, she recorded an album for Creed Taylor, on a veteran jazz label, *CTI*. It was a studio album, recorded in New York with strings and background vocals and was a huge success. Creed Taylor used some of the best jazz musicians of the time on the title track, Randy Newman's evocative *Baltimore*, including guitarist Al Shackman, adding a quality which made it a stand out track.

Simone made two albums with *Carrere Records* in the 1980s, two for *VPI* and one live album with *Verve* before making an album for *Elektra*, *A Single Woman*. She played *Ronnie Scott's* in London regularly, developing an ever-growing UK following.

Simone was bipolar and beset by personality problems. She had frequent temper outbursts and once, even fired a gun at a label manager she thought was stealing money. She abandoned her daughter when she moved to Liberia; and although they were re-united briefly, Lisa found her mother abusive and returned to live with her father in New York.

She moved to France in 1993 and continued to tour through the 1990s. Her recordings sold over a million copies that decade, thanks to CD sales and people discovering her music on the internet. In 1999, Nina gave an interview to BBC's *Hard Talk* and spoke about her life-long fight for civil rights. In the interview she speaks slowly and deliberately; and her diction is slightly slurred. Her song which opens the interview is off-key but still, there is something incredibly special. The determination and deep-centered life force emanating from her are tangible. She talks about music as being her weapon of the past thirty years to defend the rights of African Americans and third-world people with protest songs to help change the world. She said when she was on stage, she wanted to move the audience and make people understand what has been done to her people around the world. She wanted to let them know who they are and what they have done. Not anger, not fire, but intelligence. She said Nelson Mandela was the greatest man on the planet. Her success was important to her and so was being on stage.

There is much humour in her interviews and she discusses her love life with a cheekiness and honesty, as for instance when she spoke of one of her husband treating her like a horse. She marched with Martin Luther King Jr. at Alabama and Washington and knew his family. She wrote a song for him upon his death, called *The King of Love Is Dead*. His death, she said, killed her belief in human rights and she moved away. She said the FBI were after her and she was scared as several other key activists had been killed in the US. She had faith, but no specific religion and said she believed in Islam, Hinduism, Buddhism—all of them as they are necessary 'for the sheep,' she said.

She died in her sleep in France in April 2003. Her ashes were scattered in several African countries. Because of her wide and varied recordings, her cross-cultural appeal, her stands against injustice and her absolute musical ability, Nina Simone left a long and varied legacy. Her music continues to draw new listeners across the world. Ironically, days before her death the *Curtis Institute* awarded Simone an honorary degree

That so many of her songs are now standards is a tribute to this remarkable singer. They include both her own compositions and her versions of older songs. Titles like *My Baby Just Cares For me, I Put A Spell On You, Lilac Wine, Wild is The Wind* and so many more endure in repertoires today and many of her songs have been sampled, covered and performed live by many different artists. Her pioneering interpretation of music, her temper, her personality traits and her supreme stage presence have possibly no equal. She was awarded a *Grammy Hall Of Fame Award* in 2000, and two honorary degrees from Malcolm X and Amherst colleges. She was inducted in the *Rock and Roll Hall of Fame* in 2018.

Alice Coltrane 1937—2007

Alice Coltrane made more than her share of contributions to jazz music, both as a pianist, harp player, arranger and composer. Spiritual and sensitive in her approach, her music has a sweetness which

Alice Coltrane, 2006, Photograher Meylan

can break the heart or a mania which lifts the deepest of moods. Her real gift was creating music-scapes—painting pictures with her music and conjuring up images so vivid you are almost in the place. She played with

John Coltrane's group, replacing piano player McCoy Tyner. She and John were eventually married—their union creating a very spiritual and creative bond. Her chords were distinctive because they lacked thirds and so sounded empty and ethereal. It was a simple but effective and different sounding technique. In contrast, her solos were traditional and she played single lines with hardly any changes in the rhythm or linear chord progressions. Instead of taking the favoured line of using the piano as a rhythm or percussion instrument, Alice used it to add colour, texture and a firm base of sound. She was also a harp player and employed pedal techniques used for the harp in her piano playing to introduce echoey, ethereal sounds or to suddenly dampen a chord so it vanished. She also enjoyed playing the organ—something she did as a child in church. She became a band leader after John's death, before stepping out of the public eye. Her spirituality comes across strongly in her music and she had a way of gaining the emotive support of an audience and listener because of her intrinsic arrangements.

There are many who view Alice as the spiritual influence on John Coltrane during the latter part of his career, inspiring him to produce some of the most soul-searching and deeply moving music.

Alice grew up in a spiritual and musical home, her mother was in the church choir and her brother a prominent jazz bass player in the Detroit area. Alice studied classical music and then jazz, under Bud Powell. She played during the intermissions at the *Blue Note Jazz Club* in Paris, a great opportunity, but had to move back to America with her young daughter after her first marriage to Kenny Hagood broke down. In Detroit, Alice played with her own trio, a few duos, notably with vibraphone player Terry Pollard and joined Terry Gibbs' quartet where she met John Coltrane. Alice developed a stand out career in her own right as a solo performer and as a member of bands. She continued to play with John's groups as well as in her own project until his death in 1967. Alone, she continued to develop the spiritual side of her music, recording over twenty albums, each seeming to grow more in a spiritual direction, before she became reclusive.

Alice sought spiritual truth in the late 1960's and spent time in isolation. She fasted, meditated and prayed. In 1970, she met a guru, traveled to India and devoted her life to spiritual practice. In 1975, she became founder and director of *The Vedantic Center* in California.

She became intensely spiritual, taking guidance from gurus and becoming a swami herself. Eventually she took the Sanskrit name of Turiyasangitananda (meaning the transcendental Lord's highest song of bliss) or Turiya Alice Coltrane, and recorded again, filling the music with cosmic, trance-like passages alongside more traditionally-based jazz references. This music forged links between jazz and other genres and took it to a wider audience. Alice continued on her spiritual path and recorded music based on traditional chants in the 1980s and 1990s. In 2006, after twenty-five years, Alice gave three live performances, the final one of which was at the *San Francisco Jazz Festival* with her son Ravi on saxophone and Charlie Haden on bass. Ravi is one of the most sought-after saxophone players today and John and Alice's other son, Oranyan is a DJ, composer and musician. John's daughter from his first marriage, Michelle, brought up largely by Alice, is a jazz singer. Alice played with many of jazz's other greats including Pharaoh Sanders, Joe Henderson Ornette Coleman, Jack De Johnette, Carlos Santana and of course Charlie Haden. Much of her latter music explores electronic sounds as well as instrumental ones.

Alice also brought the harp into jazz in a special and imaginative way. Her *Atomic Peace* recording with Jimmy Garrison on bass, produces runs, chords and spiritual leanings from the harp; and covers the depth of the harp's range, whether in the background against bass solos or in the soaring, mesmeric solos she played.

Alice Coltrane's career is astounding for the way in which she, the widow of one of history's stellar musical minds, devotedly continued down the path where he left off while also managing to escape his shadow—carving a distinct identity, achieving artistic greatness, and becoming regarded as one of the leading figures in a male-dominated landscape of jazz soloists, composers, and bandleaders of the early 1970s by peers, critics, and listeners. She was a role model for many younger female jazz musicians.

Alice continues to be cited by many as an influence from the moment they first discovered her. Imaginative, creative and daring, she was always willing to take the listener to another place—a place where one can experiment and nothing was musically forbidden.

Aretha Franklin 1942-2018

Aretha Franklin. Photography by Gerard Rouy

Aretha Franklin was an American singer, songwriter, civil rights activist, actress and pianist. She began her singing as a child in her father's church where he was minister. She was born in Memphis but by the age of five, the family were living in Detroit. Her mother played the piano and sang; and Aretha was soon performing. Her family life was troubled with her father having numerous relationships with other women and Aretha's mother passing away when Aretha was nine years old. A series of relations and friends looked after the children in their family home, one of whom was the great soul songstress, Mahalia Jackson. Aretha had her first child at the age of just fifteen and a second at seventeen. Her father may have had his faults, but he was a gifted orator and celebrated preacher. Celebrities visited the family home including gospel musicians, one of which—the successful and highly respected artist, Clara Ward—would become a huge influence on the young

Aretha. Martin Luther King Jr. was among the visitors as well. These friendships developed between the family and their celebrity friends would be important throughout her life.

At twelve, Aretha began accompanying her father, singing in churches after or before he preached; and it was Franklin Senior who arranged for *JVB Records* to record her first single *Never Grow Old* in New Bethel Baptist Church in 1956. Three years later another track titled, *Precious Lord* was released. She also sang with *The Soul Stirrers*, a travelling group who played in the Jubilee style. Dinah Washington apparently told producer Quincy Jones that Aretha was, 'the next one'. She toured with Martin Luther King Jr. when she was sixteen and at eighteen, and under her father's management, she made her first recording for *Columbia*. These records did not do well commercially, but *Columbia* continued supporting her and in 1961, she released *Aretha: With the Ray Bryant Combo*. It featured the single *Won't Be Long* which charted in Billboard's Hot 100. She performed in many styles including jazz, blues, R&B and doo-wop. Hits followed including *Rock a Bye Your Baby with a Dixie Melody*. It wasn't until she signed with *Atlantic* in 1966 that her career really took off. She had hits with numbers including her dazzling version of Otis Redding's *Respect* and *I Say a Little Prayer*. A star was ascending in the sky. She earned herself the accolade of 'The Queen of Soul', but her voice and style was jazz-influenced. In 1968, she appeared on the cover of *Time Magazine*.

Her list of hit albums is impressive and includes *Lady Soul, Young Gifted and Black* and *Sparkle*. Her relationship with Atlantic fell apart in 1979 after albums including *La Diva* and *Sweet Passion* failed to chart. In 1980, she signed with *Arista* and appeared in the 1980 film *The Blues Brothers* before more hit albums including *Jump To It* and *Aretha*. She had a massive pop hit with George Michael in 1987 with the song *I Knew You Were Waiting For Me*. A gold album came in 1998 with *A Rose Is Still A Rose* and her performance of *Nessun Dorma* at that year's *Grammy Awards* was praised around the world. In 2014, she had the honour of an asteroid being named after her and in 2015, brought President Obama to tears with her performance at the Kennedy Honours. Audiences adored her and she inspired many musicians who followed.

Aretha's career is peppered with seminal performances. Among these we can list her command performance in 1980 at the *Royal Albert Hall*, her performance at Martin Luther's funeral, and at that of Mahalia Jackson's. Her performance for Poe Francis at the World Meeting of Families and at the inauguration of President Barrack Obama are the stuff of legend. Her later career saw her revered as an elder stateswoman of music with many artists paying tribute to her influence.

Throughout her life, from her early twenties on, Aretha was associated with the Civil Rights and women's rights Movements. She gave funding and supported many civil rights groups. She also performed at key Civil Rights events, even getting herself arrested and locked up for disturbing the peace in Detroit. Her song *Respect* became an anthem for the Civil Rights Movement and she refused to perform (along with several other musicians) at President Trump's inauguration in 2017 in a statement of musical protest.

She had several hundred hits on various charts, won many awards including eighteen *Grammys* and was the first woman to be inducted into the *Rock and Roll Hall of Fame* in 1987.

Carla Bley 1936—

Very much still here, but a woman who has influenced both musicians of the past and the present, Carla Bley is an American pianist, composer and leader and has been influential since she

Carla Bley. Photography by David Sinclair

came to the fore during the free jazz movement of the 1960s. She was born in Oakland, California where she learned to sing and play the piano. Both her parents were musicians and religious, but Carla parted with the church at a young age. All the same, she acquired a knowledge of religious and spiritual music that can be heard in the structure of her compositions. She entered a talent competition and the experience apparently opened her eyes to her own differences from the formal playing style. She gave up formal studies at fifteen and took a job in a music store selling sheet music. She also worked in her aunt's florist shop, which is said to have inspired her 'funereal music' of later years. She moved to New York at seventeen, took a job as a cigarette girl in *Birdland* and immersed herself in the jazz scene. She was a hat check girl in Basin Street where she met jazz pianist Paul Bley, later to become her husband. Recognizing her talent, she began to compose music for his group. Her work was performed by musicians including George Russell, Art Farmer, Jimmy Guiffre, Charlie Haden and Paul Bley himself who played in Greenwich Village coffee houses and in Charles Moffat's group with Pharaoh Sanders.

She helped form the *Jazz Composers Guild* (JCG) in 1964 and began a relationship, both professionally and personally, with trumpet player Michael Mantler. Together they led the *Jazz Composer's Orchestra* (JCO) which evolved from the JCG, a foundation for supporting the orchestra and commissioning new music. They began the label *JCOA*, releasing historic recordings and her own composition, the monumental 'chronotransduction' titled *Escalator Over The Hill* issued as a triple LP set. This work took four years to create and is akin to a jazz musical oratorio in free style piece. The *Jazz Composers' Guild* brought innovative musicians from New York together. Many of New York's finest free jazz musicians have taken part over the years. By 1968, the JCO featured Don Cherry, Cecil Taylor, Gato Barbieri, Pharoah Sanders and Larry Coryell. That same year, Carla released a double album of her compositions which included solos by many of these jazz luminaries. She showed that free jazz could be successful and well-received. Her work was in demand, especially in Japan and Europe although sales were relatively small. Out of the JCG and the JCO came the *New Music Distribution Service*, which was Bley's way of giving new or non-commercial records an outlet to enable small and independent music producers to sell material. It left ownership and control of the music in the hands of the musicians— something which proved innovative and provided a template for many independent labels that followed. Since the 1970s, she has recorded for her own label *Watt Records*, which she began with Mantler. Carla has worked with many musicians including Robert Wyatt, Charlie Haden, Gary Burton and Johnny Griffin. She is known for her recordings with bass player Steve Swallow who remains a close associate.

Since 1977, Carla has concentrated on live performances, many with her ten-piece band. She has collaborated with musicians from many countries including saxophone player Andy Sheppard. Her successful tour of Japan in 1984 found an ever-growing audience for free jazz.

Carla Bley's compositions added to and expanded experimentalism in improvisation and her penchant for pushing the boundaries in musical adventurism has inspired many musicians today.

Reaction to her music has been varied. She was pelted with tomatoes in France, tins of peaches in Italy and beer in Germany. However, speak with any jazz musician today and they mention Bley with reverence. She has enjoyed a love-hate relationship with the press and is notoriously hard to contact.

Bley has spoken in interviews of her belief that audience interaction is paramount. Musicians that have played with her have said she is a great leader; that she allows musicians the freedom to express themselves.

Her career has been full-on since the mid-1960s with over three hundred songs, fifty scores, and several recordings for *ECM*. Carla is known as an eccentric and definitely the walker of her own path. She remains an enigmatic woman in jazz and has a Guggenheim Fellowship for composition and several international jazz trophies. Visiting her website is an experience in itself as you navigate around a prison with rules, condemned cells and various criminal acts listed. A lady who is original in many ways.

♪♪♪

THERE ARE SO MANY influential women musicians of the recent past to whom modern players owe a huge debt and there is not enough room to cover more than a handful here. The list given here is but a minuscule number of the women who have made a difference. Trumpeters Estelle Slavia, Jane Sager, Clora Bryant, Dyer Jones (who taught Valaida Snow and was mother to Dolly Jones, who was the first female jazz trumpet player to be recorded) and Tiny Davis (who went on, after the *International Sweethearts*, to form her own *Hell Divers*); bass player June Rotenburg; pianists Mary Colston Kirk, Marge Creath Singleton; drummers Bridget O'Flynn, Rose Gottesman; saxophonists Irma Young, Betty Sattley; reeds/vibraphone/leader Peggy Gilbert— there are just too many to include here.

Others of note include the violin player Emma Smock—better known as 'Ginger' Smock—who was a band leader and TV personality, best-known for her recordings with the *Vivien Garry Quartet*. She led an all-female sextet in 1951 and the group featured for six weeks on *The Chicks and The Fiddle* show on CBS. In 1952, she featured as a solo player on the TV show *Dixie Showboat*. She not so much played the violin but jazzed, rocked and sashayed with her violin in trios, quartets and ensembles. There was trumpet player Billie Rogers, of whom Nat Hentoff in 1979 apparently said,

> *When I was in my teens, I went with some friends to hear Woody Herman's band, and there, in the trumpet section, was a woman. We looked at Billie Rogers as if she had three heads and marvelled that she could even finish a chorus.*

Billie Rogers was born into a musical family who encouraged her musical interests—she learned many instruments and focused eventually on the trumpet. She had the rare gift of perfect pitch which is either a blessing or not as people with it assume everyone hears music the way they do—all the little off-notes included. Billie Rogers played note-perfect partly due to this gift. She was apparently told by the Musicians' Union she could only play as part of a women's band. So, she played with a quartet in a bar which soon became packed to capacity every time the quartet played. She was offered an audition with Woody Herman's band and got the job, but had to start off sitting out front with a female singer before actually moving to the trumpet section. She played with the Woody Herman band for several seasons before forming her own sextet. Hentoff's reaction was probably typical of many musician's perceptions at the time. They eventually learned that women can be wonderful musicians and deserved their rightful place and respect.

Someone who influenced many vocalists who followed was Mahalia Jackson—a strong *alto* gospel singer who would sing no song which included profanity. Her place in this book is forever secured. She supported women's and civil rights and lent her voice to the support of these causes. She recorded mainly for *Columbia* in the 1950s and 60s and became the most powerful black woman in America for a time. Her persona influenced many women who saw in her the strength they needed for themselves. She sang at rallies for Martin Luther King and other civil rights leaders in the face of death threats, proving powerful women could make a stand.

There was also Lil Armstrong, a pianist whose music swayed the hearts of many, including Louis Armstrong and Etta James. Though better known for gospel and blues, Etta's deep, sensual, earthy voice which could sound like it welled up from the very depths of her being, lent itself equally to jazz. She recorded with offshoots of the *Chess* label and was in much demand during the 1960s, performing at the *Montreux Jazz Festival*. She may have struggled with addiction, but her voice was addictive in itself and after a ten-year gap in the late seventies, she returned with great success, secured a deal with *Island Records* and was back, performing again. She received six *Grammys* during her career. Her voice was incredibly distinctive. A true *alto*, she turned jazz standards into sensual numbers. She was woefully overlooked early in her career until finally discovered by West Coast's Johnny Otis. It was Otis who changed her stage name from Jamesetta Hawkins to Etta James. Her husky, whisky-riddled voice hits home still with so many.

There is Eartha Kitt, who sang jazz and other genres, had her own style of delivery and a burgeoning career in the US before she was effectively blackballed for about ten years in 1968 for speaking against the war at a White House gathering, upsetting the first lady and causing a crisis of sorts. In 1975, the CIA issued a dossier claiming she was debauched and that her fellow musicians had negative opinions about her. However, she found favour in the UK and appeared on several BBC shows including the *Morecambe and Wise* show where she deftly sent her own purring sex kitten image up and gained a huge UK following. She returned to Broadway in the US in 1978, the public support outweighing any bureaucratic opinions.

And there was Emily Remler—a jazz guitarist influenced by Charlie Christian (of the minimal three-string technique) and Wes Montgomery among others, though she also listened to Jimi Hendrix and the music of other rock artists. Emily fused the high energy of rock composition with jazz. She released an album as leader titled *Firefly* at only twenty-four and in 1985, won *Downbeat's International Poll* for guitarist of the year—some feat when you consider her youth and the competition. She squeezed every last ounce of sound through her strings and her fast-fingered playing style.

Then there was pianist Mary Lou Williams. Her real name alone is interesting—Mary Elfrieda Scruggs. She wrote and played with a huge array of the jazz greats including Duke Ellington, Benny Goodman, Thelonius Monk, Miles Davis, Charlie Parker, Bud Powell and Dizzy

Gillespie; and mentored Melba Liston. Her style will forever be distinctive. She began playing with major jazz musicians at the age of just thirteen and so was a gifted child with a passion for jazz from an early age. As well as being a great piano player, she had the knack of arranging themes and making them incredibly engaging. Rather unusually, it was her religion and friendship with a priest named Father O'Brien that led to a collaboration where they sought out new venues to play jazz music in. She also worked for a foundation which helped musicians addicted to drugs and alcohol return to playing. That takes guts and she was one heck of a gutsy lady. She lectured on jazz along with Father O'Brien at a university and made well over a hundred recordings in her lifetime. When you listen to her play, you can hear why she was a popular and in-demand player.

The UK has produced women of note too. Ivy Benson, an alto saxophone and clarinet player was from Clacton, UK. She led an all-female swing band and was important in the 1940s as a leader, solo player and topped the bill at the London Palladium in 1944.

There was Marian McPartland who had an immense influence as a broadcaster, pianist and events arranger; Dinah Washington, Shirley Horn… The list is long and peppered with notable women who all had a huge impact.

Patti Bown—another player who benefitted from an association with leader Billy Eckstine. Among her associates were Roland Kirk, Duke Ellington and others. She was not limited to jazz, but also recorded with Quincy Jones, Aretha Franklin and the inimitable James Brown. In 1985, the *New York Times* declared her "a free spirit who is not bound by traditional way of doing things". She could switch from powerful, driving numbers to gentle interludes in a twinkling and was a truly gifted player and interpreter.

There were female songwriters gaining more acclaim too—these included Irene Higginbotham, Ann Ronell and Dorothy Fields.

There was a jazz alto sax player who took playing and singing to extremes known as 'Vi' Redd. Born in 1928 as Elvira Redd, she was known mainly as a bop player—bop being a style of jazz based around strong solo work. She played with some of the best-known musicians including Count Basie, Roland Kirk, Dizzy Gillespie and Marian McPartland. She was quite the vocalist also. As the daughter of drummer Alton Redd who played with musicians such as Kid Ory, Dexter Gordon and Wardell Gray, she was heavily influenced by the jazz music she heard as a child. Vi did a lot to break stereotypical images of female horn players. She was the first female to be one of the instrumental headliners at the Los Angeles festival in 1962—a fact reported in the *LA Sentinel* as follows,

> *Another first for the Las Vegas Festival on July 7 and 8 is achieved when Vi Redd, an attractive young girl alto sax player, becomes the first femme to be one of the instrumental headliners at a jazz festival. As a matter of fact, Miss Redd, may well be the first gal horn player in jazz history to establish herself as a major soloist.*

Perhaps the first, but certainly not the last, as our next chapter attests. Women were and continue to be an important force in jazz music on all fronts, whether as band leaders, musicians or vocalists—the softening side of jazz; also the wicked, vehement, vicious and malicious side of jazz—women can be all these things and more. It is impossible to even begin to include all the important women. What is important is that these women forged pathways in the heady, male-dominated world of jazz music. They proved they were decades ahead in musicianship, talent and the ability to connect with audiences across the world. Untold numbers of latter-day jazz musicians owe much to their strengths and their musical styles. Singers like Amy Winehouse, whose clear jazz influence made her voice one of the most distinctive of its time; Lady Gaga, steeped in the jazz of New York; Alison Moyet, and of course many modern-day jazz instrumentalists owe much to these women of the past, their character, style and formidability.

When you learn more about the women who influenced jazz in the past you come to realize a few things:

First, there were actually quite a few women around jazz right from the start.

Second, many of them handled their business affairs incredibly astutely.

Third, there are names which crop up time and time again in the careers of many of these pioneering jazz women, especially early on—many of these names are pioneers themselves: Dizzy Gillespie, John Hammond, Earl Hines, Miles Davis, John Coltrane, Billie Eckstine and Chick Webb are just a few. These musicians knew talent when they heard it regardless of gender. They wanted these musicians to be included and heard—against some pretty steep odds in some cases. They encouraged them to persevere and remain strong. It is important to acknowledge that without influential and boundary-pushing musicians giving women a chance, introducing them to the people who could help them progress beyond being just a girl in the band, many women musicians would not have had the success they enjoyed. Yet for many of them, even with support, it took all the courage in the world and every bit of fortitude they possessed to put themselves out there and change the world. It is thanks to many of these early role models that female jazz musicians of today find their road a slightly easier one.

Women in Jazz Today

SPEAKING WITH WOMEN in the jazz industry is an edifying, profound and incredibly educational experience. I have been talking to musicians for years and of course, a fair number of them are women—not so many in jazz it has to be said. It is difficult to describe how much things have changed over the past few decades—or conversely how much is still to be done. People talk about the dearth of women in jazz still, misogynistic attitudes, the old-fashioned, sometimes derogatory treatment of women. However, some also talk about the abiding positivity and willingness to discuss issues which have crept into jazz and gradually changed the entire essence of the business.

Some discussions get a little heated. People feel strongly that there is this unspoken obstacle barring the way of their careers. Others claim gender is never an issue. I have felt from the heart for some women who have been frustrated and thwarted, seemingly due to their gender, whilst for others, I have shared in the elation when they establish a first, small victory over prejudice. Yet, each discussion is different, women have many differing opinions and the only way to get to the heart of the current situation is to talk to the women in depth—so I did.

Women on Women

Many women feel there are areas within the jazz industry which are challenging; yet conversely some have had few problems. Some have experienced bullying and old-fashioned attitudes from men; others have benefitted from starting their own projects, working with both men and women. Alarmingly perhaps, a few even feel it is women themselves who are holding up real progress. Speaking on tokenism , one woman said she had no problems with it because, in her words, "at least it means women are given a place, even if it is just to make an event look politically correct." Another commented, "I prefer being the only woman in the band. Women can be absolute bitches to each other." While everyone is entitled to their opinion, I know many women who would find these comments shocking and completely out of step with modern day thinking. There seems to be no hard and fast consensus.

Sexist Matters—Is Misogyny Still With Us?

A simple fact is that when your gender becomes the issue of the moment, there is little you can do about it immediately. All the laws in the world will not protect you or make you feel less threatened or embarrassed at that very moment. In the face of overt sexism, there is no weapon which you can use without appearing super-feminist or reinforcing the mindset of some men. If you argue, you are a temperamental woman; if you leave the situation, you are moody, you can't take the pressure; and if you out-play them, you might be out of the band. Men also have a physical presence which many women cannot counter in difficult situations. An angry, shouting man is scary, especially when they get you someplace alone like the green room. No one wants to feel that surge of fear which strikes then, even if the threat is perceived and not real. That line between equality and simply ignoring the fact that differences between genders exist is a difficult one to tread.

In some places there are brutal 'cutting' sessions; in others jam or sit-in sessions. One musician (male) who organizes free improvisation sessions recently told me he felt women were more suited to free improvisation where they had jam or sit-in sessions because of the sharing and collective nature of the experience. However, cutting session were definitely more of a male thing. Cutting sessions were—

and are—brutal—a question of last musician standing or, as it has been put, who has the biggest dick. Women have no tool to bring to a cutting session. It puts women at a disadvantage and although there is often talk of 'things changing', 'things being different now' and experiences for women being 'less about the fact they are female than the music they play', there are still areas where women in jazz feel gender is an issue; and it is to the industry's shame that even some young musicians have felt the presence of misogyny. I asked the women if they had experienced any problems when they were younger.

Guitar player and educator Mimi Fox says,

> *I was 22 years old when I first started in the jazz industry. I found obstacles formidable. Much derisive comments and often a hostile experience at jam sessions and gigs.*

Jazz vocalist and composer Carmela Rappazzo says about her early career,

> *I was very young when I first started and it was a very different time in NYC—much wilder, much looser. For sure it had its ups, downs and difficulties and I would have to say that as a woman in jazz at that time one was a 'chick singer' and that was about it. Opportunities opened up for me to sing and sit in and I was, and still am, grateful for them, but I did have to 'bring it' in order to be considered. Women had to be very careful. 'Never sleep with a band member' was a very good rule. Band leaders would complain that women had to visit the rest room too often.*

When vocalist Jo Harrop first started out there were a few moments where she felt her femininity was seen as something people could use. She recalls,

> *There have been times as a young, rather naive singer, that I have been taken advantage of by men who have power and know they have something you want.*

I wondered, whether anything had changed. Is it different for a young woman just starting out today? Vocalist Indira May is young but already has experiences of her own to draw on. She says,

The most common thing is just being sexualized. I've had a lot of older people (including a tutor at university) tell me, 'Oh, don't worry, you've got the looks and that's half the battle'. I think that's what people are trying to change. I've also had a lot of people saying, 'men will really fancy you if you do this...' It's always about the male gaze. I think that is changing now and women are really pushing the boundary on things. For me, I appreciate anyone who connects with me on a personal level, but the main people I think about when I'm reaching out are women—it's how women view me and what they can take away and put into their own lives. I've had a few guys who've wanted to collaborate and because I've agreed, they instantly think I'm interested in them in a romantic sense which is quite funny because if you were in the business world and someone invited you to have a meeting, you wouldn't assume they fancied you or something. So I've had a few of those,' Let's make music, oh and by the way, you're really hot, let's go for a drink.' Well, no, this is still business. I've been on line ups where I'm the only girl and to the majority in that situation, which is men, they're not necessarily going to realize how that makes you feel, and it's quite daunting at times. Or I get referred to as, 'that singer on stage' when actually I've co-written the music and had as much input as the men I'm performing with.

Carmela Rappazzo photographed by Eliot Kamenitz

When pianist and singer Wendy Kirkland started out, she noticed different attitudes because she was a woman. She explains,

> *I've been aware of it from the start but unsurprised by it as I've a degree in engineering so I thought I would be prepared for it.*

Mimi Fox puts her thoughts rather succinctly,

> *Jazz women face the same gauntlet of oppressive circumstances that other women face in many fields.*

To which vocalist Ruby Turner adds,

> *Being female can have its problems in an industry like ours.*

Vocalist and radio show host Jenny Green comments,

> *I've been working with bands for many years and I've always been 'one of the guys'. I didn't think it was necessary for them to act differently around me. But in the 80's there was a lot of teasing going on. I had to watch my back!*

Trish Clowes relates the situation in jazz music to society as a whole and hints at the insidious nature of discrimination at times when she comments,

> *Like all parts of our society, misogyny and prejudice towards women is real and in current times, often unspoken and therefore more difficult to identify.*

Another difficulty, I think, is where to draw the line at what is sexism and what is not. Sometimes, it can feel as if the lines have become blurred and gender differences or confusions can be humorous. Before I became a writer I played in orchestras, sang in shows and festivals. I found little in the way of open prejudice. When I later joined bands, some of the funniest experiences came about where people were thrown by the fact that I wore a suit, hat and had very short hair as was the fashion at the time. At one gig where I was performing with *The Razors* in North London, I ducked into the ladies' washroom before we were due on stage. Suddenly the main door burst open and I could hear a lot of noise outside the cubicle. I opened the door and a very large man stood there and said, "Oi! Come on mate, you can't be in here.... ...Oh, oh, so sorry!" Someone had told him they had seen a bloke sneaking into the ladies toilets. Then, he was embarrassed as suddenly *he* was the bloke who had gone into the ladies toilets. It was fine and we laughed later (as he handed over the cash for the gig) but my band members (all male) found it hilarious for quite a while afterwards and offered me first place in the queue for the men's washroom at our next gig. At another gig, we found ourselves surrounded by people who were from one of the area's gangs. I was frightened but also felt protected as the only woman in the band and I remember distinctly thinking how grateful I was that I had four burly blokes with me. Was that wrong? It didn't feel so at the time. In neither of these events did I sense any form of sexism though the situation definitely panned out differently for me because I was female.

Jo Harrop. Photography by Emma Acton

Sometimes women have to cope with situations which a male musician would be unlikely to have to deal with—and not always coming from men. Jo Harrop tells us,

> *I've been heckled, but actually by a woman who wanted to get up and sing on my gig, and was determined to sabotage me—I am sure that wouldn't*

have happened if I were a guy. It's important to stand your ground and be empowered with knowledge from a young age on how to deal with these situations. As jazz is largely a male-dominated industry, you come up against the people at the top—employers, reviewers, agents etc. who are male, and I have had to deal with some bullying behaviour at times, where I had to fight my corner. The few women in these roles have perhaps been a little more sympathetic to the needs of a female singer.

So my next question was about venues. Have any of the women in our conversation ever had a sense that venues expect them to be or behave in a certain way?

Jo is still surprised at some venues' expectations and says,

Certain venues—I mean hotels, bars and private clubs, sometimes want you to look 'glamorous' as a female singer so you 'fit' their demographic. Sadly, I've been told to dress sexy, walk around crowds and perhaps sing to men in the audience—have a 'gimmick'. But I tend to walk away from that kind of thing. Many events (more so for private functions) I am told quite often go for a stereotypical young, blonde bombshell over an older more talented, but less attractive singer. So that kind of thing goes on, yes. A lot of these agents are more concerned with having a glossy picture and video than listening to the quality of the music.

The more we talk, the more I realize that many of the women in our conversation see what goes on in jazz as a reflection of entrenched attitudes in society as a whole.

Trombone player, educator and composer Sarah Gail Brand observes,

I think the expectation is, men know what they are doing and people are very surprised when they find out women know what they are doing. It is a bit like a microcosm of society. People think men are brighter than women and that doesn't really change when it comes to sub-groups of society like jazz listeners, performers and promoters. I don't think men who actually work closely with women think that, but it's something men feel when they haven't worked with women. Or, it may be they have worked with a woman who is just not good at jazz (and there are both men and women who aren't) but if they work with a woman who isn't

good, it's like, 'well, there you go, that means all women can't play jazz'.
There's the usual misogynist, sexist nonsense you find throughout society.

Sarah goes on to make an important point and one which echoes the wish of many people,

I really wish women in jazz—women in anything was not 'a thing'. I wish we were at that day. We don't have books on 'men in jazz' (unless you count all the jazz books) but we don't have a specific topic of 'men in jazz' and we know why—it is because men are considered to be the norm, which is nuts! I remember chairing a panel discussion and debate at the Glasgow Improvised Music Festival and I opened the debate on this topic by saying, 'I don't really want to be doing this again'. I think everybody knows why there are few women in jazz and it is to do with misogyny and sexism at large in society.

So how about the portrayal of women in media and on TV? Do the women feel the media bear any responsibility for attitudes which prevail perhaps? Wendy Kirkland feels strongly about the portrayal of live music on TV and says,

I am always depressed when presented with live music on television and I see the only females in the band are the singers. This needs to change. Until there are at least one third of females in the band I will not be happy.

International vocalist Tina May also comments on this and the lack of role models discussed earlier when she says,

Undeniably seeing more female players on stage has taken time—I'm convinced there has been a 'lack of visibility' on television, etc. It's as if the young women just give up on being professional musicians because there aren't many role models in evidence. Understandably so—there are easier ways to make a living.

Pianist and composer Joelle Khoury comments on her experience as a band leader.

Since I had my own jazz quintet (in-Version), we played and recorded my compositions. I was the only female in the group. The male members, although I believe they respected me for my creativity, really gave me a hard time. For example, if I made a remark, they would get angry and feel offended. The same remark made by my husband (and bass player) would be welcomed. Also, in order to keep them in a good mood and willing I would have to be overly nice and 'feminine'. I would smile, compliment them, make sandwiches etc.

Joelle Khoury, courtesy of Joelle Khoury

So it seems even when they are in the position of leader, women can sometimes be assigned a supporting role. The interesting thing about Joelle's comments is that she, to maintain the peace and cooperation, played the role of sandwich-maker and mood-lifter. It is this deeply ingrained cultural rut that many feel needs to change—and yet still, many of us find ourselves falling into the trap of playing 'female' roles. The peacekeepers, sometimes put up with behaviour from men which is at best rude and at worst unthinking, ignorant sexism.

Jazz vocalist Debbie Gifford says,

The jazz scene has always been dominated by males. I found that although I was educated in the field of music and have a degree in music education and a masters in performance, there was always some guy in the band or at a gig who didn't treat me as an equal.

Talking to female jazz performers, it is clear they sense another kind of discrimination which is more subtle. Trish Clowes hinted at this unspoken prejudice earlier and now renowned saxophone player Jane Ira Bloom explains further.

> *The truth of the matter is that the kind of discrimination I encountered was not always so clear. A covert form of discrimination; the phone calls you don't get, the absence of inclusion is much more insidious. It never deterred me from pursuing the path I had set for myself, but it sure added on years.*

Kim Cypher gives another example of this subtler discrimination. Her husband Mike is bass player in Kim's band and Kim explains,

> *There have been occasions when I have contacted a booker and have received no reply. When Mike has contacted the same booker in the capacity of 'my manager' (and male), we have been offered a gig straight away.*

Kim is not alone when she acknowledges that the presence of a male band member supporting you is useful. Band leader, soprano saxophone player, flautist and educator Jane Bunnet's opinion is,

> *I have, almost all my professional music life been the only woman in the group. I have been very fortunate to have my male partner who is a trumpet player (Larry) by my side.*

It is Larry, incidentally who provides pictures, replies to inquiry emails and sorts out quotes from Jane, at least initially.

Vocalist Georgia Mancio says,

> *Personally, I have very rarely encountered difficulties of prejudices from other musicians... I did notice though that virtually all club owners, promoters, agents, journalists and sound engineers were male and this has led to some more difficult situations.*

Singer and radio presenter Grace Black is in a position of being a significant part of two different areas of jazz. She is a singer and also presents a radio show. She comments,

As a vocalist I've never come across any misogyny, but I think that it is still very hard for women who play instruments to be recognized on the same level as men, although this is changing slowly in the UK with players like Karen Sharp and Georgina Bromilow getting good recognition. In my opinion, gender shouldn't matter and it should be about the quality of the player and their ability to interpret the great music.

Georgia Mancio by Carl Hyde 2015

What about non-performing women—what do they think? Women in unique positions to observe how things are in the jazz industry without being musicians themselves? Women whose work takes them into the jazz world in roles that doesn't propel them onto the stage. It seems here, things have moved on though not much. Public relations manager and musician Amanda Bloom tell us,

I have always appreciated the authenticity of jazz as it is constantly evolving and the music is highly individualistic. Jazz musicians strive to create their own sound and style and not only push themselves, but push the boundaries of music and improvisation. For these reasons and more I find jazz to be a really rewarding genres to promote.

From where I stand on the promotional side of the music industry I have not yet experienced negative attitudes due to the fact I am a woman. I am fortunate that my boss and mentor, Max Horowitz, is socially conscious and from the beginning taught me how to have a place in this business without feeling I would be at any sort of disadvantage. I have been very fortunate in that regard, but there are, however, many women who do face difficulties and negative bias.

Press officer Ellie Thompson comments,

> *I often find that male acts are given more of a chance than women. If they have no previous credit to their name, women are dismissed frequently as being 'amateur', whilst men are given labels like 'DIY' or 'Underground'.*

Marketing manager at the London's *606 Club* and photographer Emma Acton adds,

> *I have never been victim of any detrimental attitude due to being a woman. However, this does not mean to say that it does not occur within the industry. Although times are changing slowly and it is becoming more acceptable to speak out, there will be many cases of discrimination that are left unnoticed.*

Radio station co-owner and host Anthea Redmond of *Jazz Bites Radio* was a publicist for many years before co-funding a radio station so has a good idea of how profiling and presentation can make or break careers. She offers her opinion,

> *The radio has been a huge learning curve for me and reading the history of jazz in recent years has taught me much—especially the struggle experienced by those women who both sang and played jazz right from its outset more than a hundred years ago. Things are very different today and we have seen some outstanding female jazz voices on both sides of the Atlantic, but I still feel women jazz musicians warrant a higher profile in jazz media across the board. More kudos where it's due, together with credit for their individual writing abilities, artistic skill and creativity. For me, it's a logical progression, the only direction in which to go.*

So these radio, marketing and PR women, while not experiencing overt misogyny are aware of its presence in the jazz industry.

Gender of course, is no longer clear cut either. I was recently at a *Jazz Meet Up*—a wonderful event in many cities where people who want to go to gigs meet up beforehand and go in a group. At the same venue, was a far larger LGBT meet-up, who took to loving the music. The musician playing told me that they often feel out of place at gigs so she was really pleased such a large group were here. There is a further blurring of the lines and it is no longer as simple as male and female. Trish Clowes remarks,

There are loads of different ways to be who you are in this music, and I certainly do not speak for all women. I think we should be more concerned with challenging the terms femininity and masculinity. It is not binary. Yes, women and men are physically different (and for a certain percentage of people this is not clear cut either, for reasons of genetics, or choice... as a society we are learning to catch up here), but this idea that women are essentially feminine and men are essentially masculine is madness. Ultimately, I just want people to be listening to my music and enjoying how I interact with the musicians on stage. Everything else is a distraction... Obviously, people have chosen to come to the gig in the first place, or buy the record or whatever, and why they've done that could sometimes be because I'm a novelty to them... But whatever. Life is too short.

Terri Lyne Carrington by John Watson

Echoing some of these thoughts, world-class drummer, educator and composer Terri Lyne Carrington comments,

Gender is not so binary any more. I would like to see all music forms

embrace that ideology more as well. We were socialized a certain way but that has all changed. But it still takes time to see the results of this and for some men to accept this. We are in that phase now.

Faye Patton by Benjamin John

Bandleader, pianist/guitarist and singer-songwriter Faye Patton has slightly different views and believes there are advantages to blurring the lines of gender. She says,

There are LGBT festivals, and opportunities to perform at Pride, and something called Queer and Unsigned...... For a huge majority of people gender does actually boil down to binary issues and one has to choose—how do I approach this, play this role as a man or woman and which one is society currently treating me as? I'm the kind of LGBT person that I sort of experience the world (of which jazz is just a part) from both genders' perspectives and somewhere in between. Women can benefit from saying in a situation—what would I do if I was (traditionally encultured as) a 'male'. Maybe: fight harder, get it wrong and not care, not give a f***k, never apologize or explain, command not ask, be relaxed, be nonchalant, close the deal with confidence. Whether you are male or female or somewhere in between, you need to know when to hold yourself to a punishingly high standard just to prove you can play at all—and *when to know that you are enough. Sometimes the traditional 'female' qualities win the day—for any musician regardless of gender, be that extremely ever so nice, sweet person that everybody wants to work with. It's a breath of fresh air! Fight if need be for the platform, but when you have the floor—relax, trust, enjoy, let the audience in and let the music speak for itself.*

So what do women think about the role of writer, journalist and editors? Are we doing enough to make everything about equality or should we make it not about the struggle for equality but rather just concentrate on the talent? Are editors worried about taking sides or appearing to do so? A couple of years ago I wrote a piece about women in music which was published with the caveat 'Op:Ed'—which is something editors put beside a piece to show they do not necessarily agree with what is written. The piece discussed the 'Me too' campaign and the influence it has had, namely that of empowering women to feel they could speak up about people who had bullied them. I discussed changing attitudes within the music industry—and places where work was needed. As it covered areas outside music, I also gave an example of my own experience where I would have spoken up if it had happened today though at the time did not. The piece also included positive steps that were being taken. It was read thousands of times and the feedback was incredibly positive. Excerpts are here:

The 'Me Too' campaign has empowered women (and men who advocate for them) to be able to speak out and say how they have felt discriminated against. It has also had the benefit of highlighting the power which women have and that this is growing ....

The vital roles of and injustices dealt to women has been highlighted by the campaign but actually the influence has always been there. It is just now it is acknowledged and some men—the bullies and the perverts— have apologized or been shamed. The sad truth is these men probably would be bullies wherever their power lay, getting their way however they saw fit. The only thing is now they will be held accountable ....

> *Whether that discrimination is perceived, actual, deliberate or just thoughtless and unintentional. I have heard perfectly respectable musicians talk about their mums being 'typically wifey' whatever that means and I have heard musicians discussing the physical merits of both performers and audience members.................................*

> *After all, music knows no bounds. We have made a start; the stone is rolling and momentum is being gained. One issue is on the way to being resolved in small steps—maybe. (Now, we just have to work our way through the rest on the list).*

Almost two years later—after I had parted company with the magazine who published this piece—I put out a tweet in which I made the point that when the article was first published, the editor was brave to publish but also felt it necessary to add the 'Op:Ed'; and that nowadays it would not be necessary, as more people are talking about the issues openly. The article was deleted from the site almost immediately, which I found surprising. It still takes a particularly brave editor to publish a piece which tackles these issues and perhaps they deleted the piece because they ran out of space or because I no longer wrote for them though interestingly enough they left a lot of my pieces up. So, was it deleted because it drew attention to the issue again? This led to my next questions for the women around our table—and this is, should we write and publish more on the subject? Does the press have a responsibility? Do they present female musicians fairly?

Trish Clowes' opinion is,

> *Journalists and editors have a responsibility here. I generally like to focus on my music when I'm doing an interview for a magazine or feature. It's unfair that women are the only people that get asked about gender and those interview spaces are extremely valuable for the music we are making. However, there are times when I've made comments on the debate that haven't been printed because they are not sensational or provocative enough, or I challenge 'masculinity' in some way. I have also seen other women's comments blown up out of proportion or context, twisting their meaning. So, if people want to talk about any of these*

very sensitive issues more, they have to be dealt with sensitively by whomever is in control of putting their comments out there.

Proving a Point

A frequent observation by women I speak with in jazz is the sense they have that they must prove themselves more than their male counterparts. They agree that there are more women in the jazz industry and that they cover more roles than in the past. Thankfully, they are not expected to dress like dolls or remain the ever-grateful starlet, but do female jazz musicians feel they have to outshine the men?

Kim Cypher responded,

> *I think being a woman you perhaps have to prove yourself more. I only say this because I have had incidents where people have made comments like, 'you can actually play!' Being a woman and an independent artist is no mean feat.*

Jo Harrop says,

> *As a female singer I do feel I have to keep on proving myself to make sure I can work. I think as a singer that it is perhaps not as hard trying to find work as say a female bass player or drummer but there are some wonderful ladies proving that women are just as great as the guys doing what has largely been a male dominated role in the industry.*

Florence Halfon by George Talbot

Florence Halfon is a record company executive for Warner Jazz and when I asked her about whether it is difficult for a woman to become record a company executive, she replied,

Not so much now my work is better known but I remember males in the industry being surprised I know so much about jazz. Women always have to prove everything.

Joelle Khoury adds,

Things have changed, but the road was excessively hard. I had to provide a lot more proof than any man I know around for me to be taken seriously. It takes years, then after that you can sometimes be so worn out that you don't feel like doing it anymore.

Some (men) Just Can't Get Their Heads Around It

For some men there seems to be a kind of occlusion in their brains between what they know to be true and what their entrenched mindset tells them. Despite seeing and hearing brilliant female musicians they cannot bring themselves to accept it their equality. Kim Cypher relates an incident where two male audience members were discussing her performance. She relates the conversation with some amusement:

They decided I must be miming because it sounded so good."

Ellie Thompson adds,

I feel like you are often expected to be 'lovely' as a woman; you can't have your own individual character. This means that I've had clients ask if I'm 'serious' enough to be handling their campaign even before it has begun, which is really undermining. Those kinds of reactions can be extremely discouraging for some women in the industry. I find I have to be very thick-skinned and determined to be listened to in some situations. Also, after answering the 'phone, I am always referred to as 'the secretary' in emails leading on from those conversations, while my male colleagues are not. Again, this is infuriating. Women are still assumed to be working in the most junior positions of a company, which makes everyday life in the industry more difficult and can put women off of targeting more senior positions.

Sometimes men will happily acknowledge a woman's virtuosity but can't resist the need to qualify their comments with something a little more revelatory. Wendy Kirkland tells of a couple of experiences where men have unwittingly put their feet in it and revealed a sexist attitude. A 50-something male jazz pianist told her, "I've heard you're a great singer and you play a little bit of piano". Another man, this time a 20-something bass player, told her, "You think you can play that singer's pad? It's difficult you know."; and then, from a recently retired gentleman of 60 or so, "Can I just say it's been a long while since I heard a pianist with such a great touch? Well, for a woman anyway". And which industry had this gentlemen recently retired from? You guessed it—music!

Mimi Fox shares a story which happened early in her career.

> *When I was just 28, and my first album had come out, I had a manager who was helping me. When he sent out my album to potential promoters, one got back to him and said he did not believe it was a woman playing on the album.*

Sarah Brand looks at both sides when she comments on attitudes towards women,

> *It depends on who holds the attitudes. The men I work with never consider my gender to be anything to do with my ability. In general though, there is the notion (as with a lot of art forms that require intellectual understanding of the process we go through) that women aren't perhaps bright enough to understand the technical requirements in terms of harmony, form, composition and that sort of thing. Also, in jazz you need to be confident and people don't expect women to be confident. I think, to be honest, the attitudes are held more by promoters and the audience. I have been told, 'Oh, we have enough women on the bill this year' by festival organizers, which is extraordinary. I have never had it said to me that women can't play jazz but I've certainly had the sense that some people think a woman in jazz is a pianist or vocalist and that she wouldn't be expected to understand the technical demands of playing jazz.*

I think this response includes so many of the problems facing female

Sarah Brand, Photograph by Ryan Dean Bedingfield.

performers today. Some still think women can only be vocalists or piano players. Festivals pepper their bills with enough women to be 'politically correct' and then stop at some point which makes them feel they have achieved this. Who decides where that point is? Should any decision in music be based around having 'enough' of any kind of player? Is there ever going to come the day when it is about selecting acts based on talent and not so much presenting a politically correct face to the public even when it means some acts miss out due to gender?

I have watched Sarah single-handedly transform an audience from a crowd of half-interested observers to one where they were engaged and calling out ideas for Sarah to improvise around—seagulls, ducks, tractors and sheep being just some of the ideas. The festivals who stop at a certain number of acts for any reason should pay attention.

I organized the *London Jazz Platform* in 2017—an event sponsored by the US station Jazz Bites Radio—which showcased fourteen acts from the UK, Europe and one from New Orleans. Gender never crossed my mind—I selected bands I knew would be good. As it turned out, of the forty plus musicians playing, just under half were female.

Things are Changing

Though obstacles remain, there is a real sense of change happening, albeit slowly. The number of women appearing on the jazz scene is definitely increasing and seems to have done so rapidly in the last few years. Women are aware of themselves in much the same way a person recognizes their own ethnicity or age and, while some people cling to outdated misogynistic precepts, most are simply seeking out fellow musicians who can fill a spot in the band—and many women fit the bill. It takes tenacity and a strong spirit, but women are becoming empowered and confident. From this writer's point of view, this change is positive and welcome. Now, when I go to a gig there are usually women there—and not just a few. Granted, we usually notice each other because we are few in number, but the fact is they are there. I asked the women whether they too had noticed change, and does this mean more opportunities for women in jazz?

Debbie Gifford says,

> Over the years I have seen more women jazz musicians being recognized for their talents both as instrumentalists and vocalists. I believe this recognition is helping to change attitudes and more opportunities are being enjoyed by women musicians.

Trish Clowes is also positive. She comments,

> Times have changed, there's no doubt. John Fordham's biography of Ronnie Scott details the misogyny on/around the jazz scene in the past but I've been lucky enough to play with saxophonist Pete King a couple of times in the past year and he treated me just like everyone else, and he used to book pianist Nikki Iles for his band in Ronnie's at a time when you didn't really see women much on stage. So whatever is going on generally, there are always people who just care about the music and over your lifetime, you gravitate towards them, no matter who you are. The thing is, even though it's great to be part of a moment when

these issues are being discussed more in society, when it comes to my own work on my crafting/creating music etc, I try not to dwell on these potentially negative things. I just want to focus on being good at what I do and I haven't got the time or energy to wonder or worry about what someone else might assume about me. There's all kinds of reasons why you might get a strange vibe from someone, it's not necessarily because I'm female in a mostly male environment and this person is sexist. Occasionally I encounter sexist comments or behaviour from other musicians or (more often) other people in the business, or audience members. On rare occasions I've verbally had to take a stand (that goes beyond an eye roll), but I count myself very fortunate that I have never been physically intimidated or assaulted by anyone. Perhaps one could say that as a woman, I am less likely to be working with men who have sexist attitudes, particularly as a band leader and composer. All the people I work with are open minded and respectful and when I am booked by male musicians, I doubt they have sexist attitudes either.

Jazz is often talked about as a music genre which reflects society. This comes across in conversations with both male and female musicians. When I interview musicians they often comment on how the music changes according to what is going on socially. When society become dull and boring the music reflects this until some innovator decides to add something to the mix to make it interesting and creates something new. When society is restless and lots of change is happening the music reflects this too and changes happen rapidly. Vocalist and festival organizer Beverley Bierne expresses her opinion when she says,

I think in society as attitudes to women have changed, that's reflected in the jazz world. But I have thought occasionally that jazz is like the last bastion, the final frontier. But it's finding its way. There's a lot of great women in jazz to celebrate. I think if the women who are drawn to jazz just keep creating great music, that speaks for itself. Great art always finds a way.

For many women there is a longing that gender not be seen as an issue. They want to be seen simply as musicians, pieces in a band, parts of the overall picture and gender should not cloud possibilities. For some, nothing, gender included, is going to get in the way of life.

Singer, actor and artist Patti Boulaye says about her experiences,

First of all, I don't believe anyone has the power over my destiny except God and me. No-one owes me a living as a woman. No-one can play

Beverley Bierne. Photo by Goat Noise Photography

God with my life. If a door closes, I'll search for an open door. If I can't find one, I'll create it and walk through it. I believe in the law of the jungle where each day the lion has to catch the slowest gazelle in order to feed itself and the gazelle has to outrun the lion in order to survive. I am a woman and I am black. If anyone has a problem with that then the problem is theirs, not mine. I am not a slave to man or money. That way neither can play God to me or in my life. I lived through a genocide, so I have a healthy respect for my life and my Creator, but as for my fellow man, he and I are easily dispensable. I am unusual in that I do not consider myself a woman in jazz but rather I think of myself as an entertainer in jazz. I am not precious about what I do. There have been better performers like Bessie Smith, Ella Fitzgerald, Billie Holiday,

> *Nina Simone, Sarah Vaughan, Peggy Lee and in my opinion no one has come close to the old jazz greats in recent times.*

I agree with these sentiments. Vocalist Alicia Renee *aka* Blue Eyes puts it simply,

> *I have always wanted to be seen as an instrument, nothing else.*

Body Matters & Difficult Questions:

Do women musicians ever use their femininity to their advantage and can it help being female?

Women's bodies are built differently from men's. Fact. Many instruments are heavy and being on the road is demanding and tiring. I wondered how the women I spoke to felt about the physicality of being female.

Kim Cypher thought about this,

> *Maybe being a woman in this industry is a little tougher because of the physicality of lugging all the gear around and coping with the whole lifestyle of being on the road. Sometimes I find it stressful that I have the worry of hair and make-up and need to allow time to get ready for a gig, whereas perhaps the men are a little less concerned with this (certainly the men I work with). That's not to say they don't look lovely, but they are certainly more interested in eating before a gig than getting ready, whereas I'd get ready first any day.*

I know this is a bit of a hot potato when it comes to discussing jazz. It is the elephant in the room at times. There are people who would accuse some female performers of using their feminine charms at times to get their way. Some women dress up in full regalia—make up, high heels, tight skirts, skinny jeans, the works. They look great and why not? However, some definitely change when they discuss musical technicalities with women or men. It is cringe making when you see a capable woman making out she knows very little about the technicalities of music, when you know she knows a lot. It feels like a step back, yet I have watched irascible grumpy male musicians melt when a female asks them to explain something or show them their drum kit. I wondered if this was acceptable or even if women were conscious of it.

Debbie Gifford comments,

> I don't think that using my femininity is an advantage as much as how to perform for the audiences' enjoyment and include them in the magic. I started my performance career at the age of four singing a solo in a musical theatre production and it was during that song I learned how important it is to make the connection with the audience. ...the audience is my mirror—if they reflect the emotions I convey in my performance then I feel the magic and they do too.

But some women are not helpful either. I have seen strong women play the helpless female as soon as a man turns up and some who make cringe-worthy flirtatious moves on men old enough to be their father because they want to play in their band. It is a tool, maybe, but over-use can simply affirm what some men think—that women are there to look pretty and not taken on their musical merits. A female singer recently told Wendy Kirkland,

> I like the musicians in my band to be men. Having other women in the band just doesn't look right.

Conversely, Carmela Rappazzo says,

> I was never considered one of the 'pretty girls'. I liked being considered a band member.

Kim Cypher adds, with humour,

> It (being female) does have the advantage of being able to chat up the barman for a glass of wine.

As a writer I have found that being a woman has helped on occasion. Some men react better to women than male interviewers. One musician who had not given the press anything for eight years gave me an interview after we had shared a cup of coffee and talked about life in general while he skirted the issue of music. Once he opened up, he told me he felt far happier talking to me than to a man.

Sometimes the physical differences between men and women come in to play—particularly when it comes to safety. I was at a gig a couple of years ago when a slightly drunk man decided to slip his hand into the back pocket of my jeans. As I turned away a walking stick landed rather heavily on the man's shoulder and a musician I had interviewed recently said to him, "Mate, if she doesn't hit you, I fuckin' will." I have also had my own stalker on the internet and had to jump into a taxi when I was followed to a hotel in London. Would a man be followed home from a gig? So, with the limitations nature throws our way physically, is there any thing else the women wanted to add about femininity or opportunities? This question gives the women a lot to consider and their replies are measured.

Wendy Kirkland says,

> *I think some women can use femininity in ways I wouldn't. Perhaps it might have been helpful if I'd shown more cleavage, pretended to be stupid, fluttered my eyelashes or worse but I just can't do it. I'm an intelligent, experienced woman for God's sake. Why should I behave like an inferior to get my own way?*

I asked Patti Boulaye does she feel being female has advantages and she replied with honesty,

> *My femininity gives me power and, God willing, some wisdom and better understanding of the human character and yes, I use it to my advantage.*

Jo Harrop adds,

> *There's no reason why women shouldn't do as well as the men now if they work hard and have the talent, the drive, the belief. I haven't met any young girls playing on their femininity for some time. I'm not sure if you would get a gig just by dressing up pretty and flirting with the booker!*

Composer, saxophone player and educator Camille Thurman says,

I wouldn't look at it as an advantage or disadvantage being female. I can only speak for myself but my goal every time I play is to be the best I can be—sound great, have fun and let the music speak for itself— someone who loves the music, takes command and sounds amazing regardless of gender.

Emma Acton adds to these comments by saying,

Within the jazz world there is very little promiscuity. It is about the music, the community and the people so when it comes to 'using one's femininity', it isn't really as relevant and appropriate as it is in other genres of music. I believe the only way within jazz to play on femininity is with female innocence. A delicate image. But then, every artist has a way they style themselves, so I don't believe that this can necessarily be perceived as a negative thing within the jazz industry.

Patti Boulaye points out that,

I do believe I am a superior being because I have been created with the ability to bring life into being. That's what I love about being a woman. The rest is a journey and a game and only I can choose how I want to play the game and travel through life. I bet that was not the answer you were expecting! For me, being a woman is the perfect state of being because I know no other way."

Ongoing Change in Attitudes

First some facts: I took the *Oxford University Jazz Orchestra* (OUJO) as a main reference and it is fairly typical of the current situation. The OUJO has two female musicians out of twenty members. On a tour to Bangladesh in 2017, the big band the *Donut Kings* comprised three females and sixteen males. In two of the top jazz ensembles at Oxford, there is only twenty percent female representation. This is current, and it should be different. Oxford as a whole is trying to counteract the under-representation of women in jazz, but the fact is, by the time young women reach post-school age, their numbers are already smaller than men in jazz. Still, these rates show a small increase as years ago the numbers were even smaller—it is taking that long.

As more women come into jazz, more follow. Suddenly, there are role models, women in positions of power, making the choices. The numbers both on stage and in audiences are increasing. I have observed positive changes in the attitudes to women across the jazz industry and wanted to know if the women in this conversation had also seen this.

Sarah Brand has noticed changes,

> *In my early gigs there were definitely more men than women—with only 3 players in a big band of 15 members for example. Now it is different. I see more women and younger people as I get older. There are more women. It tends to be women with men but some are on their own or in female groups. There is not a dramatic change. I did research about 6 years ago on this area and none of the volunteers were women. There are more women in the audiences than on stage.*

The ever far-sighted Terri Lyne Carrington says,

> *They (reactions to women) have changed but not enough. Some people are still surprised but if you are worldly, you see these changes and either get with it or get left behind eventually. With women's liberation I think we can do whatever job we want and pursue happiness how we want—the same as our male counterparts. We were socialized a certain way but that has all changed. But it still takes time to see the results of this and for some men to accept this. We are in that phase now.*

On the situation right now for women, Faye Patton comments,

> *It's quite good—there's organizations like Women in Jazz, (womeninjazz. co.uk) there's Tomorrow's Warriors (https://tomorrowswarriors.org/). Also artists like Georgia Mancio who are campaigning to hold the jazz industry and press more accountable and fighting for equality on the live scene. Education is improving somewhat but more needs to be done. There is only one club I know of run by women—The Green Note (Jazz club in London). Female owned clubs and venues are essential...... Many men just don't seem to like dealing with/talking to female artist or women generally.*

Interestingly enough it was at a recent Faye Patton gig in London where she, myself and three women audience members had a long discussion about how women are represented in music and other industries. The discussion was very lively and it was clear that the women felt very strongly about attitudes to women in their professions. They were amazed when I told them of how some orchestras are now choosing musicians using blind auditions and how this is changing the proportion of women in their numbers. Although their industries had made huge steps in equality issues and they felt things were definitely moving in the right direction, they had nonetheless noticed how few women jazz musicians there are compared to men and were a little bit confused as to how this could still be so in our time. They also spoke of how they enjoyed seeing women perform as well as men, they just wished there were more of them.

Kim Cypher comments

> *My general experience is very positive as a woman in jazz. I work with very respectful people and I am regarded as an equal. I think it is an exciting time for women in jazz right now. We are living in a time when anybody can do anything and women are empowered as we continue to move away from an industry that was traditionally male-dominated. It is exciting to see so many incredible female jazz musicians on the scene, especially in terms of instrumentalists.*

In America, Carmela Rappazzo has been on the jazz scene in New York and now in New Orleans for many years. She comments

> *Attitudes towards women have changed over time slowly, slowly, it's still not as easy for women.*

Vocalist Tina May adds,

> *I work with many women: Nikki Iles (piano), Karen Sharp (tenor sax), Julie Walkington (double bass), Patricia Lebeugle (double bass), Kathy Stobart (tenor sax). Gradually we see more women players on stage. I choose musicians for their playing not their gender, though. I'm happy to be with on stage with the right musician for the music—male*

or female.

Faye Patton talks of a supportive network which is important for performers, especially women. When we spoke about this, she told me,

> *I owe a debt of gratitude to singer Sue McGreeth who let me open for her many years ago and wrote reviews of me and Juliet Kelly (who dubbed me 'Nu Jazz' and booked me to play. Also Toni Kofi whom I met at The Spice of Life when I opened for the gig he played. He's been encouraging me ever since. Also Larry Batley, a double bassist, who posts lots of great stuff on social media that champions women and black history. DJ radio show host Ron Hector and Laurie at Jazz London Radio support women without making a big deal of it—which is great and most welcome. Nolan Regent of Toulouse Lautrec Jazz Club is also a firm ally of women and LGBT artists.*

So, I wondered does Faye feel men are taking her as an equal? She responded,

> *Yes and no. It depends whether you are talking musicians, promoters, bookers. Depends what age, demographics, etc. I've got some amazing men on my side. Some of the young men I work with just have a natural expectation that I will be good and are neither surprise I can play well or disappointed if I mess up, they are just really chilled out. It's a good lesson. Male musicians have been brought up to be allowed to make mistakes and even be quite average and not feel self-conscious about it. Older male promoters/venue managers/festival directors are more problematic. I've been consistently ignored and been made to feel invisible and like my stories/songs/interpretation of life and jazz is just not of interest. Also my look (suit and tie) is not anything they've dealt with before. I'm not the cocktail dress wearing 'singer', I'm one of the band, leading with an instrument and we all wear suits/ties. I dress like the guys—it's a well-known lesbian style and to have no understanding of it to me borders on ignorance at best. Potentially homophobic, but of course I can't prove it. Sometimes my male band members have to point out to the sound engineer that I am the boss. I look young and maybe they don't think I'm a serious contender in the professional adult world.*

Women Doing It for Themselves

Women in jazz tend to gravitate to bands and situations where they feel comfortable. These may be groups of their own making or ones they try out for and realize they are among people who are happy in their own skin and don't feel the need to play one-upmanship whatever the issue is. There is also a sense of support amongst most women musicians in the jazz world as well as a sense of jubilation at the presence of an increasing number of women. Many women of the past gained popularity by forming all-female bands, sometimes because there was no other opportunity for them. Ask whether this is a good thing today or not and the opinions differ. Sarah Brand comments,

There have been many all-female groups in the past and there are some today. I am not a fan of all women projects. It tends to ghettoise us and implies only women can play together. It should be more equal, 50:50, 60:40 whatever. Women and men should work together as much as possible to show that this is normal, not a big deal.

Trish Clowes says,

When I feel uncomfortable, I stay away and find situations or people that don't make me feel uncomfortable. Am I losing out? No idea. But I feel pretty fulfilled in my work so whatever challenges there have been, I've managed to make things work for me. On a slightly different note, I've always been pretty entertained by observing the change in someone's attitude towards me before and after I play.

Kim Cypher explains her delight in jazz music,

Involvement in this book is a great opportunity to celebrate being a woman in jazz. I absolutely love what I do. I am a creative person and need an outlet for my creativity. I work with some amazing people and I'm very proud to be part of a great sisterhood. Support between the women in jazz I know is incredible. We are there for each other to pick each other up after the knock backs, to support and advise each other and to celebrate each other's success.

Beverley Bierne says she finds support among other female vocalists. She comments,

> *I have a few jazz singer friends and I love them. I mean, after all, who else can understand you more and what you're dealing with than another jazz singer? We have a lot of chin-wags and giggles, especially another female jazz singer.*

Camille Thurman adds,

> *I do believe there is more attention to women players which is good (opportunities for exposure, recognition etc). It's a work in progress. I believe we still have a way to go. On one degree it's about talent, but then you still see an imbalance in the representation of women band leaders or side women in major jazz festivals/venues. In some cases, it has nothing to do with talent and is just a fulfillment of a 'fascination' which defeats the purpose of actually hiring and respecting a person because of their ability and skill.*

Terri Lyne Carrington has a vision for the future of jazz, and particularly women within the jazz industry—and she has committed her considerable influence to doing something very positive to help. She says,

> *I'm very hopeful about the future of jazz. I just feel the culture has to change to accept women composers and musicians more equitably and not render them or their contributions invisible. I think the change is happening slowly, it's not where it should be yet, so that's why I have decided to really work on this problem and dedicate a big part of my energy to this issue in starting the new institute at Berklee. There are initiatives like 'Women In Jazz' which is a collective of musicians who highlight the misconceptions female artists must deal with. They organize live events, workshops and radio shows.*

Jazz soprano saxophone player and composer Jane Ira Bloom says,

> *Over the years I've learned about the qualities of the musicians that*

help bring my music to life. It's just something that you learn if you pay attention to all your performance experiences in an investigative way. I had been working largely with men in my groups until I met pianist Dawn Clement years ago in Seattle. She connected instantly to the kind of composing and improvising I was doing. Something just clicked and I've been working with her ever since. The music connected us and it's terrific to be working with another woman.

Some found the pervading misogyny served them better than they might first have thought. For Debbie Gifford, finding a constant lack of respect inspired her to form her own band. She tells the story,

The jazz scene has always been dominated by males. I found that although I was educated in the field of music (B.Sc. in Music Education and a Masters in Performance) there was always some guy in the band, at the gig, who didn't treat me as an equal. I was looked down on as if I was not a musician, just the 'girl singer' who didn't know anything about music, just opened her mouth to sing. This attitude was wide spread and brought me to the point of creating my own big band and smaller ensembles. I built my reputation as vocalist and band leader by respecting the talents of other musicians and treating them the way I wished to be treated on and off the bandstand. I am a professional musician and being professional I always have all my music transposed into my key for every player, a set list for the performance and if needed, all necessary sound equipment.

Just the girl singer indeed!

Reactions to Successful Women

So, given the variation in how female musicians feel about the treatment they received and reactions when they started out, does this change as they become experienced and, perhaps more revealing, when they become more powerful in the jazz-world? I think from my observations, it is true that a respected musician can have a bad night and still be respected—they have history, audiences know their music and what they are capable of. For a newcomer a bad night is more risky and can kill a career before it really gets started. I wondered if this was true across the board. Have any of the women in this conversation experienced a change in how they were treated and viewed after achieving their success?

Ruby Turner says,

> *Peoples' attitude can change when you've had some success. But you must be aware that it's not always genuine. It can be pretentious and shallow, beneficial to whoever needs to be in your company. Unless you remain 'at the top of your game' as they say, then it becomes short lived. Fame is temporary so be sure you're comfortable with who you are, on the rise, peddling in the middle or struggling at the bottom. When your success and so-called power desert you, you had better be happy to be just you.*

Wendy Kirkland adds,

> *I think some men will always react adversely to successful/powerful women in any industry; those who are afraid of change or who have built their own careers using bullying or who have serious issues with their own self-confidence. It's a good job I'm a stubborn, outspoken so and so.*

Beverley Bierne agrees,

> *There are always 'some' people who struggle with successful women in jazz but maybe that's just a normal human reaction rather than a gender thing. It's a competitive business. I'd say on the whole most people in the industry are incredibly supportive of each other.*

Patti Boulaye remarks,

> *People react differently to any successful person in jazz or any other genre. I never consider myself a powerful woman as it's playing on being a god and pride always comes before a fall. When it comes to power, I will only believe someone is powerful if they can live forever. In my opinion, if they can't live forever, then they don't have any power.*

Success undoubtedly has its benefits. I asked Jane Ira Bloom to share some of her achievements which mean a lot to her personally and she told me,

> *There have been lots of highlights for me—the experience surrounding being commissioned by the NASA Art program, having an asteroid named after me—albeit with a somewhat eccentric orbit[1] and being the namesake of the first Bloom festival in 2009 in Brooklyn featuring cutting-edge women, new music artists and having pioneering work that I've done held as a model for young women leaders.*

Where Do Men Fit In?

Many jazz women of the past who gained success had behind them men who supported them. Alice Coltrane had John; *The Sweethearts* had Laurence Jones and Maurice King; Betty Carter had Ray Davis and Dizzy Gillespie; Sarah Vaughan had Billy Eckstine and Dizzy Gillespie; and Melba Liston had Dizzy Gillespie and Randy Weston. So although their talent was prodigious, their rise to fame was helped by influential men who championed them.

It is also important to acknowledge that some men are way ahead of the field, saw the signs of change years back and supported women in jazz. There is room to mention only three here, though there are many more who feel equality should not be as distant a future as it seems at times. As a writer I have rarely felt less respected because I am female. I have had people who have changed their language and approach in emails and social media posts once they realize, I am not a man (Sammy being a unisexual name) but generally, I have never felt men taking a stand against me being female. Other writers on the other hand have been protective, advising me about attitudes I might encounter when interviewing this person or that person, but I find generally, if you are honest with the interviewee or musician whose

---

1 The asteroid in question is asteroid 6083 Janeirabloom .

work you are reviewing, gender is never an issue—they are, of course, getting exposure out of it so quantifying is difficult.

33 Jazz Records is a UK record label which saw the imbalance between male and female performers as far back as 1989 and decided to do something to redress this. Paul Jolly, the label's executive producer explains,

> *During the latter part of the 1980s following ten years of the 33 Jazz Club, it was decided that Luton Community Arts Trust should form a trading arm to look after the commercial development of both the club and 33 Arts Center. Within the brief of the new company, 33 RPM, it was decided to develop a record label to enhance the programming. In 1989-1990 33 RPM released its first albums, featuring soul singer Sister Rose and Cuttie Williams. The first jazz releases followed including work by Sketch and the guitar-based groups of the New Noakes Quartet and the Kimbara Brothers. Underlining the philosophy of the label and based on the programming of the club, it was fundamental that the label should focus on bringing the work of female musicians and vocalists to a wider public. The label's fifth release featured the singer Tina May which led to a creative partnership that has lasted for nearly 30 years and involved seventeen releases from a singer who many consider Europe's premier jazz vocalist. It was obvious, at that time, that many female jazz artists were being ignored by the male dominated clubs and labels, so '33' embarked on bringing balance to the label, releasing early albums from artists including pianist Andrea Vicari, saxophonists Clare Hurst and Karen Sharp, singers Estelle Kotot, Maggie Nicols, Jamila Gorna, Louise Gibbs and Anita Wardell. As the label grew '33' maintained its devotion to female jazz artists, both UK and internationally based, releasing albums from American vocalists Deborah Brown, Leslie Paula, Shaynee Rainbolt and Joan Viskant, Italian pianist Aisha HR, two albums form Italian bassist Silvia Bolognesi (now working with the Art Ensemble of Chicago). Other UK artists releasing with '33' include saxophonists Alison Neale and Charlotte Glasson, pianist Kate Williams and vocalists Kaz Simmons, Nia Lynn, Clare Foster, Diane Nalini, Jacqui Hicks, Julie Dunn, Joanna Eden and Karen Lane.*

Non-jazz releases have also featured female artists—bassist Daphna Sadeh, Japanese pianist Taeko Kinishima, Polish artist Aleksandra Kwasniewska and UK poet Paula Rae Gibson.

I can vouch for the veracity of 33's support of female artists, which extends to social media and concerts which involve collaboration with many female artists. Paul Jolly is an advocate for female musicians and supports them in groups and as solo performers. He also supported (and played at) my own jazz event—*The London Jazz Platform* mentioned earlier.

Producer/keyboards and composer Jason Miles has produced many well-known female artists and says,

> *I have always been a great supporter of women who play music or are in the music business. If we look throughout the history of music and especially jazz, we will see that the music has truly had some amazing women expressing their musical voices. I am not someone who treats a woman who I am working with differently than I would treat a man. You step into the situation, you are judged by your talent, not your sex. I have never said, 'She's a good player for a woman.' That just doesn't fly if you are truly looking to play music on that higher plane. If you look at the history of jazz you can see where women were first introduced as mainly vocalists like Ella (Fitzgerald), Sarah (Vaughan), Carmen McRae, Billy Holiday. As time went on we were introduced to women players who could hold their own with any man like bassist/guitarist Carol Kaye who played on so many hits with the Wrecking Crew, to pianists Marian McPartland and Barbara Carrol to now a line-up of some very serious ladies like Terri Lyne Carrington, Tia Fuller, Allison Miller and a new younger generation like Hailey Niswanger and Linda May. It is not about if you are a man or woman it's about dedication to your craft.*

> *Right now in the business we need more female recording engineers and producers to break through the male dominance of the craft. It will come but it has taken too much time. Diversity has always brought*

great creativity. Women bring a different and welcome perspective to the music. We've had great female singers for decades. This next phase brings them full circle to band leaders and players who can stand toe to toe with men. It's how music is supposed to be—always evolving.

Similarly, event organizers are becoming more aware of the need to include women while avoiding the dreaded tokenism which can happen at some festivals, where female musicians are included for the sake of political correctness and once the quota is reached, they are told, 'We have enough women on the bill now, thanks'. John Russell organizes the legendary free jazz *Mopomoso* events at London's *Vortex Jazz Club* and also co-runs the *Weekertoft* record label. He told me,

I feel there is still a long way to go but certainly the atmosphere at concerts is much less stern and far more welcoming and I feel that is in large part due to the increased interest in the music from women both as performers and members of the audience. At Mopomoso we try to actively not discriminate without appearing tokenistic. There is still some way to go but in general it is possible to make sure there are some women on each program and I am convinced this influences how the music is perceived by an audience.

There are so many good female players around on the free improvisation scene these days and new ones seem to appear on an almost daily basis. I think this shows both the strength of the scene as well as the strength of the players, creating a two-way win–win situation for the music and musicians. There are also women musicians involved in organizing events which again is a very healthy sign of a flourishing scene.

Equity & Women—What They Give Us.

Equality in jazz will bring huge benefits to the music and the industry. Men and women have powerful assets which are put to good effect in successful societies and there is no reason why this should not apply to jazz. When women are excluded, their talent is excluded too. Both

Jason Miles and John Russell spoke about qualities they feel women bring to events and jazz music. But what do the women think?

Singer, producer, multi-instrumentalist and composer Arema Arega says,

> *The strength of 'The Feminine' as I see it, is tenacity and constancy, because we are making our way in a world many times contaminated by the stereotypes of what one should do or be as a woman. The music producer role for example is conceived to be only for the male figure and I have found myself in situations where they call me, 'the singer', when I have been the producer, arranger and composer of music. I love the fact, that every time there are more women, who are tracing their own path, like being a front-woman, or a band leader without the need of being supported by the patriarchal figures, sweetening the content of their art, which could end up destroying their essence.*

Wendy Kirkland observes,

> *I see younger women than me speaking their mind, being confident and I think, 'good for you'. I don't wish it had been that way for me as that was not how things were back then. I'm a stubborn, indignant person when I think injustice is being dealt out, so I've dug my heels in. It sometimes hasn't helped me gain friends I can tell you.*

Jane Ira Bloom says,

> *The thing that heartens me most about watching young women entering the jazz world today is how comfortable they are in themselves and their ability and who they are as women. They seem at ease with themselves and their status in the music world. That's the way it should be.*

It seems that some women, especially those of more recent generations, are bringing with them confidence, an assuredness and an unquestioning belief in their right to be present. Many of them are also very aware that this generation is benefitting from the groundwork laid down by the women who came before them.

Camille Thurman says,

I know the generations before me spoke of having harsher experiences (out-front encounters making it clear that women were not wanted). Some spoke of the scene being much more challenging to play due to harsh interactions with male musicians at sessions. When I first started, there were a few women out and about on the scene. Some of these women were respected for their playing (Tanya Derby, Tia Fuller, Sharal Cassidy, Lauren Sevian). I was shy and hesitant to jump in and just play at a session because it was really about who you knew. If you knew a musician there (who was respected) and you were seen in their company, and heard playing with them, it was more likely the situation would be a little easier for playing and in your favour. I always tried to keep my head up despite how I was feeling inside and keep a straight/confident face whenever I was out and about at sessions as my armour. It was helpful having male figures like Abraham Burton, Eric McPherson, Charlie Persip and Valery Ponomarev hiring women or allowing them to share the bandstand with them at concerts and sessions. I believe these actions helped people to see and understand that these women could play and were respected by these men (and the public should respect them too).

Many times I might be the only woman in the band. I don't feel out of place now. I just try to claim my space via my playing. When I was younger, I felt out of place and intimidated (and it was made clear to me by others I was not welcomed). I was very self-conscious about being a woman and what others thought of me or what would be the 'right' way to present myself etc. Now that I am older, I realize the value is on the player, not what other people think of you because of your gender. I believe this gives an opportunity to look at how you can bring yourself into the situation and make your own niche, not shape/mould yourself to society's expectations. Seeing it this way gives me hope/confidence to walk my own path in my own way without pressure.

Mimi Fox adds,

I am heartened by all the young women who are making their way in this very competitive, male dominated industry. Society changes. Hopefully it will get easier for women jazz musicians.

Of course, underlying all the above is the fact that jazz is an industry. It needs to sell music, whether that is live shows, CDs, vinyl, books, radio contracts or whatever the product may be. Carmela Rappazzo puts it simply when she says,

> "I think the industry is about who makes money, what sells, what is marketable, no matter what the gender. It is a business. What we are discussing is why certain things sell and why certain people feel they are not yet allowed into the shop either as a seller of a buyer. There are still plenty of people for whom the gender issue is a real and present thing, which makes trying to put it into hard business terms difficult.

Jenny Green adds to this when she says brutally,

> To be honest, I did have problems in auditions. Although I had the voice, it was always the blond, long-legged one that got it over me even though my voice was better. Sex sells and nothing has changed.

Women are present and are taking the opportunity to push jazz forward—perhaps kicking and screaming a little, but still forward—in the pursuit of equality. Yet they do not want to scream the feminist line or be overtly aggressive—jazz is not like that. Women are challenging some of the old-fashioned attitudes. Many are creating their own collectives, providing platforms for women players and getting noticed. There have been female-focused shows including in 2018 workshops for women at the *London Jazz Festival*, and exhibitions dedicated to women in jazz such as the 2018 '*Women In Jazz—A Celebration of The Past, Present and Future*' exhibition at the Barbican Center in London—which was pitifully small, occupying just one wall in the library.

An interesting aside: if you are searching for books on jazz music at the British Library in London, it is not kept in the music reading room. Jazz is found in Humanities 2—almost hidden beside a rather large cabinet. The section is all of four shelves or so and of the couple of hundred books present about half a dozen are on women jazz musicians and singers.

Radio stations like *Worldwide FM* have hosted series concentrating entirely on female musicians and the US station *Jazz Bites Radio*, has had several series dedicated to women in jazz through the ages, curated by Anthea Redmond and myself. Attitudes may have some way to go but the age-old assumption that women in the bands must be vocalists is disproved on all fronts. There have been several festivals where women have been prominent on the bill and many women are part of the boundary pushing, innovative and original jazz showcases. There is an ever- growing list of important female musicians appearing—and staying—on jazz venue's line-ups and we are heading towards that day when jazz will be music first, gender, background, colour or politics secondary.

Jazz continues to reflect those changes we witness in society at large. Attitudes towards gender are changing, sometimes aided by legislative victories, but more and more by attitudes gained from peer groups and the essence of the music itself. It is sometimes difficult to find the dividing line in a natural increase in women entering the jazz industry and a 'token' inclusion, creating a potential for accusations that women are getting spots simply because they are female and not on merit. It seems people acknowledge things aren't ideal and need to change in terms of the male/female balance, but they are not quite sure how to go about it the right way.

Wendy Kirkland sums it up perhaps when she says,

> *As there are more women in the jazz industry, I hope the questions around women in jazz will become obsolete.*

Jenny Green adds,

> *It's a male dominated world in Jazz but some great female musicians are rising through and we won't be ignored. I think because there are more women in jazz earning awards, we are a force to be reckoned with.*

Ellie Thompson points out,

I think the awareness of sexism within the industry has meant that efforts are being made to create more opportunities for women as well as education resources, which is helping. I think young people are beginning to realize that they don't have to fit into the traditional bracket of a genre to succeed, which is also wonderful.

Help

There are a number of innovative programs and events which seek to ensure the inclusion of more women in jazz continues.

THSH (Town Hall, Symphony Hall) is an arts charity based in Birmingham, UK which has a specific arm to encourage the development of women in jazz. Their *Women in Jazz* program aims to support young female jazz musicians (16-25) in their musical and professional development. It is a year-round program which offers participants the chance to develop their skills through master classes, workshops, and high-profile performance opportunities. It also includes mentoring and professional development sessions focusing on essential career and industry skills and, best of all, if you are based near Birmingham, it is free. Most supportive events happen in London, so it is inspiring to see events like this. There is also the *Women in Jazz Program*, funded by the *Esmée Fairbairn Foundation* based in London. This foundation offers grants for various projects including music and social change projects.

The *Women in Jazz Organisation* is a collective of professional jazz musicians who identify as women or gender non-binary. *WIJO* works to empower members and create equality in Jazz.

Some believe one way is to get legislation to enforce equality. Faye Patton comments,

Festivals, clubs, promoters, programmers, should be legally required to have a 50/50 representation on their books at any given time, which

means booking and rebooking female artists so we stand a chance of sustaining momentum in the public eye. If venues say they don't know any female jazz artists that's just lazy, ignorant and sexist. I say—do your research.

The US has regional support bodies as well. The *Seattle Women in Jazz* features concerts with talented female artists. *SWiJ* is fiscally sponsored by *Shunpike* and is the first organization of its kind to specifically highlight some of Seattle's best jazz artists and bands led by or comprised of women. It also connects with youth and aims to reach new audiences and help those who otherwise might not come to a jazz concert. The SWiJ holds concerts throughout the year including *Jazz Shout* every March in recognition of Women's History Month.

Women In Jazz—known as *WinJazz* is an international project to promote the growth and mobility of young women jazz musicians in Europe. The project was created and directed by the Italian association, *Mulab*, in partnership with *Collage Arts* in the UK, *Prostor Plus* in Croatia, *Fundacja Arteria* in Poland, and funded by the *MIBACT* – the Ministry of Culture in Italy.

Kim Cypher sums it up,

Women are definitely claiming their place in this industry and with this growing acceptance a new generation of exciting, talented female musicians will be born.

Getting the Break

THAT MOMENT WHEN you firm up your first run of bookings or cut your first album can be life-changing. Getting your first review means there is documentation of your music. It takes a certain combination of timing, the right people and the right place, often along with a dose of cash and it goes without saying a shed load of talent. For women, is this more difficult?

Some women have found recognition and achieved the highest accolades the jazz industry can give. Getting the break is the first and often hardest part. Searching social media provides an overview of how many would-be jazz musicians are seeking their first contract. Many women are professionals and a few have made the breakthrough into becoming internationally famous. For some, the road has been easier than for others. I asked women why they chose jazz and how they got their break. Many of the musicians I spoke to play other genres as well as jazz, but for an equal number, jazz has become their specialist music. This was an area many women wanted to talk about. They seemed eager to share their experiences with others and help them on their own journeys.

The journey to getting a break in jazz can take different routes. Some go straight from college to performing, promotion, managing or another role; others work their way into bands via friends, jamming along, sitting in and networking socially as well as musically. I have witnessed collaborations spring up when a social media network message has gone out from a band asking if someone can turn up and play at such and such an event because their bass player got sick or something similar.

A bass player sees it, does the gig, fits well with the band and a new professional relationship may evolve. In the upstairs jam sessions at Ronnie Scott's, musicians meet, play together and network. Spaces like this are vital for new collaborations to happen. In some gigs, players will sit in for a while. I have been at some events where members of the audience have been invited to bring instruments and the band have called on them to play for a number or two. Sometimes, wonderful things happen like when I watched as a quiet young lady was invited on to stage by a band. After a less than confident start, she took a deep breath, closed her eyes and dived into a full throttle engagement with the tenor sax player. She was amazing and stayed on stage with the band for the rest of the set while other musicians came and went. I later heard that same violinist had been invited to tour with a Spanish jazz ensemble whose drummer was in the audience that night.

I have always suspected there are different circuits in the jazz world, each interacting but largely, each operating as almost separate entities. Some musicians play a local circuit, others nationally, and yet others still who play across the world. In local circuits the same names crop up at venues, perhaps with different visiting stars—our locality has one George Double, a drummer who plays at many events and as part of different house bands. Then there is the national circuit where bands might tour for a summer or a year with some musicians popping up in London, then Exeter, Bath or Colchester. In the United States, there are bands who have played widely in America but never come to Europe or the UK, they remain American-based. Then there is the international circuit with musicians playing all over the World. Players like Gilad Atzmon, Claire Martin, Barb Jungr, Camille Thurman and others are in this circuit. Musicians may prefer one circuit or another—sometimes it suits to stay local at different times in their life. Debbie Gifford confirms my suspicions when she explains,

> *The jazz scene is divided into local, regional and international performers. The local and regional performers are usually booking their own performances and do not have the same opportunities that*

international performers have who are being represented by agents and managers. They wear many hats. Not only are they up on stage , but they also have to manage, booking agent, accountant, music director etc. It's a labour of love but extremely time consuming and doesn't leave much time for what you really want to do and that is work on your music and perform.

Some have other jobs before taking the plunge and throwing everything into their music and a few have been 'spotted', but nearly every musician I know in jazz has been given encouragement by other musicians. In most cases, opportunities exist for talented musicians regardless of gender. A musician in need rarely has the gall to be sexist.

Just hearing the different roads taken by the female musicians I spoke to for the book is both inspirational and shows the many ways this journey can be made.

Faye Patton comments on her own journey to jazz.

Music is what I always wanted to do since childhood. I got derailed as a teenager and did a theatre degree. I retrained in a very practical, vocational way in my mid-20s and got my guitar grades 1-8. I became a teacher of music, (voice, piano, guitar). A student then teacher then course leader/designer with Community Music Ltd—a grassroots organization for those excluded from the mainstream, and a singer in a world music choir. Getting my own band together was a natural evolution and I found them through my educational contacts in East London. The line up has changed but I have worked with the same drummer for twenty years! My band mates are soul mates, friends and family too.

Vocalist, lyricist and producer Georgia Mancio relates,

I started about twenty years ago, semi-professionally at first, then turning fully professional two years later. I had been studying and intending to make a career in film-making. I knew some great musicians from my part-time waitressing job at Ronnie Scott's and I started doing a few gigs. Ironically, though I was largely untrained and inexperienced it was

*easier to build on this than to really find my place in the film industry.
I was very lucky to have guidance and encouragement from generous
musicians who never patronized my lack of knowledge and allowed me
to learn on the job. I had no idea at the time, but this approach fed into all
aspects of my career. On one hand I have always been self-sufficient—I
have always been my own manager, agent, copywriter, photographer,
record label, producer, graphic designer and publicist, but on the other
hand it is all about my connection with and respect for other musicians.*

Since her waitressing days, Georgia has become an influential musician
and someone who moves mountains to make change happen. Her
Hangs sessions feature bespoke collaborations between stellar musicians
including a large number of women. Her annual *Re:Voice* event is an
international voice festival held at the iconic *Pizza Express Jazz Club* in
Soho where vocalists as diverse as Gregory Porter, Karin Krog, Georgia
herself, Lianne Carroll and many more have performed since its
inception in 2010. Georgia is becoming known as a supporter of fellow
female performers and in a gentle but profound way, Georgia is making
change happen. She is showcasing a huge number of female performers
including pianists Kate Williams and Nikki Iles, cellist Shirley Smart,
harp player Alina Bzhezhunska and many others. By showcasing them,
she gives them as much exposure as the men who also perform at her
events including flautist Gareth Lochrane, accordion player Maurizio
Minardi, guitarist Luis Morais and drummer Dave Ohm.

Vocalist, broadcaster, producer and composer Emily Saunders says,

*I grew up in an intensely musical family, so sitting down at the piano
and writing songs was a way of life since I was a little kid. Improvisation
was the same; if we went on a long car journey for a family holiday,
we'd end up doing four-part harmony on the way just to pass the time.
So improvisation, song writing, and composition in jazz was a really
natural thing for me to fall into. My debut album received four star
national press coverage, and radio play round the world, which took me
by surprise, and I've never looked back.*

Emily has established a career as a broadcaster, vocalist and event organizer. Her innovative *Jazz Connects* is a free shop front hosted on the web where artists can showcase their music, connect and collaborate not only with other musicians but also with agents, writers and venues. This platform has had a profound effect on how musicians and other people in jazz connect with each other already; and allows people direct connections without having to wade through umpteen different contacts to reach the right person. It is a brilliant concept.

Joelle Khoury comments on her journey, which was different again,

> *My start in music in general was very difficult, since I had come from the Middle East (Lebanon) to the states in order to study engineering. I had never studied music before and my parents did not appreciate the move.*

Trish Clowes took a route which many musicians will identify with:

> *I came up through gigging in Shropshire with people older than me. I'd always played musical instruments because I had been encouraged by my family (including instrumental lessons), but I was naturally a bit of a song bird I think. I was fifteen when I played piano in the local big band (my dad's friend ran it) and I worked really hard to be able to play the music (I also played piano and saxophone in groups with my own peers at school). I started doing small band jazz gigs as a vocalist at first and then as my saxophone playing got stronger, I sat in on local gigs and eventually started to lead duos or quartets. I also wrote my own tunes and played them on gigs when I could. I'd been introduced to loads of fantastic music by these older players and this guided my listening— although I very much had my own tastes too! I loved the music so I worked really hard to be a part of it, and I had nothing but support from those around me, and yes most of those people were men. It didn't feel weird or difficult because I was a woman. To be honest, playing jazz felt like a slightly odd thing to be doing in Shropshire! I'd always wanted to move to London, so eventually I decided to study music and auditioned for jazz courses. I moved to London to formally study in 2003 (aged nineteen). I loved being at music college and surrounded by so many people my own age who loved music as much as I did—a*

new experience to me. Throughout my entire undergrad I was the only woman on the jazz course (there were sometimes women on the post grad course however). After that it was a question of gradually, bit by bit, integrating myself into the playing scene in London. Ultimately, you have to find your own community of people to make music with.

Sometimes, the path chosen can take unexpected turns. Gail Tasker is a successful PR representative for *Gearbox Records* in London, but it is not where she originally saw her jazz journey going. She explains,

A couple of years back I began an MA in jazz performance. I'd had classical flute lessons at school and, after completing an academic undergraduate degree, I had this idea of becoming a jazz musician. Going to jazz college was an interesting experience; there was a definite boys' club. Myself and one other girl were the only jazz instrumentalists on the course at the time. Due to a host of reasons, the gender imbalance included, I didn't feel comfortable during my performance studies. At the same time, I was writing for London Jazz News and Tina Edwards' EZH magazine and was interested in the jazz that was taking place in London. By chance I got a call from Gearbox Records (who I'd previously interviewed), about working for them. I started working for them during my studies and found it liberating. I would call this part a 'smooth run'.

Sarah Brand had a different journey again and describes her route to jazz:

I played trombone as a kid and joined the Midland Jazz when I was about fourteen or fifteen. I gained experience in different kinds of music and joined the Birmingham Schools Big Band—which played swing. At university I studied jazz and I found free jazz and improvised music. I started to gig and a few people began to want to work with me, notably Phil Durrant and Veryan Weston. I tried different genres but preferred jazz both as a performer and composer. I got picked up by people like Billy Jenkins, the guitarist and others who made jazz music enjoyable and I started a small club as soon as I left college.

Where the musician lives and their socio-economic situation also plays a significant role. Arema Arega is a Cuban living in Spain. Her route into jazz was different again. She is also a mother and for her, this had immense impact. She comments,

> *I started composing at the age of fourteen and at nineteen, I decided to join the music school. I needed the tools that allowed me to communicate my ideas to musicians, because I didn't feel like one of them. Rather, I was a messenger containing melodies drawn in the air. Despite this, I only set out to show my work as a singer-songwriter when I had my first child. This honed my vision and gave it dimension. It was almost like extending my roots deep down into myself. That was a time to fight for what I really wanted, where priorities changed completely and I began to discover my path.*

Arema Arega has certainly created her own path. She has made recordings, videos and eventually released an album on which she plays a range of different instruments. I first heard of her when she contacted me saying she liked how I wrote and telling me of her project to create an album of music with different sounds. She was very engaging and I replied saying I would be willing to listen to her music when the album was complete. Late last year, almost two years later, I received a CD. I loved the music. I reviewed the album and got airplay for her music on *Jazz Bites Radio*. Others picked up the quality of her music and she got the exposure she deserved. Meantime, she was on fire in the creative sense and her film score was used at a film festival. Arema would just not give up and though it took two years for her original album to be made, she persevered and created something special and unique.

In my experience, it is this tenacity which is often present in successful performers and an understanding of the importance of quality and attention to detail that leads to great achievements, regardless of gender.

For Debbie Gifford, her early times in jazz were a mix of good and bad. She explains,

> *It was difficult in many ways. At the beginning there was lots of competition among the musicians to get work. One of the reasons was that at the time I started to perform jazz (1999) the era of performing a*

steady gig for six or seven nights a week had diminished. Live music was being replaced by DJs and pre-recorded music. Previously, the mainstay for musicians had been hotel, high-end restaurant and club gigs and now there were lots of good musicians but not enough opportunities to perform. As the new kid on the block gigs were hard to come by, but fortunately, I was being mentored by two of Cleveland's seasoned jazz veterans, Hank Geer and Dick Meese. They not only introduced me to the world of jazz musically but also to other great players. This helped open doors to many local and regional performance opportunities. My second big break was being chosen by Patricia Adkins Chiti to perform in Rome in the Donne Musica Concert Series which opened the door for me in Europe.

Ellie Thompson, now working in PR tells of her route, via some slightly less glamorous jobs.

I was struggling to find a route in. I actually worked in a café/record shop to try and get closer though I mostly ended up washing dishes! I found an apprenticeship course on Digital Marketing which placed you for work experience in a music PR company. I qualified for the course and, after a change in company, settled at Prescription PR. As I pointed out to the academy running the apprenticeship course at the time, Digital Marketing and PR are not the same thing! This meant I couldn't complete the qualification for my apprenticeship but I did get offered a job at Prescription PR so that is how I found my way into the industry!

Sometimes, it takes a brave woman to pursue a career in jazz music, particularly when they have a perfectly respectable and alternate means of making a living—and additionally so when your partner needs to commit too. Before becoming a full time musician Kim Cypher had a career as head of music in a primary school while her husband Mike, also a musician, ran branches of a national bank. Gigging at week-ends and working hard during the week became their life until they reached a point where they both decided to put more into the music. Kim explains,

We became increasingly frustrated, wanting to follow our musical dreams and ambitions. I wanted to create my own music, record albums, work with exciting musicians and achieve my full musical potential. So,

one day after a lot of consideration, we made the brave decision to give
up our day jobs and pursue music professionally.

Within four months the pair had done just that and, though they
had support from family and friends, most of them considered them
mad. Kim found life as a professional musician to be hard. As an
independent artist she had to do promotion, arrange gigs, recording
sessions, manage the finances—everything in fact at first and for Mike,
it was a change in direction too. Kim says,

> *Finally, being part of it brought a sense of belonging. We were where*
> *we were meant to be and other musicians will relate to that. To us, the*
> *thought of now working Monday to Friday 9 to 5 in the same place with*
> *the same people would just be weird. Starting out in the jazz industry*
> *was pretty tough. If you want the good gigs you have to prove your worth.*
> *So it was a definite journey, working my way up the ranks and proving*
> *myself as a musician and composer. The difficulty with this is that you*
> *need to build up the 'evidence' of your proven track record and venues/*
> *bookers will expect to see professional videos and hear your professionally*
> *recorded music. They need to select you over all the competition. This takes*
> *time and money.*

Debbie Gifford adds,

> *I think it is very difficult at this time for a musician in any musical*
> *genres to have their sole income from performances alone—especially*
> *jazz. If they are also willing to combine performing with other musical*
> *fields like composing, writing lyrics, teaching or arranging they may*
> *have a better chance at making a living as a full-time musician.*

Mimi Fox says,

> *I feel it is difficult for young women in particular to break into jazz*
> *because of societal constraints. Women face the same gauntlet of oppressive*
> *circumstances that other women face in many fields. However, I am*
> *heartened by all the young women who are making their way in this*
> *very competitive, male dominated industry. Society changes. Hopefully*

it will get easier for women jazz musicians.

Joelle Khoury echoes some of this sentiment when she says,

> *It is not too difficult if you want to play standards in pubs. It is extremely difficult, at least here where I live, to go for something new because number one—people don't easily accept change and two—the musicians would rather play easy gigs and get paid for them instead of long complicated rehearsals.*

Georgia Mancio adds,

> *I think it is always difficult—at any stage—to make a living from this music. Arts in general are still undervalued and underfunded and music is becoming increasingly more disposable. The great jazz vocalist Sheila Jordan told me she believed you work most when you're either very young or very old and there is certainly a truth in this. In a sense an artist's first album, first tour, first statement is more enticing than their second, fifth, tenth, etc. but it's a short-sighted approach because sustainability is the real key to professional development.*

Some entrepreneurial women are fortunate to see their jazz projects and experiments bear fruit. *Jazz Bites Radio* has been a success because the adventurous co-owners put their heart and soul into jazz music and promoting mostly unsigned and under-exposed artists, while at the same time trying to uphold a level of quality. From a small podcast, the station has grown to three channels, each broadcasting different jazz genres. The audience has also grown with time. *Jazz Bites Radio* are also the holders of the *Jazz Repository*—a collection of over 59,000 rare and vintage jazz tracks bequeathed to the stations' founders by a private collector. I am lucky enough to have been asked to curate the collections—something which is an ongoing task.

Jazz Bites Radio now reaches over 500,000 listeners across the globe as Anthea Redmond, co-owner of the station told me,

> *After a lifetime working in Public Relations & Media in the UK, I*

moved to the United States in 2011, married the cutest guy in the world, and began using my skills to promote jazz artists, gigs, albums, and jazz festivals for free via my alter-ego @Jazzigator on Twitter. Over a short period of time, the service I was offering garnered thousands of followers along with multiple requests from unsigned musicians asking me to listen to their tracks and help with some advice as to how they could get their music played on the radio. This led to an experiment and the creation of The JazzBites Show—a chat and music show in the form of a podcast where I asked artists about their influences, inspirations, and to candidly bear their souls about their individual journey and experience in the music business. The show was an overnight success, and twelve months later the next step seemed the natural way to go: creating a broadcasting medium with the widest reach possible: a medium without barriers, where elitism and fame weren't conditional to being accepted; an international radio platform where unsigned artists could be heard alongside their more famous peers. Ultimately JazzBites Radio was born. It's been a most joyful ride. We love what we do, and over half a million listeners can't be wrong.

Why Jazz?

Many of the women I spoke with could be successful in any genre of music, but they speak with a profound passion about jazz music and come alive when talking about it or playing it. They have made jazz their preferred genre and I wondered what drew them towards it.

Georgia Mancio comments,

As I was growing up my parents listened almost exclusively to classical music until one day my dad brought home some jazz records. One was the Frank Sinatra/Nelson Riddle classic 'Only the Lonely' and the others extensive compilations of leading instrumentalists and vocalists. I think the combination of the story-telling and the feel resonated deeply and instantly. Jazz seems to be the purest expression of self and I love the freedom and individuality. Repertoire is extremely important to me and being able to pick and shape my own as I develop as both singer and human being means that art and life co-exist symbiotically.

Wendy Kirkland comments,

I sometimes play other genres, but my first love is jazz. As a pianist, I'm fascinated by the sophisticated sounds of the chords, the vast variety of feels, sometimes cool, sometimes sad, sometimes lively and sometimes downright raucous! I think no other style of music is so broad and that's probably why I've never been bored with it.

Joelly Khoury explains her experience.

I just like music that represents who I am right now, and I use any means I possess to create it. I am mainly a composer. I am as much into contemporary classical music as I am into jazz and electronics.

Tina May explains the magnetic pull of jazz for her.

My career in jazz began in Paris in 1983 when I was a student studying for my BA (Hons) in French. My father had been against me reading music, so I decided to read French (but spent more time in the music department and theatre). I loved Paris and within a week was 'sitting in' and making music with musicians on the Paris scene. I found everyone very friendly. Of course, I spoke French, which made it easier. I also knew the repertoire as I had listened my parents' record collection all my life (Ellington, Basie, Ella, Sarah, Sinatra, Waller, the list is comprehensive). I knew my keys and could count the band in, so I was already useful. I found myself singing with the great Kenny Clark in the Roger Guerin Big Band, amongst others.

In Paris I met young musicians who have become life-long colleagues—they included jazz pianist Patrick Villanueva and tenor sax player Pascal Gaubert with whom I recorded live at the Club Lionel Hampton years later. I have always found jazz to be quite egalitarian really. I know singers are always a slightly special case (I might feel different if I was a sax player) but if you 'knew your stuff' you were accepted. I think this is generally the case and musicians are generally supportive of 'new recruits'. Certainly in Paris this is the case—to this day. There were not so many female instrumentalists at that time in Paris (mid 80s) excepting Rhoda Scott. This has changed. Now there are many female jazz musicians, all instruments in Paris and elsewhere. I went to London after university once I had fulfilled my contracts as an actress in a couple of touring productions. I missed jazz so much.

I was fortunate to meet some great musicians pretty much immediately. The 606 club and Ronnie Scott's became my regular haunts. I have never ever felt anything but warmth in a jazz club—anywhere in the world. In my experience, a woman can feel at ease and talk to people who share an enthusiasm for the music without fear of being propositioned.

There were a few awkward moments (professionally) however. I remember my first BBC Big Band broadcast session of three songs. As I entered the studio the drummer started playing the 'stripper' rhythm on the bass drum. I felt it was a test—to see if I had a sense of humour mostly. So I walked to the microphone with 'a bit of a wiggle' and pulled a funny face. We all laughed and it never happened again.

Mostly older jazz musicians were rather sweet and 'avuncular' towards me. Ray Bryant, Bobby Watson, Dany Doriz (the Lionel Hampton 'Français'), Don Sickler, Humphrey Lyttelton, Ronnie Scott —have always been very kind towards me.

Vocalist Barb Jungr says,

I have played across music of many kinds, but my leaning is towards some level of harmonic, and also rhythmic improvisation around the melody, along with the words. Consequently there is a strong jazz element in my work, and for the most part I perform with jazz musicians in the UK and USA. They too play across genres. Jazz allows creative impulse as part of the form and that's exciting and also makes the experience of live music a beautiful thing. I was talking the other day to Simon Wallace (British composer and pianist) about how, in the old days, you would go and see an act at Ronnie Scott's the night they started their three week run and they'd be raw and clawing for ideas. Then you'd see the same band a week later after they'd played eight sets or more together and they'd be cruising and floating and then you'd go on the last night and they'd either hate each other or be on fire. The music grew and evolved through being played, and through the musical interactions of the players who may have come together for the first time for the run.

Mimi Fox talks of the freedom offered by jazz when she adds,

I love and have played many styles of music and continue to do so. However, jazz gives me the most freedom and is the most challenging/ stimulating music I play.

Jenny Green reacts almost in surprise when I ask her, 'Why jazz?'

Why Jazz? I suppose I love the freedom of expression and to improvise on a tune. It's exciting when you are singing with a live band- something you just don't get singing with a backing track (don't get me started on that one!) My repertoire reflects the years I have been performing through the genres. It's important to sing tunes people recognize to draw them in. So singing pop tunes in a jazzy way is good. If I'm singing at functions I offer all types of music because having had years of experience I am able to do that; from light country tunes to swing jazz, ballads, rock and roll to back where I started in the early 80's with the Abba anthems. It was a banjo player in my local jazz club where I was waitressing who first said to me, 'learn Billy Holiday tunes and then come and up on stage and sing some'. So that's what I started to do whilst getting to know some fabulous Jazz musicians.

Jenny is now also a broadcaster, co-hosting a weekly jazz slot on 107 Meridian FM Radio. I asked her why she began to broadcast, and why she specialized in jazz. She replied,

Presenting a jazz show idea came out of my wanting to hear and learn more about instrumental jazz, to not only educate myself but others too. I was always being told, 'I don't like Jazz' from folks but there is a great variety in jazz. It's not all be-bop! Jazz is a melting pot I think. From the radio perspective our jazz show 'Jen and Sooz Jazz Mix Up' (Meridian FM) reflects this, from jazz-soul/blues to big band right through to the new stuff coming through with all the classical hip hop and experimental jazz.

Jenny's co-host is Susie Homes from *Red Carpet Entertainment* and as the show is broadcast, Susie manages media platforms, adding links, videos and other information about artists featured on the show, which serves to link the show's playlists to media—another innovative idea.

Indira May is young but is a rising star in the world of jazz. She explains what drew her to this music,

> *Jazz is very emotional, especially instrumental jazz. You can hear the emotion in the instruments—horns, piano. Someone will take a solo and it goes from loud to quiet to staccato—it takes you on a journey. Sometimes when I listen to sad rock music, it can feel a bit dreary and one dimensional but when I listen to jazz and I'm feeling sad or sombre, it still makes me feel good on some level. It's more complex and I think that reflects human emotion more accurately. Because when you're feeling sad, it's not just one emotion- and jazz captures that. Jazz is also very inclusive. What I love about newer artists like Ezra Collective, Moses Boyd or the female saxophonist, Nubia Garcia, apart from the energy, is that you can hear the different cultural references in their music. Like the Afro-tinged stuff, Ezra Collective have their reggae-type song. It's good to get different perspectives like that. It's fun to dive into someone else's world.*

On her jazz discoveries, Debbie Gifford comments,

> *I had done many years in musical theatre beginning at age four. After graduating with a degree in Music Education, I pursued a Masters Degree in Classical performance and only sang opera. One evening someone asked me to sit in and do a jazz standard and I was hooked. I love the freedom of jazz, being outside the box. My performances are also sprinkled with pop music but with a jazz arrangement. Ten years ago, I was fortunate to meet a local jazz pianist, John Trzcinski who writes my arrangements which cross genres. This gives our performances a special uniqueness. I use the talent I was gifted with as an opera singer and mix it with jazz and the result have been very well received thanks to these great arrangements.*

Sometimes fate lends a helping hand. Emily Saunders, tells her story.

Initially I got a scholarship to music college as a classical clarinettist, but I damaged my hand. This was a wonderful twist of fate and was strangely the best thing that happened to me; it gave me the space and time to get back to my first loves: singing, song writing, composing and improvising music. I went back to studying, doing a Masters in Jazz Voice at Trinity Laban Conservatoire and my career as a singer-songwriter and composer in jazz took off from there. Growing up I listened obsessively to the jazz greats, and they will always be close to my heart, but what I create is my own sound within this genre. To me jazz is a process, and an environment that gives you the freedom to express what you want to say, in the way you wish to express it. It's a melting pot of your musical voice, musical environment, social environment—wrapped into so many fundamentally important creative processes. Growing up in Brixton in a musical family, I was surrounded by many fantastic varied genres, as I still am today. All these musical influences continually evolve in one's life. You absorb them and evolve them to create your own sound. It's a combination of both conscious and unconscious internalizing, reflecting, and creating, and that's what has come together to create my sound today.

Gail Tasker adds,

I chose to do PR in jazz, solely because I like the music. I don't think I could do it in many other industries. Though I don't generally see PR as a fulfilling job role, trying to get people listening and talking about good jazz is. The best part of my job is talking to fans and those passionate about the genre.

Amanda Bloom says,

I have always appreciated the authenticity of jazz as it is constantly evolving and the music is highly individualistic. Jazz musicians strive to create their own sound and style and not only push themselves, but push the boundaries of music and improvisation. For these reasons and more I find jazz to be a really rewarding genres to promote.

Many women speak of jazz being played in their homes as they grew up. This seems to be true wherever they are from. Indira May tells us,

"I first encountered jazz through my mum and dad playing it at home – artists like Herbie Hancock, Miles Davis, Charles Mingus and Ella Fitzgerald. But also my Granddad played a lot of old 30s jazz on his vinyl player. I remember that resonating with me and I enjoyed listening to it. When I was very little, my Dad used to play a 78 record of Charlie Parker on an old player he had too and I used to crazily dance around the kitchen to it. Then when I got to the teenage years, the internet was more of a thriving place, and websites such as YouTube were really key because I could search anything, and it would send me off on a trail. You would find one artist and it would suggest another one. So I used to trawl through hours and hours of jazz music. I already knew Nina Simone, but I discovered people like Peggy Lee, Bessie Smith, and Billie Holiday. At that time, I was also learning at school about the Suffragette movement, and women not having a voice, and I realized that these songs were so important to those female jazz singers because they were expressing how they really felt which was a rarity back in the 1940s and 50s. I remember listening to 'Strange Fruit' by Billie Holiday and being blown away by it because it was so truthful and there was so much pain in it. Growing up in Gloucestershire, in the countryside, it wasn't like being in a city. There was very little diversity. In fact, there weren't any black people anywhere – just maybe one girl in my school. And I think the music and the struggles those singers expressed resonated with me even more because of that – that lack of diversity. Because no one else I knew was into that kind of music—'old music'. I didn't know anyone who was passionate about jazz. They just listened to what was on the radio."

Vocalist Claire Martin says,

I love improvising and with jazz you can make each night different which is very exciting. I improvise with the phrasing and lyrics mostly and not with chorus after chorus of scat singing, which I'd actually really like to do, but I'm pretty rubbish at it sadly. I have only sung jazz for over thirty years as it's the only style of singing I want to do. I like rich, complex harmony, swing and heartfelt ballads. I love jazz!

Indira May adds more.

The teachers at my school were classically trained, and we'd sing lots of hymns or old folk songs. And I do love folk, but it wasn't until I bought a Corinne Bailey Rae song book and just sang the whole book back to front with my singing teacher, Kate, that that changed. Then a younger teacher called Jack Mizzi came on the scene in my school and he was really into jazz and really pushed that in me. He'd only ever do jazz standards with me, and jazz scales. He was the one who got me to trying out scatting. I remember doing it for the first time and feeling a bit stupid because you're making lots of weird sounds, but also it was that point of just letting go. That's what's cool about scat singing—it's improvising and having fun with it. Jack used to let me miss the same lesson every week so we could have a bit longer to sing. No wonder the PE teachers hated me!

For Alicia Renee it was through her father. She says,

I guess you could say (I came to love jazz) because of my father's love for the music, singing me jazz lullabies and him playing the music when he would come home from work at General Motors. I grew up studying opera, classical and singing gospel in church. Throughout my life, I have sung many different genres of music, from recording with Bill Laswell (Electronica), Easy Mo Bee (Hip Hop and R&B producer and incidentally the only producer Miles Davis won a Grammy with), Jessica Care Moore (International Poet), singing with New Orleans legends Kermit Ruffins, Shannon Powell (King of Treme), French Music, The Last Poets, Shaquille O Neal (pop and hip hop). I have been singing jazz since the age of two, basically singing back to my father the songs that he used to sing me to sleep. Nat King Cole, Sarah Vaughan, Ella Fitzgerald etc. My transition to singing jazz for the public began at the age of 6 singing the songs in plays, schools etc. For me, it was a natural thing as opposed to an industry thing.

Many musicians play across genres like Alicia. Patti Boulaye comments,

I have had the great fortune of plying across many genres of music

including pop, stage musicals, opera, rock, blues and standards but simple and straightforward jazz sits comfortably with me. My first performance of live jazz was in the 1980s when I was cast in 'Blues in The Night'. Then recently I wrote a one-woman show, 'Billie and Me' featuring the music of Billie Holiday, Bessie Smith and Alberta Hunter. I find great ease comes with singing jazz. It feels very natural, very carefree and second nature to me.

Terri Lyne Carrington is a world-class drummer so it is natural She has played across the musical board, but of jazz she says,

I play other genres, but I feel jazz is part of me, where I am most at home. I play funk, rock but it is not the same feeling. I feel I grew up playing jazz (her father was a saxophonist and president of the Boston Jazz Society) and from a perspective, it is my culture. I love folk-rock, R&B, hip-hop and I love the merges with jazz. Jazz therefore feels very fertile as many people are mixing genres and making some very interesting music.

Words of Wisdom & Encouragement

There are many people who want to play jazz and some of the established women in jazz wanted to provide advice on the journey, share what they learned and helpful tips for those entering the jazz world. They have made the journey, or are on it and they want to make the road a smoother one for those who follow.

Camille Thurman shares her experiences,

The hardest thing was developing the confidence and belief that I could play. I was more frustrated about not having mobility on my instrument and not understanding harmony. I had perfect pitch and could hear everything but couldn't get to it on my instrument to explain what it was. It wasn't until I got to high school that I started to understand the harmony behind the things I loved to listen to and why/how they worked. Once that understanding was there it opened the door to me loving jazz even more, giving me confidence and the want to develop a deeper understanding of my instrument.

Claire Martin has some honest advice,

It's very hard because there are not enough jazz clubs and smaller venues often don't have the budget to pay even Musician Union rates. If you can make your living out of only playing jazz you are a rarity and I don't know many musicians who don't teach, play in West End shows or have other side lines to make up their income. When I first started, I was a new face on the scene and so for the first few years all the gigs wanted to book me. Keeping the diary busy is and always has been notoriously hard for most musicians but especially for jazz musicians as it's a specialist music.

Alicia Renee aka Blue Eyes says,

Maybe I was lucky, but for me it was never a financial or difficult issue, singing in New Orleans, Switzerland, France, Italy, Garment, Holland etc. The financial compensation has always been a respectable one for myself. I never had the desire to be the wealthiest woman in the world, just comfortable in doing what I love and that is what it has been for me.

Occasionally one comes across musicians who have just graduated. They have three years of experience playing in a protected environment, in clubs affiliated with their schools, and to family, friends and sometimes large audiences as part of their training. Some graduate with a sense of entitlement, but they quickly learn that jazz doesn't work that way. International vocalist and writer Barb Jungr comments on whether it is easy for a young musician to come into jazz.

Honestly, in our current climate, no but that's nothing to do with talent. It's to do with expectations.

And this is true. Beverley Bierne expands on this,

I'd say it can be difficult for newcomers. Even the super talented can have find it tough out there hustling for gigs. Since jazz became part of the curricular at Universities worldwide there has been some phenomenal talent coming onto the scene and the reality is there are only so many gigs and festivals. Also, I'd say most musicians and singers have another source of income alongside performing; teaching, writing, or something else entirely. I know a few musicians and singers that have gone into alternative medicine, learning Reiki, aromatherapy, or become a Pilates instructor to supplement the jazz income. I believe a famous jazz singer used to sell her home-made preserves at gigs so I guess this is not a new thing! Jazz artists have to think out of the box a bit to make it work. I think it can get really tricky once marriage and kids come along too.

Gail Tasker says,

I think these days, you've got to have more than just talent. You've got to be entrepreneurial, have a handle on self-promotion, a good network of talented musicians to play with, possibly income from another profession such as teaching. Also, having a positive presence on social media has become crucial.

Amanda Bloom adds,

I do feel newcomers face difficulties entering the jazz scene. Many people assume that you have to reach a high level of fame or wealth in order to be considered successful in a music career. The reality is there is a vast middle ground of people who have sustainable music careers though they may not be a household name. Coming into jazz for a living often means having various streams of income in order to support yourself. Talent is absolutely vital but it's just one part of the equation. Being business savvy, easy to work with (preferably) and creative in monetizing your musical abilities all contribute to a higher chance of making a living from music as a new comer.

Offering advice to women coming into the jazz scene, Carmela Rappazzo says she would tell them several things.

> *Look after your instrument or voice, know how to run the gear in the studio as well as on your gig. Respect yourself. It's a marathon, not a sprint.*

Jo Harrop adds,

> *Have an identity, tell your story, believe in yourself and find your own voice is my advice to a young singer starting out. Celebrate the other women in the industry and work together, help each other. Don't take any BS!*

Terri Lyne Carrington has seen many young female musicians come and go. Her advice is,

> *It is a difficult art form. You need a desire to learn plus talent and an aptitude for jazz. You have to be good. No, you have to be great. Natural talent helps but it is not easy at all. Lots of people study jazz but end up playing other genres—which is fine and makes better musicians. The pedagogy of jazz is important at music institutions as it makes you stronger in other genres.*

Kim Cypher gives this advice:

> *There is no manual to follow as a guide on how to do things correctly. It is a case of learning from mistakes and researching each project as you go. Some techniques work for one person and totally backfire for another. The gigs won't come to you, you most definitely get out what you put into this industry. If you are good at what you do and are prepared to work very (very) hard and can cope with the knock backs and have the determination to succeed, then you stand a chance.*

Amanda Bloom gives some simple advice:

> *Be genuine and surround yourself with people you trust and respect.*

Gail Tasker expands on this advice when she adds,

> *I'd say for any young girl looking to get involved in the industry, it's always helpful to find an icon to look towards. When I was studying music I thought Emily Remer was the coolest girl ever. She was the only*

female guitarist I could think of who had any status in the jazz world, and that made her an icon for me.

And Georgia Mancio gives this advice on being realistic and practical,

My suggestions for women (and men) going into jazz is to acquire and experience as many skills as you can. Yes, we all want to just be artists and focus on the music but that is not realistic, certainly not at the beginning. Learn and do everything and then you will have a better understanding (and even advantage over) those who book the gigs, write brochure copy, do accounts, graphic design, produce records, tour manage etc etc. And always be professional, even if those around you aren't. I would also say, do call out unacceptable behaviour, don't be afraid to put your head above the parapet and be part of a team—offer solidarity and support where you can.

Barb Jungr adds,

I think it's about why you come into anything. It's best to come into music wanting to make music, wanting to play, to sing, to write. The other stuff is icing. If you are lucky you will earn a living. Most musicians do another job or have other strings to their bows, no pun intended. They teach, they do music therapy, they make radio or podcasts. It's the few who make their living only by playing. So I think, don't come in with making a living being the reason, come in because the music calls you. Then be happy for the chance to live making music. It beats hands down everything else.

Wendy Kirkland gives advice based on her experiences,

My number one suggestion is—just don't give up. Don't give them the satisfaction of seeing you pay attention to prejudice and bullying. It can be very hard, but you just have to keep going if it's something you want. Don't pay attention to the advantages that some people are given when you are discriminated against. Just keep striving, and don't underestimate the amount of time it will take. 'Nil carborundum illegitimae!' (don't let the bastards grind you down).

It is not just jazz musicians who need to find ways of getting a break. Emma Acton is a photographer as well as being marketing manager for the *606 Club,* one of London's iconic and prestigious music venues. She has a growing portfolio of musicians and is making her way in the world of jazz photography. Some of her candid portrait photographs are included in this book. She has had to be resourceful.

Emma Acton informed me,

> *I was lucky enough to learn from my Dad who is also a photographer. Due to my background in marketing I was able to make educated decisions as to where I would focus my efforts. Due to my lack of a professional portfolio I sought out opportunities to change this. I scrolled through Eventbrite (an events platform) and contacted organizers to see if they were interested in having a free photographer at their event—on one condition—if they used my images, they would give me credit and if they were happy with the work they would compose a testimonial that I could use for self-promotion.*

Her approach worked and two months later Emma says,

> *I had my portfolio and a handful of wonderful testimonials. In the two weeks that followed I built my own website and was ready to go. Since then I have worked on a range of events, but my role at the 606 Club has opened up the opportunity to take photos of wonderful musicians.*

Jazz vocalist Beverley Bierne says,

> *I started out singing in a rock band and musical theatre. As we all know, most of the great American Songbook heralds from musical theatre. On my latest album 'Jazz Just Wants To Have Fun' I draw from the music of the 80's from my school days but the album is definitely jazz. I'm quite open when it comes to genre, I think it's a lot more fluid now and there's a lot more original fusion material that is still within the realms of jazz. If it's good music and it resonates and you want to sing it or play it then I think go for it.*

It does not always go perfectly though. Debbie Gifford told me,

> *During one of my first quartet gigs as a new singer and band leader in the Cleveland jazz scene, I was fortunate to perform with a local jazz pianist Larry Meuhling and bassist Dick Meese. Both of these seasoned musicians had tons of experience and were now up in years. The gig was going smoothly and I felt a bit more at ease. As an added bonus the butterflies in my stomach had calmed down. The next song I called was, 'I got a Crush on You' (Gershwin) in the key of C. Larry played a beautiful introduction and then I sang the entire song. Now it was time for his piano solo and to my shock he was playing, 'When I Fall In Love' (Victor Young). I didn't know what to do so after he played half way through his solo I stood next to him and whispered, 'Larry, I got a Crush On You!' He responded, 'I know Deb but let's get through the song first.'*

The audience apparently were none the wiser as Larry returned to the original song and Debbie sang it.

Joelle Khoury adds succinctly,

> *Women must be ready to put up a fight with a smile on their face.*

It is difficult for some to be the one putting themselves out there, to be the one asking for gigs; but starting out, that is exactly what most musicians must do. Talent most definitely comes into it but, as Joelle further points out,

> *Talent will get you places, as long as people can see your talent—the right people! So you need to have a good business head too to push yourself and promote yourself, or at least have good representation. Many artists do not feel comfortable with self-promotion—me included. It's knowing the effective way of getting yourself through the right doors to the right people, and if you are talented then that should get you the success you need. There are a lot of talented people who aren't where they should be, and some who are less talented but are making it work for them! It's a balance of being confident, talented and making good decisions. As a girl from a working-class background, to boast about ones talent is not*

the 'done thing', so it's hard for me to say, 'I am good, please give me a gig', without feeling guilty for self-promoting! Do men feel that way? Maybe!

Debbie Gifford adds to this,

Share your gift with however will listen. Not everyone has to be a superstar—that is not my measure of fame or success. If I perform and see someone in the audience is connecting with my music, that is my success. Your music is a gift that should be freely given to anyone who wants to listen—whether on stage or singing a lullaby to a baby- just as long as it comes from your heart.

When I was talking to women before starting the book, Beverley Bierne wanted me to understand the range of different hats a working jazz musician has to wear. Beverley is a successful recording artist and regularly gigs across the UK and at festivals (she runs Ilkley Jazz Festival too) but even an established musician has to work hard at different areas of their career. Beverley sent me an example from her diary of a day in the life of a working jazz musician and it makes salutary reading for anyone interested in entering the jazz industry—this what it is like in reality.

This morning's been busy, with all kinds of things. My producer Jason is mixing the second album we did together 'Dream Dancer' and we're emailing back and forth with ideas and sounds. I'm also knee deep in planning the Jazz Just Wants to Have Fun, (her last album) tour. I'm organizing promo for 'The Ilkley Suite' (the record I sing several songs on that Jamil Shariff wrote for the Ilkley Jazz Festival's 5th year) and trying to get a distributing deal for it and also casting an eye on next year's festival and I ask myself if women are better at juggling than men—as I get a little flustered trying to do several things at once! Aren't women supposed to be much better multi-taskers? But this is really what being a professional jazz singer/musician is all about. This is the stuff people don't really see and if men do have a better handle on this then they're keeping it to themselves.

Today I thought about the wonderful effects of synchronicity, that has without a doubt been a huge part of my career. Jason Miles, my producer on these next two records, sent me ideas for Old Brazil, the song Duncan Lamont wrote which is on the album and actually the theme tune from the adored children's program' Mr Benn' from my own childhood. Duncan wrote this and all the incidental music and it's the first time it has been recorded like this with lyrics as a jazz standard. Being a fan of Mr. Benn and the tune I was thrilled to do this. But it only came about because of working with Esther Bennett's project 'The Duncan Lamont Songbook' and Duncan sprang this on me the night before recording (we were doing another of his songs 'Now We're Just Friends' that I sing in the show). Coincidentally, Duncan did a big band version of the Mr Benn music and recorded it in the same studio I was in. (this was called As If By Magic *and I reviewed it in December 2016). So, this had a touch of destiny about it. Having Jason on board was also synchronistic, as we were looking for a producer for this next album and my husband, Mark, saw a random post from Jason about producing so contacted him seeking advice. Next thing we're chatting and the rest is history.*

I suppose it made me think that being in this is industry is not a linear career. You don't have an A-Z guide. Things come up and come at you and you have to be ready to go for it. I can honestly say though that me being a woman and an older woman at that, has ever been a factor other than in my own head, sometimes my own personal fears. In actual fact, I'd say both men and women alike have admired me going for it and have embraced the fact that I'm an older woman and actually quite like what that brings to the table. Women do bring 'something else'- women of all ages, talents and abilities and isn't that great!

Passing It On

Sometimes a successful woman can empower others. Many of the women in this book have used their positions to empower others, particularly women, who often need support. Jane Bunnett found herself in Cuba and decided to help female Cuban jazz musicians. She formed the ensemble *Maqueque* (which means 'the energy of a young girl's spirit') and the album she recorded with them in 2014 won *Best Group Album Juno* award. Until then, unknown musicians such as drummer Yissy Garcia, pianist Danae Olano, bata/conga drummer Magdelys Savigne, Violinist Elizabeth Rodriguez and bass player Celia Jimenez did not have anyone as their advocate—until Jane Bunnett came along. Yissy Garcia has been a member of the band *Bandancha* and part of many projects expanding knowledge of Cuban music. Danae Olano has gone on to win many awards and played festivals and major events. Magdelys Savigne is part of Bill King's *Rhythm Express*. Elizabeth Rodriguez moved to Canada and has a successful career teaching and playing. Many of the other musicians who have come into *Maqueque's* orbit of influence have enjoyed success and recognition. Jane explains,

> *With my partner we dreamed of musical situations that were musically exciting to us and then pulled them off with a pretty good success level... When we discovered the Cuban music scene in 1982 our musical course took a bit of turn. I was always drawn to the 'Latin Tinge' as they call it even when I was playing classical music. The open Afro jazz sound of Coltrane and Pharaoh Sanders were extensions of modern jazz with a new open sound. I heard that in Cuban music too of course because they are connected. For many years I continued to visit Cuba mixing up this Afro Cuban thing with jazz and then it started to influence my writing style. This was now the music that seemed to catch people's interest as not many people were doing this. We made our first Cuban recording in 1992 but I already had 3 recordings out but of a totally different nature, 'In Due Time' with Don Pullen and Dewy Redman, 'NY Duets' with Don Pullen and 'Live at Sweet Basil's, NY' with Billy Hart, and Don Pullen.*

> *For many years we kind of alternated. More straight-ahead jazz recordings with our Cuban projects. I still see myself as a jazz artist and that is what I love more than anything. Being from Canada I was able to take full advantage of the good relationship our two countries*

have. In the end this is what has taken us all over Cuba to work, record and collaborate with different Cuban artists in various regions and to make two documentary films.

Always in Cuba I was the only woman artist amongst mostly men. My husband, Larry decided to start an all-women ensemble as we were never seeing them out there playing even though they have superb training. We recorded two CDs. The first, 'Maqueque' received a Juno award in 2015 and our second received a Grammy Nomination 2018. We are now working on our third CD. Once again this is what has caught people's attention. They are all young women instrumentalists that sing and compose too. Even though the touring is difficult with the travel restrictions for Cubans we manage to plough on. The group has been named one of the top 10 groups of the year by Downbeat magazine and I hope the sky's the limit. We try to keep our sound highly original and this way we cannot be compared to anyone else.

We have heard advice on different parts of the journey from many jazz women. As a reviewer and writer, I would offer this advice: In order to get your music heard, you need exposure. Do the homework. Target the right reviewers by reading past reviews. Make sure the music is absolutely top notch. Also, be honest and open about what motivates you. I get a lot of messages from people wanting me to review their material. The language used will often determine whether I even open the correspondence in the first place. A subject line in an email like, 'you gotta hear this' is a turn off. Same goes for a musician telling me where to place a review. What is important is to approach a reviewer politely and ask if they would consider listening to and reviewing the music. Online reviews are generally unpaid to avoid bias (and many professional writers find internet review sites offer them the freedom to write about music they choose in their own style). A review takes time and a good reviewer listens intently and gives their opinion. So be polite, respectful and open. If the reviewer is too busy or can't listen to your music for another reason, simply thank them for their time and move on. If a reviewer agrees to listen to your music, give them what they need. Most sites need artwork, a personnel list and the reviewer may ask for details to make their review different from others, so be cooperative. After all, it is exposure for your music.

Jo Harrop comments,

> *It's a competitive industry as a female singer, and often people love to compare us all, which can lead to negativity, but I think as women we need to all stand together and celebrate and support each other as much as possible—I think many people like to think that there's a need to put other singers down in order to succeed, but we are all individual and there's room for us all.*

Kim Cypher's advice is

> *I think succeeding in this industry is based on getting out there and learning how to cope and make things work in the 'real' world. It is all very well and good studying music and achieving a music qualification (which is a good thing), but that does not guarantee success. Success is definitely based on your ability to promote yourself, getting yourself out gigging and to having enough resilience to survive. So, there are a lot of factors to get right.*

Education, Funding & Innovation

"We must remember that intelligence is not enough. Intelligence plus character-that is the goal of true education. Martin Luther King Jr, 1947

EDUCATION, FUNDING and the future go together. While we enjoy the women of the past and those of today, there is another layer—the musicians of the future. They need funding, education and opportunity if there is to be a future in jazz music for them.

Education is a gift. We are fortunate when we have the opportunity to learn. It expands our existence, our being; it opens doors. Education can be theoretical, practical or academic. Learning from those who are both skilled and willing to teach us is something special when it happens. Some abuse the formal education system, not taking it seriously; and for others, education is cherished and personal and communal sacrifices are made to give people the chance to learn. Women in particular, have had to fight hard for education in many cultures.

If you look at statistics charts from the US, Australia and the UK, just under half of music students are female while only about twenty percent of artists registered to receive royalties at organizations like APRA AMCOS, ASCAP, BMI, PRS (bodies which license music) are female. The figure is just over sixty percent for male performers—three times that number. What does this tell us? It tells us that while many women study music, not many go on to professional careers. The statistics cover music as a whole, so it is not possible to draw conclusions about jazz alone, though it provides an idea of the comparatively low number of women in music who make their living from it. Women are still low in numbers in some jazz bands—perhaps two out of twenty musicians in some cases—a ten percent participation rate versus twenty, so it can be seen how the statistics for jazz music might be even worse.

In the UK, students can study jazz at many institutions: Trinity College, Leeds Conservatoire, The Guildhall School of Music and many more colleges offer jazz-centered degrees. Also, several London venues have *student days* allowing jazz students to get a taste of performing in front of an audience. However, if we look at the number of students playing at these concerts, again the proportion of women is less than twenty percent.

Without funding for this education, places where people can learn jazz music would not exist and it would be almost impossible for new projects to get off the ground and for jazz to develop.

In some schools, music is part of the curriculum in early years and there is opportunity for children to learn instruments. They learn by group lessons or one to one tuition and many children grow up with a love of music. Then something happens where music become formal, constrained, with only a few genres available and the choice of instruments limited due to costs. Music has less funding than other disciplines even where education is provided by the state or is mandatory—and in these schools, jazz is rarely found in curricula. Add to this the emphasis on religious, classical and folk music in schools and it is easy to see how students could pass through the education system and never come across jazz.

Jazz was never part of formal music education early on and was even thought to have a detrimental effect on musical education. There was the general opinion that musicians who played jazz were unschooled and classical music was the better path. But we need to remember that the education system is necessarily rigid and conservative; it teaches subjects which are historically important and have been established for decades. It reacts slowly and takes time to adapt, to acquire the experts, design the programs and so on. Jazz was not included in the curriculum for decades. In the 1930s and 40s it was still considered 'new' music. There were few maestros in jazz and those who were at the top of the jazz tree were themselves largely uneducated people with little social influence. Finally, parents were not going to go to colleges to demand the instigation of a jazz study program. Also, much of early jazz was played without scores, apart from some orchestral arrangements. So they had the added difficulty of discovering how to teach this new form of music that was not even written down.

Without set books, developing a method of instruction was difficult. Many musicians like Buddy Bolden, Joe 'King' Oliver' and Jelly Roll Morton were self-taught. Jazz musicians learned by playing with more experienced jazz players, picking up techniques and to a large extent, mimicking their style. Formal teaching methods were not laid down.

Jazz also had its own traditional ways of educating new players. Brutal as they were, cutting sessions and jam sessions were in their way the first group education activities—comparable to today's performance master classes, but far harsher. They provided opportunities for new musicians to learn from experienced ones and upheld the African traditions of knowledge passing orally from one person to another. Even today, jam sessions or 'sitting in' are key ways for musicians to share aspects of style and musical knowledge. I was recently told how, early in the UK's *People Band's* career, the great John Surman came and sat in on a couple of sessions in the late 1960s with the less experienced members of the band. This was common and with jazz music, most musicians learned by working their way through the ranks of a band, or on occasion being spotted and asked to sit in, guest and then become part of the band or orchestra. It was often a social progression as well as a musical one. Jazz education was obtained at the side of more experienced musicians. For schools and colleges, classical music was easier to teach and had a more defined methodology. Some colleges went as far as to ban students from practicing jazz. However, as jazz developed, it attracted people from all backgrounds and proved itself commercially viable. Those who wanted to study the history of the music and then the different styles and genres as well as jazz music itself began to emerge. Slowly jazz became incorporated into the education system, initially as part of study programs or summer schools, but later as fully jazz-centered programs. The first jazz program students were overwhelmingly male. Women began appearing in minuscule numbers though these numbers have been growing steadily to reach today's proportion of around thirty percent.

In the meantime, we ask what effect this has had? Has jazz education delivered a raft of players who can outplay others? How do those already ahead in their career feel about graduates and in particular women? Has increased education opportunities led to more women coming into jazz and does the jazz-degree-holding woman fare better than her non-degree-holding counterpart in getting work?

Jazz came into the education system through the back door via classical tutors who liked jazz and introduced it as another style of playing. From the early 20th century, the first jazz recordings meant the music could be heard by a much wider audience. Radio play helped even more. Many schools developed jazz and swing bands and jazz bands proved extremely popular as entertainment at school events.

As more recordings were available, experienced and young musicians could use them as templates to play against and emulate the styles of. In the 1930s and '40s conservatory-trained musicians who also played jazz began teaching jazz in New York, Los Angeles and Boston. This gave jazz acceptability and sure enough, books began to appear on how to play jazz. The influential music press like the *Downbeat* magazine began to publish columns with jazz lessons.

In Boston, Heirick Schillinger began to teach improvisation and arranging at Schillinger House (this later became *Berklee College of Music*). In the military, educators like Len Bowden taught African American military service personnel jazz music for dance bands. Jazz pedagogy was born and Bowden and a few other educators began to outline curricula to include jazz ensemble playing, arranging, improvisation and rehearsal techniques.

The school system gave rise to a few exceptional bands including the *International Sweethearts of Rhythm* (see earlier). Major events like the 1939 World Fair in New York featured the *Casa Loma Orchestra* that played classical music alongside jazz and swing. Swing music and jazz in particular, proved popular. With such massive interest from the general population, it was not long before colleges felt they should offer jazz programs in their music studies.

In the meantime, classical purists saw jazz as diluting the quality of music students were being taught. But students themselves were seeking it out. First because it was new, popular and rebellious. Later because they had discovered the musicality of the genre and the different ways of playing—and they liked it. It was not encouraged in every college however. Recently Steve Rubie, manager of the *606 Club* in London, told me that when he was a music student in the 1970s you could get a two-week ban or a fine if you were heard playing jazz at Trinity College. Of course, this meant students played jazz wherever and whenever they could and it became the 'underground music' of the music colleges in London, adding to its power and mystique. Students formed jazz groups, played in clubs and composed jazz. Now these students are teachers and jazz is part of their musical teaching. Because many of them have had success in jazz, they impart their instruction to their students. They share their experiences, talk of the clubs, the players, the social history and inspire the next generation. Schools now have their own jazz clubs, groups and orchestras. Jazz is seen as a distinct discipline, with its own complexities, style and methodology—and is offered as part of the curriculum in many colleges as complete programs or jazz-specific degrees. Trinity College, where Stevie Rubie witnessed jazz being banned, now offers jazz studies.

One of the keys to the change was that becoming a jazz musician became a viable career path for college students. In the 1950s and 1960s jazz had become a commercially significant industry in the US. Musicians made money—maybe only a few made real money, but many made a decent living as jazz pianists, members of jazz orchestras and session musicians. This happened a little later in the UK than in the US and continental Europe, but colleges could no longer ignore jazz.

Today, formal jazz education continues to grow. It is still difficult for a student to study a baritone saxophone, double bass or flugelhorn formally at school, but there are ways and means. There are grants to help also; and competitions like the *BBC Young Musician of the Year* expanded to include a *BBC Young Jazz Musician of the Year*. This shows jazz is increasingly popular and with growing acceptance in the mainstream. Seeing the *Albert Hall* filled to the rafters at the Mingus Proms and hearing young musicians like Leo Pelligrino move the entire audience with his version of *Moanin*, pianist Hiromi or saxophone player Jess Gillam play jazz and the audience lapping it up is wonderful. In fact, the *Albert Hall* have their own jazz events regularly allowing Londoners and people from further afield to enjoy jazz in a semi-formal setting.

Some UK venues like *606 Club* and *The Vortex* in London support students by giving them the chance to perform in front of a mix of friends, family and paying audience members. A very different experience from playing in college halls. As a group of newly graduated musicians came off stage, one of them told me,

> *"This is great because playing in a small group is nothing like when you are on stage. On stage it feels like there is a vast open area between you and the audience. Then you look up and they are like, right there, way too close." Another added, "the first time someone who is not part*

of your family or friends stops you as you are going to the green room after playing and says something like,' you know what? I really loved your style' or even, 'why don't you look up a bit more?' It is like 'wow, they actually noticed me enough to engage with my music! It shows they care enough to comment which is great. And we do learn from these experiences. For some of us, it even shows us performance may not be our forte so we might decide to go for doing something else to do with the music!'"

Yet, for all this increased education, encouragement of students, and venues offering them a chance to try out, where are the women? There are still far fewer women in colleges studying jazz then men.

The first universities to offer credit for jazz studies included *Berklee Music College*, Boston, *North Texas State University* and *Los Angeles City College*. After World War II, some colleges saw the need for G.I.s needing specialized training and offered jazz studies as part of this.

In 1941 the *New School of Social Research* in New York became the first to offer a jazz history course. This viewed jazz from an academic, scholarly perspective, giving the music and its history an 'academic' status. By the early 1950s more than thirty colleges and universities in the US were offering jazz courses while music publishers provided arrangements for jazz playing. Instrument companies sponsored jazz in schools and funded school jazz festivals. This added *kudos* to jazz as a mainstream genre. Summer seminars and jazz schools began to be popular—there are now numerous summer schools across the US, UK and Europe.

In the 1960s, jazz's popularity grew both in secondary schools and colleges. Many schools had a jazz band, gave jazz classes and programs became faculty led rather than student-directed—a major step forward in jazz's credentials. Professional musicians were invited to visit schools to give master classes and the demand for jazz education materials soared.

In 1968 the *National Association of Jazz Educators* (NAJE) was founded with an aim to create standards, set goals, authenticate materials and assist those involved in jazz education. From one hundred initial members it now has over eight thousand educators, students, performers and industry personnel.

The 1970s saw jazz becoming more popular in education facilities. Many teachers had learned jazz by other routes, but understood the value of jazz techniques. Suddenly students were no longer denied this additional musical area. Jazz performances on campus proved very popular, making it a more attractive genre for students.

By the late 1980s more than five hundred colleges across the US and a good number in the UK and Europe were offering jazz related courses. More than seventy percent of junior and senior high schools in the US had at least one jazz band and over three hundred summer camps operated offering jazz. In addition, there were regular high school and college jazz festivals and schools expanded their jazz programs to include vocals, performance, jazz theory and harmony and more.

There have, since then, been even more developments in jazz education. Computer programs have been developed to allow home education in jazz techniques, play-along books and discs have grown as popular home education tools for playing techniques and most music teachers will offer jazz specialization with other techniques. Jazz is no longer on the periphery, but is part of music education as a whole.

In Europe wholly jazz degrees are a relatively new thing. *Leeds College of Music* was the first in Europe to offer a jazz degree in 1993, nearly three decades after the first jazz study courses were offered in America. With jazz degrees simply not being available until the mid-1990s in Europe, we now have the situation where there are many musicians who have come up via the college route and many who have not. Given the fact there are musicians of renown in both camps, the discussion on whether jazz degrees are useful continues—often deep into the evening after a performance. In the UK, more music colleges offer jazz degrees and you can attend summer schools and specialist weeks of jazz study in locations as far apart as London, Wells and Falmouth.

Today jazz is widely accepted and taught in most music colleges. From 2009 there has even been a world-wide network—*The Jazz Education Network*—which "inspires collective improvisation in music, action and word". They have a yearly event which continues an on-going conversation between students, teachers, pros and enthusiasts to connect, learn, and jam. All in the name of jazz. The first JEN conference in 2010 was attended by twelve hundred educators, industry personnel, performers, students and enthusiasts and now there is an annual conference.

The techniques of playing jazz can be learned in school and at university. The exchange and dissemination of knowledge, jazz's historical context, its cultural importance, influential players and more can happen in a distilled and rapid manner.

Many still believe that in jazz, just as in most genres, true 'education' only happens when you play and hit the real world. Getting gigs, finding your character, deciding where you sit as a solo or ensemble player, whether you play just jazz or cross into many genres—many believe none of this can be learned in a formal setting. Jazz is still full of players who have never had formal training in jazz. Some have not had formal music training at all and there are a good few who believe in the old way of 'paying your dues'—which means you need to have started small—as a 'sidesman' in a band—and worked your way up to solo spots. Some musicians actively resent people coming straight out of college, getting solo spots because of their talent and never having to work their way up.

Patti Boulaye puts it like this,

> *I would really like to think that jazz degrees would improve chances for future jazz musicians and though I have met some amazing young*

graduates and worked with a few, I can't help feeling that jazz has a human side that cannot be taught even at degree level. It sounds like teaching a person how to fall in love.

If you ever want to start a discussion at a gig, mention jazz education and see the different reactions you get. Some musicians shrug and say if a person has talent they will get the gigs, others laugh and say the kids coming out of college have no way of being prepared for the harsh reality of jazz; and others say they don't really care if a person has a degree, they just want to hear how they play. Many musicians feel education should also include how to get gigs, sell your music and market yourself to make money from the talent you have rather than just learn about the history, musical idiosyncrasies and theory of jazz. Actually, this crops up frequently in discussions because musicians feel that young people coming into jazz need to understand that they need to keep records, pay their taxes and work out how to make it pay.

There are some young people fresh out of college whose talent is prodigious and obvious yet fail to make a connection with the audience. Others might not have quite their technical ability or talent, but can make that connection with an audience that makes a gig feel great or interpret the music in ways one might never have expected. I have been at gigs with an entire orchestra comprising students and felt a lack of connection. They play well but something is missing—it feels more like a concert orchestra playing at jazz. I have been to solo performances where the freshly-emerged graduate has come on stage, played brilliantly, left and the audience hardly knew they were there. I have also been to one or two performances where the newly-graduated musician delivered a unique performance, played something entirely new, different and completely engaging. It is still largely down to being able to play well and engage people with your music no matter how educated you are or how you came to be that educated.

For female jazz musicians, education used to be something of a difficult area as they were so greatly outnumbered by men. They also found the competitiveness of the jazz arena difficult. Very few female performers had proved in the past they could hold their own in the brutal field of the cutting session. Most had learned from jam sessions and sitting in with bands and ensembles. College and a jazz degrees were very much a male area until the late 1970s. The collegiate setting was less animalistic than the cutting sessions. Women became accepted as a presence at jam sessions or sat in with established musicians. Education slowly became another door into the world of jazz. However, women are still in the minority at most colleges.

Matters appear to be slowly changing and as graduates become successful performers, later maybe turning tutor, they become role models for women to follow into the jazz arena. Many performers, even some who have not been part of the college system themselves, are becoming educators and some of them particularly support women.

Emily Saunders says,

> *It's fantastic how education in Jazz has massively developed for quite a few years now, both through jazz expanding into conservatoire degrees, and in supportive centers and educational environments like Tomorrow's Warriors, the Julian Joseph Academy, and the National Youth Jazz Collective. These places are fundamental in the recent explosion of energy in jazz—as it puts kids and young people in touch with top musicians and composers, passing on their wisdom in a bubbling environment. It's this that really supports great new talent to burst onto the jazz scene. In the classical world, the impact of conservatoires on the classical tone can be seen as limiting in the sense of unifying people's 'sound', but jazz is not a vessel that the sound travels through, in the way in which classical performance is. Jazz is a different process of creativity, where both performance and composition are tightly knit. To me, the essence of jazz is about gaining harmonic knowledge, technical skill, improvisational freedom and compositional skills, all within the context of developing your own musical voice and creating your own sound—meaning: what is it that 'you' want to say? Therefore within jazz degrees, with the right tutors and the right guidance, people can be supported to find their own*

musical voice. I think that as jazz develops and strengthens within its current revival, expanding opportunities for work will also naturally evolve with this.

There are some drawbacks to education in field of jazz music. People speak about the newly graduated students being very similar in style, with just a few variances depending on who taught them and where they studied. Gail Tasker comments,

I think jazz degrees have definitely institutionalized the genre. The fall back of jazz education is that the genre becomes more homogenized.

There is also a lot of discussion on the atmosphere in jazz studies. Some people talk of an aggressive atmosphere which does not suit women, while others say this has changed. When I speak to young musicians what comes across powerfully is how they support and protect each other and this does not seem to have anything to do with gender. It is about like-minded people bouncing ideas off each other and being creative. Previously, I mentioned that there are some graduates who have a sense of entitlement and I think jazz is probably the best genre they can go into which knocks that misconception out of the park. Jazz musicians 'qualify' in so many other ways than just getting their degree, or not as is the case with many performers.

Joelle Khoury is not so impressed with degrees in jazz. She says,

I think it gives them a chance of getting a teaching job, probably but a concert audience does not care for degrees.

Many people now, musicians included, believe education is part of the musical journey. Unless you are from a musical family, who will teach you about jazz if not tutors at college? Secondly, colleges encourage people into what was for a time a dying industry. The injection of young talent, fueled to a major extent by graduates and those with college experience— has been wonderful, bringing new energy into jazz music the like of which we have not seen for decades. I have been told by many musicians that it was a teacher who inspired them, and not always via college either.

In London during the late 1960s, teacher Mel Davis curated sessions at *The Starting Gate* in north London where students and young people interested in jazz could come and play. Under Mel's direction several ensembles developed and went on to be seminal performers in free jazz and improvised music. Many musicians talk about people who have mentored them early in their jazz career. The great thing for women is that now there are more female role models and many of them are more than willing to encourage other women into the jazz scene.

Studying jazz at university means you spend time learning your instrument inside and out, understanding jazz history, influences, world jazz and much more, including different genres as well as playing with other musicians in varied settings. Jazz program graduates are often well-rounded players—they just choose to specialize in jazz. The problem arises when newly graduated players face the transfer from the protected playing and showcase concerts provided by institutions to having to find gigs themselves.

People studying together often end up playing together also and trying new ideas. There are a few spaces such as *Jazz Re:Freshed* in London where you get, not only young people fresh from college with energy and enthusiasm, but the opportunity to play alongside experienced players like Evan Parker and those who graduated before them. The recent recordings of Moses Boyd with Evan Parker are examples of great collaborations happening between veterans of the playing arena and younger musicians who need experience. For some, these experiences can be a baptism by fire, but are also probably some of the best education experiences a young jazz player can hope for. An example of this can be found on Delfeayo Marsalis's live album recorded in concert in Michigan. In the audience were two University of Michigan students Delfeayo had invited to the concert—for a reason. He called them on stage. One was vocalist Christian O'Neill Diaz, the other drummer, Madison George. Delfeayo asked Christian if he normally sings big-band style, to which the answer was "yes." Marsalis tells him,

"We don't do that, but can you scat?" It turned out he thought he could—sort of. Delfeayo then asked him which key he preferred to which Diaz answered "F or B flat". Marsalis told him he would play in D flat. Marsalis had tricked these young musicians into performing unrehearsed, in unfamiliar keys and unfamiliar styles—in front of a packed theatre. They did a fine job on the subsequent *Blue Kalamazoo* considering it probably felt like walking on coals. Diaz could scat and George certainly proved he could drum. The audience loved it as they were part of the process. Delfeayo commented,

> *Part of maturing is being able to not only assist, but to also challenge the younger generation. If we had performed a song that Christian sings all the time, he would have probably sung in auto-pilot mode. Creating a song together spontaneously forces you to reach deep inside and stay committed to the moment. It's an African tradition.*

Barb Jungr comments on the importance of learning while playing to an audience, and the lack of opportunities,

> *Three-week runs don't exist anymore, or very rarely, and that's had an effect. Young musicians, male and female, are unable to grow and create in front of an audience in that way. Institutions do not give that possibility*

As I mentioned, education is something which always starts discussions—sometimes heated ones—among jazz musicians. Some believe education should be gained by working hard, doing gigs, getting experience and making your way in the music business. Others believe the way forward is jazz degrees, courses and studies into particular playing styles. They believe you only really get to understand an instrument and genre by studying it, having uninterrupted time to do that and getting the opportunities to play with other musicians in your peer group; and that only an institution can provide that.

Terri Lyne Carrington comments on her experience. She learned the business of jazz from the age of seven when she began playing drums.

She got her Union card at age ten—the youngest person in Boston to do so. Her father was a saxophone player and president of the *Boston Jazz Society* and her grandfather (he gave her the drum set) was drummer for Fats Waller—so her route into jazz was not too difficult. Her father was already collaborating with a lot of musicians and she was allowed to sit in. From the time she was ten until she was sixteen, Terri Lyne gained a reputation as a player and never thought this was different or unusual. She gained a scholarship to Berklee when she was eleven and attended part time until she was seventeen, attending full-time for three semesters at eighteen when she moved to New York. She played with Clark Terry and was mentored by Jack DeJohnette and Wayne Shorter. So in Terri Lyne's case, education came both from college and experience with great musicians. She told me,

> *Things fell into my lap, I always worked, paid my bills so I have no complaints.*

Wendy Kirkland comments,

> *I would say it's more difficult now as the education system is producing newcomers at a rate of knots. This wasn't the case when I started out – not to the same extent. There's a feeling that to become a musician you have to have studied at an establishment and passed a qualification. I'd liken this to the driving test – once you have it, then the learning begins! I'd say self-taught and self-directed musicians would have a harder time getting on the 'ladder' now if you like, because there are so many graduates of jazz courses doing the same and getting more acceptance, regardless of their talent or abilities.*

I agree to some extent but I would add that, from what I have seen, jazz soon finds you out. A graduate with exceptional playing skills will maybe do well post graduation in a classical orchestra but in jazz, if you do not engage others you are sunk.

Jenny Green advises,

> *If you can afford to, go to the music colleges for your grounding but it's*

getting out there and playing. There is no guaranteed work out there, you have to go knocking on doors and you have to be pretty determined. It's a long road! You have to do a lot of networking.

Faye Patton comments,

Education for girls needs to be better obviously but we need stuff for the elders and mature artists too– lifetime infrastructure, not just stuff for youth with 26 as the age limit. Some of us take until into our 40s/50s to get heard—that needs to be respected.

Jane Bunnet talks about a different education—that of learning first hand by experience. She explains,

I have had the great opportunity to meet my musical heroes and work alongside with them, learning first-hand the magic of the music. Don Pulley, Dewey Redman were two of the most important figures and I have toured and recorded with both of them. I have found that all the musicians I love have encouraged me to try to be myself on my instrument and form a unique concept for myself.

Jo Harrop agrees. There are more ways to get a jazz education than a degree in jazz music. She says,

Firstly, I was told at school that I wasn't really musical and rarely got the chance to learn music or an instrument, so I danced instead. However, I loved singing, so I learned the words to all the songs in the charts, the jazz standards that my parents played in the house, I joined musical theatre holiday clubs and so was quite obsessed with singing and writing little songs. As I didn't study music in a school or academy at all, I have very much learned by listening, watching, more listening. Most of what I have learned has been on stage with the fantastic supportive musicians I work with. It has been a journey from song writing and performing my own original songs on a very different scene, into singing jazz standards with jazz musicians in jazz clubs. I often feel frustrated that I didn't get to study an instrument as a child or go on to learn the theory side of things, as I have had to overcome quite a few hurdles. What I do though, everything I sing, comes from a natural place. It's very real and from the heart. There's still time to study!

Sometimes, a degree is only the first step. Emma Acton graduated from university with a degree in Music Technology (first class). She wanted to find a role which combined her love of music, her work experience in marketing and event photography. She says,

I think music education is very important regardless of whether you see yourself becoming a musician. I wrote my university dissertation on how music effects the emotional development of children and the positive effect it has is totally undeniable. Musical opportunities for young people are so important to encourage, inspire and also aid the development of other academic areas. The 606 club hosts jazz club performance exams as well as monthly gigs for those studying at the Royal Academy of Music.

Jenny Green adds,

It is great to have jazz streams in music colleges and universities and there are some great music departments. Some secondary schools have jazz bands these days. Graduating and then finding work? Jazz jams are a good way in getting experience connecting with musicians learning to perform to an audience. I don't think it makes much difference really. If you want to perform you'll find a way degree or no degree! Learn an instrument at school, sing in your choirs, go to music college— then go and do it. Learn from the grass roots up.

Andrew Lloyd Webber said in an article in *The Stage* that,

It is vital to keep music in our schools. It is absolutely ludicrous that the government does not understand. Because it is not about turning children necessarily into musicians. It is about empowering them in all sorts of different ways.

Terri Lyne Carrington runs education programs herself and is a professor at Berklee. She comments,

It is interesting in education. There are lot more young people studying jazz but they are people who have resources so in the US, jazz has come a bit out of the community it started in and moved into jazz education. A

lot of urban/inner city schools do not have funding and resources for jazz programs so it has moved into the suburbs as far as education is concerned. This affects the demographics of the genre—players and audience. Young people aren't that interested in traditional jazz. More are interested in the new forms of jazz where styles (from hip hop, R and B) merge. I think that is important because it keeps a jazz audience and it may turn some on to going back and listening to the classics. It is all important.

Claire Martin has a very successful career without a jazz degree. She says,

Offering jazz degrees is amazing and I wish I'd done one. I'm not sure having a degree or not will guarantee any work on the scene though. To meet a jazz musician who hasn't come through onto the scene via this route is unusual now but it's like any job. You need some luck and you need to network.

For Kim Cypher, it was not about getting a degree or not, it was about her love for jazz and the saxophone. She says,

Following classical training and progressing though grades on the clarinet fulfilled a purpose in terms of gaining qualifications and mastering techniques but it did not ignite a passion in me. I was looking for an instrument that excited me and that would allow me to express myself in a more creative, funky style. So, later in secondary school I took up saxophone and I have not looked back. I absolutely love this instrument. It is in my soul.

It is wonderful that jazz is part of the curriculum at many colleges and universities, young people realize there are other young people playing jazz, they have time to spend on their instruments, they network and build relationships, some of which last many years. However, a dose of realism is also necessary.

Georgia Mancio says,

Jazz degrees have raised the level—many students graduating with immense skills but I do wonder where they will all find work and whether the expectations of what that work will be are unrealistic.

Georgia and others touched on the 'real' world in what they say. Having a degree and being cosseted in university or college is not the best way to prepare for the knocks and shocks of the jazz industry. Carmela Rappazzo comments,

> *I wish the business of jazz and the music industry in general was also being taught. I know that Juilliard has a course in it. One course. How to make a living as a musician, how to pay taxes, balance a check book, get a mortgage, practical matters that musicians don't think about. So important. I was lucky, my mother was a stickler for women knowing how to be business minded. As a result I get to live in a house, have health insurance. Practical things matter.*

Jo Harrop comments,

> *There's more music education out there now than ever. You can do courses in singing and music management. I think it can only be a good thing to empower yourself with an education, but I think as long as you are then able to find your own voice, have your own story to tell. There's no reason why the women shouldn't do as well as the men now if they work hard and have the talent and the drive, the belief.*

Terri Lyne Carrington says,

> *I do not think you will get hired for gigs because you have a degree, but it does maybe help you to teach and find other ways you can use your knowledge of studying jazz to better society. There are a lot of people who graduate but not many that are 'cream of the crop' players as it is so competitive but you can for sure use your degree to be creative because I think studying jazz is creativity. I have a few students who have done other things. They are happy and may still play a bit but it's not the main source of their income but when you study creativity, it makes you creative no matter what you do. It's all connected.*

Barb Jungr expresses her views on jazz degrees.

> *I think they've affected people's expectations. If you have done a three-year intensive degree in 'jazz' (and what does that mean in the first place?)*

and everyone's told you you're the bee's knees, and you can play Coltrane solos faster than he could and then you come out into the world and find there's another ten players who are mirrors of you and guess what? They can play as fast an nobody cares, that's harsh. But if you make the playing of your music your priority and developing your own 'voice' on your instruments, your mission and learn and play whenever and wherever you can and look down on no-one and take what's on offer, make friends and don't think you're the bee's knees, then maybe, maybe.

Camille Thurman says,

Education is critical in getting our society to adapt practices that encourage and allow young women to pursue music (jazz). Constructs about what it means to me 'male' or 'female' start within our community (schools, home, television etc). If we can start the discussion at an early age and break down these constructs, we can teach the youth to respect and appreciate each other based on character and not gender. We have to commit to being conscious of how the language we use and actions we do contribute to upholding these principles of what it is to be male/female. Representation is key. If girls could see more role models playing instruments, playing jazz, taking positions of leadership, then it would encourage them to pursue this career or have an interest and appreciation.

One thing I have often observed is that people find that going to university or college to study jazz music—or music of another genre—opens their minds to other possibilities. There are areas within the music industry which remain somewhat inaccessible unless you have the chance to meet the people in the industry yourself. This seems to be a benefit of the degree course—it opens other areas of the music industry to people which they may not have considered before. A good example of this is Amanda Bloom of *Crossover Media*. Amanda's route to music promotion came after she graduated from the *Peabody Institute of Music* at John Hopkins University with a degree in jazz vocal performance. While working as a musician, she began to do social media promotion for a few artists and connected with Max Horowitz at *Crossover Media* who offered her a job. She found she loved that side of the business—and stayed. She says,

> *I would recommend if you go into music to really keep your options open as to what you will ultimately do with your degree. While I was studying jazz vocal in college, I would never have predicted I would be passionate about a career in music promotion. Many students getting jazz degrees are stuck in a practice room and assume they will only teach and perform after graduating but that kind of mindset can be very limiting. There are so many fulfilling things you can do in the music industry in addition to performing.*
>
> *For me, it was a seamless extension of what I was already passionate about. I am constantly exposed to new, exciting music and really enjoy communicating with my radio and press colleagues. I have also been very fortunate to have a wonderful mentor in Mr Horowitz, who has been in the business for over thirty years.*

Funding and education are often discussed in tandem. Funding itself is an issue many of the women I spoke to feel very strongly about. Jazz is enjoyed by millions of people a year and yet it largely funds itself at the higher levels. This is fine on one hand, but it can limit the audience as prices go up for gigs and funding needs to be put in at entry level, helping create the jazz musicians of the future. Opera gets far more funding per head than other genres due to costs like costumes, sets, orchestra, large venue hire and so on. Jazz gets very little funding and finding the funding that does exist can be difficult. The creation of bodies such as the *Durham Commission of Creativity and Education* will hopefully help influence those that enforce policies within England as well as support Arts Council England with their development. It won't be easy however, as funds are increasingly limited in the UK and even more so in some European countries. Others, like Norway and Germany offer more in the way of funding jazz. In an article in *The Guardian*, Professor Colin Lawson, director of the *Royal College of Music* expressed concern about the knock-on effect of cuts in creative budgets in schools. He argued that the combination of cuts to school budgets (arts candidates are down twenty percent since 2010) and loss of specialist teachers has resulted in a skills loss.

Many women I spoke to also believe that music, and in particular jazz music, teaches young people so much more than just the music itself. Because of its connectivity and collective concepts, jazz can help develop creative minds and social skills which transfer to a role in society. Yet education surely begins at an early age—how we are raised and where we come from. For example, a child growing up in Harlem is far more likely to be exposed to jazz music than a child in Nurnberg or Guildford (UK). So, does this mean gender definitions are etched in our minds by parents, teachers and so on from a very early time in our development?

It is interesting to try to understand when and how children identify as one gender or another and also when they associate particular behaviour with their gender. I wondered how women saw this and whether they felt children were still to some extent tethered by expected behaviours? Was this holding their developing talent back? If so, are we missing something? Do we need to change attitudes in the school or in the home?

Sarah Gail Brand shares her observations,

> *It is at a young age when things get instilled. I see when I've worked in youth jazz with kids of 10 years and up the boys are confident and club together whereas girls will stand on the sidelines. In breaks, boys jam together and girls look on. In teenage years girls and boys don't want to know each other in terms of just being mates. Jazz is a social music and often mates will join together, so bands tend to be friends and girls are partners or girlfriends. It is getting better but we are still basing our cultural and artistic decisions on our social grouping and our understanding of group dynamics and this is going to be very hard to shake.*

Terri Lyne Carrington echoes this when she says,

> *I feel there is a problem with jazz education in middle school and high school and that's where women drop off. We have to educate the educators.*

So schools like Berklee and other schools that have music ed. majors have to look at this seriously inside and do the work now in creating a new generation of educators that won't operate form a platform of patriarchy. When it is equitable, the music will have another dimension to it."

Sarah Gail Brand comments,

I imagine young people these days have more of a grip of what they want to do. Young people I teach at Guildhall often have their own scenes going, doing function gigs etc and are determined to pick up teaching work. They are very realistic but there are also a lot of students from families who do not have to worry too much. Some come through Gary Crosby's 'tomorrow's warriors' or through the Junior Guildhall Academy jazz programs so have a good understanding of what is required in jazz. So already these students have a good idea of what they need to work on to become a performing, working jazz musician. It's a bit different than in my day when we stumbled into it somehow.

Camille Thurman adds,

Funding is important for allowing children to have access to programs that expose them to music at an early age (lessons, seeing concerts, having opportunities to talk to artists etc). If we can provide more opportunities to see talented men and women working together and performing then we can inspire the next generation to do the same.

Claire Martin says about funding,

I think funding is available to all jazz musicians through the Arts Council. It's just a case of applying and often re-applying if it's turned down initially. I have had good success with the South Coast Jazz Festival funding and so it's there if we ask for it, but the forms to fill in and the application process is brutal.

The going can get tough in the US. Terri Lyne Carrington says,

There is not enough funding in the US. Not much national or government funding. There is some from the National Education Association but it is mostly private funding. I have sat on meetings to discuss who's going

to get the money. Not enough goes to women or African-Americans—
both minorities but the good news is a lot of organizations are looking
at this, seeing where the money is going and trying to be more diverse.

Faye Patton adds,

> *Funding needs to be more in terms of amounts and more easily accessed.*
> *Some of the awards for women are derisory. Amounts like £5000 which*
> *amount to nothing once the studio time is booked and the band/engineer/*
> *personnel paid. Women have to demand more and not be so grateful for*
> *small concessions. We need support and mentoring networks, data bases*
> *and information hubs.*

Wendy Kirkland echoes some of this and adds her own thoughts,

> *I think some of the jazz funding could be better directed, e.g. to develop*
> *audiences rather than being put solely in the hands of musicians, who*
> *might not have the business skills to deal with it efficiently. I'm not*
> *involved at present in music education but I do have friends who*
> *are, and they tell me that their students are not taught any business,*
> *management or personal goal setting skills whatsoever.*

New ideas like crowdfunding have allowed many musicians to raise
funds for projects—perhaps a particular album project or summer
school—but it is the rewards offered to contributors that attract the
funding, so profits can suffer severely. There is also a slight snobbery
from those who take the position that if you need to crowdfund,
then it is because there is little value in your project to begin with.
Crowdfunding, however, has meant projects which large record labels
pass over can get done. Sometimes funding sources are surprising. For
example, the inaugural *Walthamstow Jazz Festival* of 2018 in London
was sponsored by Adnams—a small brewery in the East of England.
Occasionally the matching of clever marketing ideas and a creative
curator can prove beneficial to both sides.

There are many innovative programs taking jazz to young ears. In the US
students can take part is many jazz workshops held in libraries, schools

and colleges. Daniel Bennett, a hard-working performer and recording artist, takes time to go to schools and present workshops and master classes. Numerous states and cities offer music and jazz workshops for young people in school holidays and in the UK, *Serious* who organize the *London Jazz Festival* have a fairly extensive program of activities for schools, both in term time and during school holidays; even pre-school classes for toddlers to hear different rhythms and genres including jazz. So opportunities do exist, just few and far between. Many believe the key to encouraging potential musicians is to introduce them to music at a young age. As jazz is still not widely taught at school level, there are many initiatives where children as young as two or three are given the chance to hear and take part in jazz.

At a recent gig in a pub at lunchtime for Mother's Day, four world-class musicians played to around a hundred people, including children who were running around, almost getting knocked by the saxes. The musicians told me that, apart from the danger of hitting a child with their instrument, they loved the fact that the children were moving to the rhythms and dancing along with their parents.

Education appears to be something jazz players value. The women I spoke to certainly value it. Yet this education takes many forms. One can enroll in a music school or study jazz at university, but it seems to be of more value when it is part of music education as a whole.

It is an encouraging sign that the interest in jazz has become far greater than what it was just a few years ago. Summer schools often have a jazz program now. There are opportunities for young children to learn jazz methodology and several academies have a junior program. Another noticeable thing, in London at least, is that jazz, which was seemingly the domain of white, middle class, has again become the treasured and loved music of the communities which create it. Young, black, female, male, or non-assigned gender musicians are finding jazz performers they can relate to—and it speaks to them because once again, jazz is reflecting societal changes right back at them—and they love it.

Beverley Bierne argues that, as well as developing their talent and ability, self-promotion needs to be something musicians learn. She explains,

Without a doubt there are a lot more talented people out there on the jazz scene than ever before with the universities worldwide turning out some phenomenal talent, which on the one hand creates a fantastic, vibrant, diverse scene. But of course, each year there's the new alumni and competition is fierce. I'd say most of the students, by the time they graduate, have pretty realistic expectations, as they're probably already working on the scene by then and getting clued up to how things really are. It can be really tough hustling for gigs and I think learning the business side of this is so important, having all the promotional tools, great photo's, accessible sounds, making things easy for promoters. With so much talent out there, you want to give yourself the best chance possible and it seems very sad to me not to have this down and to lose a gig for your great music because you just didn't get organized and I'm not just saying the youngsters here. Running a festival, it's amazing how many people send you so little and you have to either chase them or if you're interested you have to start googling for information, instead of having everything sent to you and easy to access. It's actually really important stuff and it's all part of it.

In spite of the programs, opportunities and degrees opening doors for women, there are still far fewer women than men competing for college places. Inspired by this dearth of women coming into jazz education Terri Lyne Carrington began a new institute at Berklee called *The Institute of Jazz and Gender Injustice*. She explains,

There are more women playing jazz for sure. I started a new institute at Berklee called The Institute of Jazz and Gender Injustice to try and encourage even more women to play and I think that will affect the audience as far as gender. Gender too is not so binary any more. I would like to see all music forms embrace that ideology more as well... Bringing the female aesthetic into the music will be beneficial to all. I want to make sure there is an environment at the college where women will feel supported, safe and able to thrive. It's not the NFL or the NBA—not a sport that men have to play with each other in a segregated way. Women should not feel like outsiders or that they are being let into a club or invited to a party. I want women to feel real ownership in the music, to feel they are throwing the party. It is a long and tiring road I'm sure, but I'm up for it.

The headline for the BIJGJ website asks the question, "What would jazz sound like in a culture without patriarchy? Without bias?" From their mission statement, the BIJGJ is focussed on "equity in the jazz field and the role that jazz plays in the larger struggle for gender justice. The institute will celebrate the contributions women have made in the development of the art form as well as frame more equitable conditions for all pursuing careers in jazz in an effort to work toward a necessary and lasting cultural shift in the field." It outlines, as part of its directive, that one of its goals is to do corrective work and modify the way jazz is perceived and presented so that the future of jazz may be different than its past without rendering invisible many of the art form's creative contributors. These aims may, at first glance, appear wide ranging and a massive undertaking, but break it down and the ideas are simpler— they want a level playing field for all men and women of all cultures and backgrounds. Furthermore, it seeks to create a safe and nurturing environment for people of all gender identification to study jazz. Terri Lyne is fervent about the BIJGJ and says,

> *The Berklee Institute of Jazz and Gender Justice will focus on equity in the jazz field and the role that jazz plays in the larger struggle for gender justice. The institute will celebrate the contributions women have made in the development of the art form as well as frame more equitable conditions for all pursuing careers in jazz in an effort to work toward a necessary and lasting cultural shift in the field.*

Again, there is that reference I hear so often to the effect that dealing with issues in one area also assists others. Many musicians feel this— that when we address sexism in jazz, we will also bring on an entire generation who will deal with the issues surrounding this at large and so help educate society. Entry-level funding too is vital.

Terri says,

> *Funding is important for allowing children to have access to programs that expose them to music at an early age (lessons, seeing concerts, having opportunities to talk to artists, etc.). If we can provide more opportunities to see talented men and women working together and performing, then we can inspire the next generation to do the same.*

There are other opportunities to study jazz provided by colleges which encourage people other than their students. *Trinity Laban* in London offer courses for students of varying levels and ages. Their *Taste of Jazz* and *Young Women in Jazz* courses are specifically aimed at young women. Last year, they offered young female artists the chance to take part in interactive workshops exploring and playing jazz. There were groups to suit different levels and young musicians were given opportunities to be creative on their instruments. They worked alongside world class teachers to create, play and perform as an ensemble, share new musical ideas and get support from professional jazz musicians already making their living in jazz. Aimed at young women aged eleven to sixteen, this was an incredible opportunity for them to learn with the support of *Trinity Laban* professors and professional musicians in a safe environment.

There followed a *Young Women in Jazz* Day which was aimed at women from sixteen to twenty-five and offered a more intensive opportunity to experience studying at the conservatory level and working with professors, professional musicians and Trinity Laban students. The day finished with a group performance for the public. For some, this was their first taste of playing to an audience.

Days like this are huge opportunities for women seeking a way into jazz. Contact with students, professors and professional musicians gives them the chance to understand the industry, how much work they need to do and find out what it is really like. What's more, it is free.

One might wonder why it is necessary to have courses specifically for women? It is about that safe environment which the BIJGJ gave as part of its mission. In the past, studies showed that women feel intimidated and uncomfortable in mixed ensembles until they find their feet in jazz. It is a powerful music and men tend to dominate playing groups and sessions. Until female musicians feel comfortable, women-only sessions may just be the way ahead.

There are musicians who travel in the US and UK and go to schools presenting programs for children to listen and learn about jazz music. Daniel Bennett in the US, a hard-working performer, also takes time to go to schools and present workshops and master classes. Numerous states and cities offer music and jazz workshops for young people in school holidays and in the UK, *Serious*, which organizes the *London Jazz Festival* have a fairly extensive program of activities for school children, both in term time and during school holidays. They even offer pre-school classes for toddlers to hear different rhythms and genres including jazz. There are also wonderful jazz musicians like the amazing Tuba Duo who go into schools with huge brass instruments and introduce children to jazz alongside other genres.

While we understand that being introduced to jazz at a young age is a good thing and having the opportunity to go to university and study jazz is also a good thing, I wondered if education at any level was having an effect on the jazz industry and if any of the women had comments on that .

Wendy Kirkland did and funding comes into it too. Wendy says,

> *Absolutely. There used to be no such thing as a jazz degree. The great jazz icons, who today's graduates try and emulate would never have studied that way – some of them would have a basic knowledge of music, some would come from a classical background, some would have nothing but their ears and tons of experience to guide them. I really wonder how many jobs there can be when audiences are dwindling and venues are closing or changing their focus to other, more profitable genres of music.*

While there are pots of arts funding money to help graduates get gigs in venues and help them on their way, one year on they are going to be just like all the other jazz musicians trying to make their living.

What any graduate is unrealistic to expect is the right to have a job doing what their degree has trained them to do. Do all History graduates become historians? There will always be other talented people out there who do things their own way, the unofficial way, and who deserve equal respect, or perhaps more, as it is much harder work that way.

In terms of funding, is there enough of it going into jazz? In the UK the main providers of project funding for musicians are the *PRS for Music Foundation* and the UK's arts councils (*Arts Council England, Creative Scotland, Arts Council of Wales, Arts Council of Northern Ireland*). Arts Councils offer many different funding schemes. Specific grants will have different rules, but funding can be sought for assistance with research and development, creating new work for production or touring, training, mentoring and continuing professional development, and business and market development. All of these are open to music projects, including jazz; and there are other potential sources including the *Momentum Music Fund,* the *BPI Music Growth Export Scheme* and *Sky Academy Arts Scholarships, Help Musicians UK,* the *Emerging Artists Fund* and the *Help Musicians Develop Fund.* The criteria and deadlines for each of these bodies and for all funding schemes can vary from year to year. Funds are always limited so competition is strong. Jazz musicians can also make use of crowdfunding sites like *KickStarter* and *Pledge Music* to get small amounts of money in return for rewards if the project gets off the ground for those who donate. *Jazz Services* offers a number of routes including tour funding for emerging jazz musicians with exceptional talent, though the service is limited due to restricted funding from the Arts Council post-2015. Jazz in the UK receives less funding than other music genres, partly because it does not require the vast costume and sets budgets that opera or a classical orchestra need and partly because there is still the sense of jazz being a niche genre with few people attending concerts compared to other genres.

Given that over 100,000 people attend the annual *London Jazz Festival* and on any night many gigs across the UK host hundreds of audience members, this assumption seems difficult to justify. The hard facts are that funding is very limited; and the good news is that jazz musicians find ways of putting on concerts and getting the music to people.

Several smaller festivals benefit from sponsorship from breweries and other organizations and one-off's like *The London Jazz Platform* showcase find sponsors in radio stations (in this case *Jazz Bites Radio*). The *Manchester Jazz Festival* and others benefit from several sponsors, all funding a little but adding up to enough. Jazz promoters are diligent and passionate and this often leads to funding being found.

In the US, organizations like the *Jazz Foundation of America*, the *Arthur Jordan Foundation* and organizations specific to areas offer limited funding to jazz musicians. Some even help in times of need with housing, rehearsal space and other necessities. In Europe, there is the *Senate Department for Culture and Europe;* in Berlin, the *European Jazz Network*, which is a multi-nation organization which receives funding to support the development of jazz music by giving awards to musicians, commissioning studies, supporting conferences and similar activities. Funding exists and there are organizations that support the development of jazz music, but competition remains fierce and funding limited.

Carmela Rappazzo comments, when I asked about finding.

> *This made me laugh out loud. There are some grants and foundations. Is it enough? No.*

Barb Jungr comments,

> *I don't understand funding at all anymore. I'm literally flummoxed by who gets it and doesn't and why. There's not enough of it for sure. But then, who decides where it goes? I think the arts should be heavily funded and*

in appropriate and equal ways, but I'm aware we are in a society where there's little money for housing, health and education and that affects how people feel about arts funding in general. If we fund jazz, which jazz do we fund? By how much? Do we only fund things we feel have 'artistic merit'? Who decides what that is? It's complex and unresolved. The political climate does not help. We live in a country where the arts make a lot of money and yet we are treated as pariahs for the most part, as idiot savants. It's unhelpful. Try saying, 'I'm a jazz singer' to people at a party. Responses are often hilarious. In a not good way.

Gail Tasker says, on a more positive note,

There's been quite a few gigs I've been to where the band have been funded by the Arts Council. I can't imagine the same being said for many other styles of music, except classical.

Emily Saunders says this.

I've been incredibly fortunate and have had a fantastic reception of my music across the board—I'm so grateful to those who've supported me. But the Arts industry all round has been having a tough time for a while due to lack of funding. However, jazz seems to be fighting through those barriers—maybe it's the honesty in the music—but it's really exciting how the impact of jazz in the music world is going from strength to strength right now.

Whether jazz gets enough funding is a subject of heated debate. Georgia Mancio says,

Absolutely not and there is very little guidance available in securing that funding. Applications are overly involved and more concerned with the way music or a project is described than its actual quality. Bandleaders bear the financial brunt of albums, tours, gigs, often playing for a share of the door takings, with no guaranteed income. This is a corrosive and unsustainable business model when the difference between profit and loss is small (relative to larger classical productions for instance). It is deeply frustrating there is not more help available.

Debbie Gifford adds,

> From what I have seen and heard funding for musicians in the United
> States is very minimal. Some funding is available with grants but these
> are for specific projects. I have heard funding is much better in some
> European countries. The arts in general does not receive enough funding
> and among the arts the funding for jazz unfortunately is at the bottom
> of the list. But this doesn't stop jazz artists from being creative and
> finding their own way to fund their projects. Isn't creativity what jazz
> is all about?

Applying for funding seems to be a bit of an 'Alice in Wonderland'
adventure too. Kim Cypher recently explained to me that when she
applied for funding she was refused. One of the reasons provided was
that she had not applied for funding before and so was lower down
the funding ladder than others who had. Kim had funded her own
previous projects, but it felt like she would have been better applying
and re-applying for grants. Many tell of their frustration at the forms
and the need to show progression—recordings, big bookings and so
on when the grants they may be applying for are just so they can make
quality recordings. It seems to have more to do with following protocol
and being able to produce evidence so the funding body can track you
than about what the funding is actually for.

One important factor in achieving fair compensation for musicians
(jazz musicians included) was the recent passing of the *Music
Modernisation Act* by the Senate. The act ensures all musicians of all
genres get paid for usage of their music in all formats. It also assigns
random judges to decide royalties paid by bodies like ASCAP. Also the
CLASSICS Act (Compensating Legacy Artists for their Songs, Service
and Important Contributions to Society Act) benefits artists who
recorded before 1972, previously not covered by the laws, by paying
royalties for playing their music on digital radios, internet streaming
sites and so on. At the moment, only post-1972 recordings get royalties
on play. The Act also enables producers, engineers and others to claim

royalties for their contributions to the creation of music. The days of using pre-1972 recordings and not paying the artists are over it would seem. Will that mean artists will see compensation for their work if they recorded before 1972? Or will advertisers opt to use more recent music, including jazz? We shall see.

Jenny Green comments on funding,

> *Jazz definitely does not get enough. It all seems to be going to the more classical route at the moment but it will change I'm sure of it if we keep shouting about it long enough. There need to be more development programs locally and we need to find sponsors.*

> *There needs to be more women in jazz in the educational side of things, more funding for women in jazz touring. A women in jazz award I'm sure this is a good start.*

Beverley Bierne considers this,

> *Opera gets a lot more funding when they have a lot less people in the audiences. I believe it's much better in mainland Europe than it is here. The Ilkley Jazz Festival (which Beverly runs) simply wouldn't be able to exist without the funding and at present I'm organizing a tour for my new album JJWTHF and funding would be great to help out with this.*

Wendy Kirkland adds this:

> *Some of the established regional and city jazz organizations are not generally run by businesspeople—they seem to spend inordinate amounts of money on badly-directed promotion and uber-niche music that does nothing other than turn off new audiences, to satisfy their own personal tastes. If you look at the ACE (Arts Council England) website you can see the amounts of money they receive and perhaps ask yourself where it is being spent; especially someone like me, who runs a jazz club with no funding and although we don't profit, we don't lose. The amounts of money I spend on promotion are tiny compared to some clubs and I still manage to get audiences of a similar size on most occasions. What I could*

do with the money they get would be incredible! NB as an aside I've been told by no fewer than three unconnected punters who came to Chesterfield Jazz Club that they walked out of Derby Jazz concerts (three different concerts) half way through because they couldn't stand it. Pots and pans jazz, one called it. This is unprintable (no it isn't) I suppose but that's my evidence for stating the above, about turning off new audiences.

Emily Saunders says,

Funding for the arts seems to have been hit in a massive way for a long time, not only funding for jazz, and other arts, but also the fundamental basics such as instrumental lessons in schools and music education in general. It's really heart-breaking knowing so many talented people are just not getting the education they need and deserve. The process and advancement of artistic self-reflection and communication seems fundamental to the psychological health of society. The Arts is known to reflect a society and looking at our society as it is right now and the neglect of the Arts is sadly in-line with the funding neglect of many areas of our society at present. There clearly needs to be more funding support for jazz and the Arts in general.

Love, Life & Relationships in Jazz

Jazz can be all-consuming. Composition, performing and arranging can be tiring and not just for those performing. Many jazz musicians have families and partners who have to deal with them being away for long periods, engrossed in what they do and so on. Besides which the hours of work are unsocial. So how do partners feel? How does it work when you are on the road with your partner and how do those who can't travel due to other commitments feel? I got the view from both sides.

Kim Cypher comments,

My musical journey has definitely been a partnership with my husband

Mike. Although it is my name and my music that gets the recognition, it is without doubt an equal joint success and my identity has been shaped by this. We are a team and we work to each other's strengths. Between us we have naturally gravitated to the jobs each of us does best. For me, that's the creative side of things, composing the music, coming up with projects, driving things forward. For Mike it's the business side of things, dealing with all the finances, working out the logistics etc.

Wendy Kirkland:

I love working with Pat (her guitarist husband and fellow band member). With regards to equality, he's totally unprejudiced towards women. When he cites his musical influences, he always includes Emily Remler. He loves female as well as male singers, seeing them as musicians on an equal footing. He owned loads of albums featuring female musicians I'd never heard of at the time: Emily, Kristin Korb, Terri-Lyne Carrington. There are lots of other men like that out there too, the good guys I call them! I work with them, they are inspirational and positive and I avoid anyone who isn't these days. Pat is always very supportive and makes constructive suggestions too, with regard to arrangements, performances, techniques. We are always exchanging ideas in this way. He's always treated me as his equal.

Tina May commented,

If you have children—then it is almost the end of your playing unless you have supportive parents and in-laws. I was fortunate that my father became my great supporter (after his initial doubts about a career in jazz music). He regularly moved in and took charge of my two children if I had to do a lot of travelling. He was an amazing supporter. I had lost my mum while still a teenager.

Gretchen Bennett is HR director for a technology company and the wife of Daniel Bennett of the Daniel Bennett Group who tour regularly.

Gretchen tells me what it is like for her.

I met Daniel when his band was performing at an event my company was hosting back in 2005. He was working as a freelance musician and bandleader in Boston MA at the time—he had moved there a few years earlier for graduate studies at the New England Conservatory. I was working at a consulting firm in Rochester NY, which happens to be his hometown and a place where he still had a lot of musical connections. I was watching his jazz group perform and we recognized each other from undergrad school years earlier. (We had mutual friends but had never met!) I loved listening to him play and watching him perform and entertain the crowd so easily. I knew he always wanted to tour and I really encouraged him to go for it. Early in our marriage (before kids), I was able to join him and the band on most of their trips. Some of my favourite trips tagging along were when he played with a group who travelled into Italy and Switzerland. When we lived in Boston I also loved going to NYC with the Daniel Bennett Group on weekends. Those trips helped inspire our move to NYC a few years later! Daniel tours quite a bit but it is definitely balanced with downtime as well. I help plan the logistics for some of his tours, which is a great way to stay connected to his trips even though I can't tag along anymore. While sometimes he does trips that are a week or longer, the majority of his touring is in shorter stints. For example, a couple of times a year the band performs throughout the US in places that they've gone to year after year. San Francisco/LA, Florida, PA, summer jazz festivals in VA and upstate NY, etc. Each of these "regular/recurring" tours are typically spread over long weekends, 4-days max, which makes it manageable. Trips to Europe or other places are longer but less frequent—so we can plan ahead and make it work.

So, with her own career, I wondered how it was when Daniel Bennett was away. Gretchen told me,

I work full-time as HR director for a company in NYC. Thankfully my company offers a flexible schedule and my mom lives nearby and often helps babysit. We miss Daniel when he travels, but we're also grateful that he's often able to spend more time at home during the day than most other dads can, since he doesn't have to follow the typical 9-5 schedule when he's not touring. Many days he is able to help take the kids to school and be available for fun things like joining field trips with their classes. When I come home from work in the afternoon, Daniel is typically heading off to rehearsals, private teaching (he is on faculty at a few music schools in NYC), or he's getting ready for a concert later that evening (that's where he is tonight as I write this!). He performs regularly in the city, several steady gigs each week—jazz clubs, theater pits, etc. We've been able to get into a pretty good routine even with the unusual schedule!

I asked Gretchen if she ever felt like Daniel Bennett's wife rather than Gretchen Bennett? She said,

No, but sometimes I do feel like I'm married to the 'Daniel Bennett Group' rather than 'Daniel Bennett'. Daniel is so passionate about what he does, it seeps into every moment. Daniel is an extremely hard worker and is always working on things related to his music, performing, promoting his band, planning tours, etc.

I am aware the Bennetts have two young children and wondered how everything fit around them. Gretchen explained,

Our kids are quite young (three and five), and so far they have been very understanding. They miss Daniel when he is gone but we try to explain that just like mommy has to go to work every day, sometimes Dad has to do work in other places. They love to listen to his music, and of course when asked what do they want to be when they grow up, a common answer is, 'I want to play instruments like Dad!' Daniel is good about bringing them little souvenirs from his travels, which makes the reunions even sweeter. DBG recently performed in Denver CO, and Daniel got the kids little toy cars which they loved! And when he played in Pittsburgh PA a few months ago, they both got souvenir t-shirts. We've also been able to combine a family trip with his tours a few times—where he might fly out first and then the kids and I come later to a few shows and visit family or friends in that area of the country.

I asked whether Gretchen had experienced any attitudes to wives/ partners/girlfriends? She replied,

> Sometimes I've been the only wife/partner/girlfriend coming along. The attitude from the guys has always been very friendly and positive. Sometimes people are in different phases in their lives, and that's fine. Some are single, some divorced—and others are attached but their spouse or partner are not able to get away. We try to be very welcoming. Daniel and I have had many band mates over to our apartment for dinner or for Christmas parties etc. over the years. It's also been great to meet girlfriends and wives at those events or at concerts throughout the year. Many times, I'll meet people at 'noteworthy' events. Every time DBG plays at the Blue Note, I always seem to meet loved ones from Daniel's band mates. We have a lot of friends with a-typical jobs. A close friend of ours also lives in NYC with his wife and 3 small children. His wife works full-time in consulting and he works as the CEO for a toy company. He has to fly to Honduras for four days a week and flies home to NY for the weekends. That makes Daniel's travelling seem mild! It's amazing how you can make things work when you both set your minds to it. I'm proud of Daniel and his music, and love to be a part of his journey with the Daniel Bennett Group.

I have reviewed the music of the Daniel Bennett Group over the years and can vouch for the quality of the music, so the Bennetts' way of doing things seems to be paying off.

Sales

Recording your music is expensive and there is a lot of free music available on streaming platforms. It seems there is an expectation to be able to listen to some or all of an album before buying it, if you then decide to. Digital music can be sold but the pittance for each listen is pitiful. Paul Jolly mentioned to me that one of his artists had got over 95 000 listens on a streaming platform and was paid a measly £40. So to make decent money from streaming platforms, artists need to get hundreds of millions of hits. On some platforms, the artist receives less than half a penny per stream. Had the same artist sold 90,00 singles a few years ago, he would have made thousands of pounds. Good quality digital recordings still cost money to make as well.

Many people still buy CDs at gigs and festivals as having something physical—particularly if they are signed—is important for their fans; but the overall market for CDs is slowly shrinking. Having made a CD, musicians need to be playing festivals and gigs as this is where most copies get sold now.

It is clear that things have changed, not only where but also how music is being sold. I remember not that long back when musicians would tell me that CDs were their main income. Now, they tell me live playing is where they make most money—and sell some CDs. Streaming and downloading have eroded the livelihood of musicians. Even when a track gets sold, people share it. Even if many people listen to a track, often it may only get an actual sale a couple of times; the rest of the listens coming from illegal sharing.

Gail Tasker says,

> *I don't think the record industry as a whole is in the greatest position at the moment. Yes, people talk about the revival of vinyl (Gearbox, where Gail works, specialize in this) but the majority of people are getting their music from digital platforms (and not paying the artists much for it!) Shops are really struggling to compete, especially the independents. I think people would be surprised how difficult it is to make money from recorded sales.*

Jazz performers now need to be switched on business-wise. They need to be able to find gigs and gain a place to play live.

Jenny Green says,

> *The younger generation are used to free downloads, but those of us that*

remember holding our first vinyl appreciate the CD! With its info, pictures and liner notes. You mostly sell them at live gigs I hate this pay for play business or donate in a hat especially in pubs. Frustrating with venues expecting you to do all the media and rent a crowd! When I was performing in the 80's there was plenty of work. You can't just wait for the phone to ring, you have to put the work in via networking making the right connections. If you don't get a gig, make one yourself. Okay it's a risky business but if you don't try then what? There are so many backing track singers out there people have lost the meaning of live music!

Beverley Bierne:

There's obviously been a huge difference in sales of physical CD's for everyone since the advent of streaming and digital sales. It's worth pointing out that many people don't even have CD players anymore, so we're definitely onto a losing game here. We've all had to start to re-think things. I think this is why vinyl is making a come- back. I think it makes listening to music a special experience again instead of being just instant gratification, it's something to savour. I don't think there's a right or wrong thing to do here to be honest, I think we have to just get inventive and think out of the box as I say. Being both a jazz singer and a festival organizer I see things from both sides so I'd say as it's all actually really positive. There are some superb artists out there and the scene is actually thriving and evolving daily.

More positivity from Georgia Mancio when she says,

Producing, releasing and sharing music is more affordable than ever without compromising the quality. The world has become smaller thanks to the internet and social media so it's easier to reach new and varied audiences. There are certainly some very successful and creative festivals and venues with healthy attendances but many regions suffer from a lack of funding and arts cuts which takes a toll on promoters and the bandleaders who are often at most financial risk. As a self-releasing artist I have noticed a drop in CD sales over the last few years and fees are pretty stagnant from ten years ago or more.

Debbie Gifford's opinions is,

> *Record sales have suffered because of the ease of online downloading. The number of people who want a physical product is decreasing but there is still a certain sector of the audience that find it exciting to purchase a CD at a concert.*

Vocalist Barb Jungr puts it briefly:

> *Well, record sales are through the cellar floor across the board as anyone in music will tell you. So that's not where positivity floats right now.*

The Importance of Social Media

Kim Cypher mentioned the effect social media has on getting bookings, particularly for festivals.

> *A musician who the venue has not used before will find their social media sites, if they have them, scrutinized. Venues can check how many followers you have, how many likes you get and the likelihood that these people will come to your gigs. This is understandable as festivals need to make sure people will come to events and they need to check a band is as popular as they say they are but it also brings into the equation that it is about how many people follow you than the quality of what you are bringing to an event. It could also mean that bands who don't have the time for social media may find some venues lose interest.*

Festivals are another place where bands play, sell their music and products and get paid for performing, These remain very popular. Not only do you get to hear bands you know, but also ones you don't or have only heard about. You are also in a place where everyone is there for the music. There are many small festivals in the UK, either taking place in one hall in a town or across several venues. Of course, the large ones like *Love Supreme* and the *London Jazz Festival* are still winners in terms of attendance and visibility stakes.

Jenny Green comments,

Gosh you have to be so 'on it' these days with social media and all the music platforms, particularly if you are on an independent label. There are very few jazz festivals now in Britain but loads of fringe music festivals if you have something different to offer. It's all about getting your name out there but it's how to do that in the first place to get noticed. An album is just a calling card having produced one myself in 2014. There is no funding left for young artists or any artists for that matter wanting to tour!

The *Love Supreme* festival on the South Coast has many opportunities has various stages and are very encouraging booking emerging artists, but how do they find the contacts?

Barb Jungr says,

Barb Jungr photographed by Steve Ullathorn

There are still venues and there are still festivals. Fees are lower than they used to be except for the very top name international acts. Nonetheless, people still come out and want live music and that's fantastic and we have to keep them coming out and wanting live music. But we are un-supported by mainstream television and radio. The few hours dedicated to any kind of other music than mainstream industry fod-der are pitiful, as are the boundaries. When Desmond Carrington left us for the great bar in the sky, he took a major opportunity for many of is for Radio 2 plays with him. Thank goodness Jools Holland is back on BBC radio 2 and Clare Teal consistently supports our homegrown talent on her big show. With-out Radio 3 and Jazz FM—it doesn't bear thinking about!

Social media also gives female musicians the chance to post comments about events, their thoughts on jazz and many other matters. It allows people to see how strong they can be, what they are actually thinking and hopefully also blow away some preconceptions.

The Way Forward

There are some conclusions which can be drawn after speaking to women across the jazz industry. It is difficult to separate many issues such as education and funding; but certain conditions persist that make a women's position less advantageous than for male musicians. Firstly, sexism is deeply entrenched in the music industry as a whole so it is perhaps wrong to highlight jazz as the root of all evil. However, it does appear to persist in jazz while other genres are distancing themselves. It is far rarer to see a female-dominated ensemble in jazz than it is in classical music. At jazz gigs, you still hear phrases like 'chicks', 'come on boys' (leaving the female musicians open-mouthed) 'good for a woman', 'she's one of the guys' and so on. So many women tell me that when they say they are a jazz musician, the initial reaction is, 'Oh, so you sing?' It should be noted that many of jazz's famous performers were women; but switch to instrumentalists, and it is a male-dominated history. This means role models are fewer for women. Something else to consider is that when you play an instrument, it affords gender anonymity unless you see the musician playing. The smaller number of women in jazz has nothing to do with women being musically inferior, but indicates a difference in judgement when you are able to see a performance. Women are judged differently than men.

I think some of this difference can be explained by confidence and assurance. Because women are judged on different criteria, they feel less assured and this comes across in their playing. Intuitively, women are more pragmatic and reserved as a whole and so feel less confident standing out on stage. Critics and other musicians also know how to take away confidence from a woman. Women may feel a greater need than men to be socially accepted. During auditions women put energy into being likeable and approachable, which may make them less confident and therefore affect their playing. Men of course are nervous at auditions as well, but do not appear to exhibit the additional anxieties attached to female players.

There is definitely a sense of change in the air, however. Oxford University appointed the first female president of OUJO which was, at the time, a major achievement. The number of females auditioning for the jazz bands rose to thirty percent. Female set-ups have come into being such as *Sisters of Funk* and the *Sisterhood Festival*—an event for those whose identity includes female. While not specifically for jazz, this event showcases female groups—including jazz. Oxford is a microcosm in the larger universe and is a fairly representation of how change is coming to the world at large.

A surprising effect of these events which support female artists and female jazz festivals is that, perhaps for the first time, men are excluded. It is a case of either being unable to take part in a growing number of events or including women on equal terms in others. Most musicians, when it hits their pockets, will choose the latter and hopefully also come to understand people who identify as female are just as much part of the jazz scene as those who identify as male.

It is women who have spent many years advocating for change and it is finally happening thanks to their efforts. Women I speak to, tell me of more and more women entering jazz. A large part of this is because they have role models, mentors, other women to play with. This opens doors for men and women to perform as equals.

Given where women are in jazz today—possibly at the point where equality is just a few more positive decisions away—and that change is happening and the way is clear for both men and women, how do women see it going for them and jazz? They tell me, they feel positive, like the journey has only just begun. Their starting point in jazz has come later because of the difficulties women have faced in the past, but they are certainly making up for lost time and closing the distance quickly. This has been helped immeasurably by events which have made a concerted effort to include more women. The 2018 *Monterey Jazz Festival* (the 61st) was just such an event, with that year's festival's objective to include more women. It was an incredible success. As the world's longest continually running festival and one which draws audiences from across the globe, this was a major call to attention to the jazz hierarchy stating women are now pivotal in the genre. The festival delivered a huge diversity of female band leaders, solo artists, composers and arrangers, each with visions going far beyond simply playing or churning out recordings. According to the San Francisco *Classical Voice* magazine,

> *For every trail blazed on stage, an alternative direction seemed to open up, offering a different perspective on how to get to a similar destination.*

The festival featured saxophone players Tia Fuller, Kristen Strom, Jane Ira Bloom and Melissa Aldana, trumpet players Ingrid Jensen and Bria Skomberg, other female leaders including bass player Lisa Mezzacappa, flautist Jamie Baum, vocalist Cecile McLorin Salvant, guitar player Mary Halvorson, and many female musicians from across the globe as well as many men of course. The festival proved a ground-breaking success. It also proved that it was easy to fill schedules with female players of world-class expertise. Instead of a festival offering female artists an opportunity, it was more a case of female artists offering the festival a chance to show off the wealth of talent it could put on—men and women.

Georgia Mancio echoes this positivity,

> *The great news is the scene has never been more vibrant or diverse; with so much talent out there is feels very much alive and kicking.*

Gail Tasker says,

> *I'm absolutely positive it's going to get better. Arguably the world is*

moving forwards at the moment. We're seeing more and more female instrumentalists on stage and people are questioning it less.

As proof of the vibrant scene, new projects spring up regularly including in the UK Georgia's own events called *Hang* which are a series of bespoke collaborations and new writing featuring the cream of the UK's jazz, Latin and improvised music scenes at one of Europe's most iconic venues (*Pizza Express Jazz Club*). There are numerous small and large jazz festival across the UK and more festivals include jazz stages with a noticeable increase in the number of female musicians. The UK has a burgeoning list of talented female musicians who attract large audiences including every women in this book, but also musicians like harpist Alina Bzhezhinska, pianist Nikki Iles, Cellist Shirley Smart, singer Kitty La Roar, cellist Hannah Marshall, trumpet players Laura Jurd and Sheila Maurice-Grey, guitarist Shirley Tettah and many more.

There is a lot of talk about increasing diversity in music. Many people comment that the very fact we have more women, LGBT and other non-defined genders means the diversity increases and by consequence creativity itself increases too. Jazz developed as a genre out of a real mix of cultures, styles and rhythms so if anything, it should be the genre which appreciates the change that different dynamics bring. We have departed the period where most women performed on piano or vocals. Today, the list of stellar female instrumentalists is incredible and continually growing. Musicians like bassist Carol Kaye who played on so many hits with the *Wrecking Crew* or Emily Remler prove women can hold their own against any man. *Every* woman in this book is proof of that.

Change is happening even if at a slow pace. Producer Jason Miles says,

It is not about if you are a man or woman, it's about dedication to your craft. Right now in the business we need more female recording engineers and producers to break through the male dominance of the craft. It will come but it has taken too much time. Diversity has always brought about great creativity. Women bring a different and welcome perspective to the music. We had great female singers for decades. This next phase brings them full circle to band leaders and players who can stand toe to toe with men. It's how music is supposed to be-always evolving.

John Russell conveys the change in atmosphere when he says,

I feel there is still a long way to go but certainly the atmosphere at concerts is much less stern and far more welcoming than back when and I feel that is in large part due to the increased interest in the music from women both as performers and members of the audience.

He also mentions that fact of the dangers of having women in the line-up of *Mopomoso*—a free jazz regular event—just for the sake of it. He says,

At Mopomoso, we try to actively discriminate for women without appearing tokenistic. There is still some way to go but in general it is possible to make sure there are some women on each program and I am convinced this influences how the music is perceived by an audience.

Beverley Bierne comments on the festival she runs:

Running the festival you get to see what attracts people more and what demographic come to certain types of acts. It can actually be really surprising. We've got a mixed bag, but I'd say the general overall trend is towards younger people checking things out. It is worth pointing out here is that we have without a doubt more women in the audience that there ever used to be at jazz gigs.

Kim Cypher adds,

I couldn't even imagine doing anything else and for that reason I am truly grateful to be living my dream with my husband well and truly by my side (well, behind me on drums actually)

Gail Tasker,

I do think the live music scene is taking off in London a bit more. A lot more venue are putting on jazz across the city, while it used to just be Ronnie Scott's and a few pubs.

There appears to be steady, but slow progress in terms of more women playing, taking roles in media and management and attending concerts, though there is still some ways to go. There are reasons for this progress and reason for it being slow.

Georgia Mancio says,

> *I am aware that I have certainly deferred my ego to my male counterparts but that has been down to me own lack of confidence or self-belief. My confidence has changed and this has been a very real and organic process from grafting, not just as an artist but in all aspects of the business. If someone has issues with their ego they will probably be threatened by a successful woman, not least because she may find it easier to voice her opinion. There are many allies who truly want talented men and women to succeed and be treated equally. Then again, globally wages (for women) are still too often inferior, women are still overly sexualized and the terrifying rhetoric of Trump and now Bolsonaro is in danger of normalizing misogyny. There is still a lot to fight for.*

In an interview with *London Jazz News* Georgia said,

> *I think we are making progress, yes, and I'm really excited to see so many more women playing the music, working in production and getting accolades than ever before. I've talked to a lot of musicians, some press/industry people over the last year and appreciate it's a nuanced subject. Being conscious is the first step and I think there are still too many sleepwalking. Festival and club programs still need more balance. There are very few female journalists (why is that?) and particularly outside London fewer women than men going to gigs. The biggest change is probably that there are more female musicians now and women working behind the scenes, although there is still a way to go before parity. Where there is a fear of change it's good to remember that if we keep doing things in the same way, we'll get the same results. We need to look beyond our own experiences, elevate our consciousness to imagine another's scenario and then make active improvements. Some of this will happen organically over time but that time is also very much now.*

Debbie Gifford comments,

> *Over the years I have seen more women musicians in the field of jazz being recognized for their talent both as instrumentalists and vocalists. I believe that this recognition is helping change attitudes and more opportunities are being enjoyed by women musicians.*

Something which is noticeable as we move ahead in jazz is that young musicians call out bad behaviour, especially when it comes to comments which are racist, ageist, misogynistic or anything showing disrespect. These young, amazing players seem to be suddenly 'here', though I am guessing they have been around for a while. Some are male, some are female, others are neither one nor the other—and that is important too. Some young musicians see gender as a side issue, nothing to do with talent or how you play. The young players are creative, developing new projects, they play alongside older statesmen of the jazz community like saxophone player Evan Parker playing with Binker and Moses, cellist Hannah Marshall playing alongside veteran Davey Payne of the *People Band* and many other collaborations between older, young, men and women. Jazz is definitely having a revival and the young are leading the way. There is a powerful energy right now in jazz.

Kim Cypher says,

> *I think it is an exciting time for women in jazz right now. We are living in a time when anybody can do anything and women are empowered as we continue to move away from an industry that was traditionally make dominated. It is exciting to see so many incredible female jazz musicians on the scene, especially in terms of instrumentalists.*

Present & Future

Changing Demographics & Youth in Jazz

THERE ARE A LOT MORE WOMEN coming in to jazz and, coincidentally or not, more young people. Not long ago an ex-Sony executive told me in conversation that he felt young black people had very little association with jazz music. Now, things have changed and young people of all backgrounds are popping up at jazz gigs—sometimes in large numbers. I recently spoke to a group of young people at a gig and they told me they loved jazz and that it embraced music they could relate to. They were at the gig to see one of their peers play and one of them said it was also important that more young people were playing jazz music because they could relate to them and that music played by their own age group felt more accessible. Funnily enough when I ran the *London Jazz Platform*, there was a hip-hop event going on next door and several young people came to have a look at the young performers at our event—and several stayed awhile too. Across the world many musicians tell me that audiences are young and very enthusiastic, especially in South America apparently. Mats Gustafsson recently played in Colombia and he told me the gigs were packed with young people.

Debbie Gifford says,

> *It depends where you are performing. Our performances in China were sold out with young people who knew every word of every jazz standard*

I sang. Our performances in Europe are a mixed age group and the same is true for the States. There are many jazz clubs closing their doors world-wide but new clubs opening in Europe but they seem to be quite small. That doesn't stop the jazz lovers filling them to the brim.

A couple of years ago, I covered a gig for the BBC at London's *Cafe Oto* where most of the musicians were in their 60s and 70s. Around half the audience however were under thirty and I was intrigued as to why. I interviewed a few of them and they told me that for them, jazz *is* the alternative music. They are finding jazz and improvised music in particular, to be a complete departure from the popular music they are bombarded with. They are, they told me, also realizing that there is a lot more to jazz than the music played as background in restaurants. One twenty-five year old informed me,

I used to call jazz 'lift music', like in John Lewis, there would be jazz always in the lifts—you could ignore it and think about your next purchase, or in a café, it might be playing in the background and the only parts you would notice were when a sax solo came on.... But this music I heard tonight is so different—mad, slightly angry, it kind of hit me in my soul department.

A lovely way to put it, I thought. A couple of weeks later, I went to see the late Hugh Masekela at *Snape Proms* and once again the audience was decidedly youthful. A few weeks later, I saw Wayne Shorter with the *Jazz At The Lincoln Center* orchestra led by Wynton Marsalis. The audience was a mix of young and old with lots of women. Next came Gilad Atzmon at *Ipswich Jazz Club*, a small but popular venue. Lots of women, older men and loads of young people. Then, Peter Brotzmann at *Cafe Oto* and yet again, loads of young people and quite a few women. Delfeayo Marsalis and his Big Band at *Snug Harbour* in New Orleans—lots of young people and lots of women. I wondered then, whether jazz was not only attracting more young people, but also more women. Young people tell me jazz is very much a 'thing' at the moment and they are particularly liking the newer kind of jazz which cross references hip-hop, street music and other jazz, played by musicians like Kamazi Washington and Soweto Kinch.

Georgia Mancio says,

> *In the last few years promoters such as Jazz Re:freshed have definitely brought in younger audiences with artists operating more cross-genre.*

In New Orleans, the jazz venues are packed with young people alongside middle-aged and older ones. So, is change happening? Are young people finding jazz again? Venues *like Cafe Oto, Iklectic Art Lab, The Vortex, Club Karamel, 606 Club* and numerous US clubs and ones in Europe like *Sunset* in Paris allow younger players to take the stage. Players like Dominic Lash, Sam Leak, Elliot Galvin to name just a few, share stages with established older players. I have seen a seventy year-old saxophone player improvising alongside a twenty-something cello player with huge success. The young players bring young people and it seems they love the jazz they hear. Many of the musicians and audience members are female and I wondered if the women I was talking with felt this change in demographics too. It seems it is varied and may depend on where you play. I asked Carmela Rappazzo about this and she said,

> *When I lived in L.A. there was a well-known jazz musician who would bemoan the fact that the audiences for jazz were 'geriatric'. I have really seen that change. There are most definitely younger people in my audience now and more people (this might be a NOLA thing).*

Emily Saunders, notes

> *I think there's a new wave of Jazz listeners opening up the previously thought limitations on age and gender—it's really exciting, there are loads of new listeners and new things happening. To me, what's fundamental in this is the opening up of contemporary mediums that people can access, communicate and connect within, to discover jazz and all related music. This was the reason why I created Jazz Connects—an independent online digital platform for people to search, connect and*

collaborate in Jazz and related music. Being online it's totally open to all, from national and international, to local and regional, where people in the Jazz world can create partnerships and eradicate boundaries. Plus new audiences can easily access everything there to find out what's happening.

Ellie Thompson comments,

I think I have seen a younger audience begin to understand that the arts, in general, is something that is worth your time and money. I think there is more of an understanding that it isn't something you can expect for free all the time without it being detrimental to the quality.

Tina May is in a great position to comment, given that she plays across Europe and the UK. She says,

I do see more women in the audience these days. Also, quite a lot of young people, too are getting the jazz bug. Recently, I was singing at the Caveau de la Huchette *in Paris and was so happy to see a lot of young people—dancing to the music! Apparently, the success of the film 'La La Land' had given a real boost to student attendance. This gig has always been a place where they gave student concessions, too. I was reminded of my first visit to the* Caveau de la Huchette *as a student. I loved it then and still do. Live jazz is so exciting. I worry about jazz clubs that are too expensive for young people... this is obviously going to stop them 'taking a chance' on jazz. We could do with a few more women in management, though. I'm always aware of the maleness of booking agents, festival programmers etc. This would affect real change and, I dare say, in the journalistic world of jazz too.*

Jazz, in general, is not too visible on mainstream TV / Radio and therefore women are even less visible.... we have a way to go yet. This is especially true as producers are younger and probably know very little of the music 'before the Beatles'....

In Ecuador I went to several jazz gigs in the capital, Quito. The audience was mixed; but what struck me there was the engagement of the listeners with the performers. Many times, people got up and danced in the aisles, self-unconscious and showing their enjoyment of the music. The jazz there was subtly different too—big names like Lizz Wright or more local bands like *The Garbage Men* who had a Latin twist in their music. The audience enjoyed them equally and with a passion.

But in Europe, the UK and the US, there seems to still be a divide between the demographics of older audiences and young ones. It seems older audiences are more likely to be male, but younger ones will be a mix of male, female and others.

Jo Harrop agrees, and informs us:

> *I think that most older audiences tend to be older males as a general rule—the older male generation tend to be okay with going out alone to see jazz gigs, drink on their own etc than women of that generation do—but there are women, and couples who come out to see jazz, especially vocal jazz. In younger generations I think there is a more balanced male:female ratio—I certainly go out to gigs alone and feel comfortable.*
>
> *The 606 Club is a pretty well-balanced audience as far as my experience goes. As is Pizza Express, Hideaway, etc. Perhaps the venues are more accommodating to the needs of people of all walks of life and age groups now?*

Georgia Mancio says,

> *In the bigger cities (certainly London where I am based) the age range is more varied and the gender more balanced. In the regional clubs the average age is older and there are still probably more men than women attending concerts. The biggest change is probably that there are more female musicians now and women working behind the scenes, although there is still a way to go before parity.*

Gail Tasker says,

> *It was strange moving from Cardiff, (to London) where the dominating demographic was 50+ and white males. I feel like the UK jazz scene has*

split into two: there's the prevailing demographic I mentioned and then there's this younger, much more diverse audience.

Barb Jungr comments,

> *Festivals get audiences. There seem to be young and older people at everything which is appropriate. I'd say that demographics also reflect the genre. If you've got a tribute to Ella your audience is going to be substantially older across the board than if you are Annette Peacock at Cafe Oto or The Bad Plus at the Festival Hall. The younger players and the cult names attract a much more mixed audience.*

Claire Martin adds,

> *Clubs and festivals continue to book jazz acts if they are jazz clubs and jazz orientated festivals but I think it could be better because we need more venues to play jazz and we need festivals that claim they are jazz festivals to stop booking pop bands. ... In London, the audience are younger for sure, plus there is the tourist factor but on the whole the audience are white, 70 plus and the numbers are dwindling. It's always been this way as long as I've known it. It depresses me to see hardly any younger people in the audience. I've grown to accept it.*

I would add a personal observation to Claire's comments and this is that I recently saw Claire perform at a school—she was the headliner for the school's yearly music festival. Ipswich School in Suffolk, UK nearly always finish with a headliner and usually it is a performer from the world of jazz. Claire sang to an audience whose age ranged from the older to a far younger section made up of the school 's older students—aged from sixteen to eighteen and their forty-something parents—and they loved it. It just goes to show that where schools encourage people to hear live jazz, it is a popular and perennial show stopper choice.

In Beirut, the audiences are getting younger and Joelle Khoury says,

> *Here in Beirut I am glad to start to see younger people interested in jazz music.*

And it is one of the great things about the era we are in. Young people seem to suddenly have found jazz. For a few years, it is true, jazz appeared to be the domain of the white-haired, beard-stroking die-hards—people who virtually shut the door on newcomers because of their jazz snobbery and unwillingness to embrace change. It is clear jazz is having a bit of a moment in the UK and further afield with young people coming to the music in large numbers. It is not traditional jazz, but jazz infused with elements of other genres like hip-hop and street music. Musicians like Kamazi Washington, Soweto Kinch and Courtney Pine are attracting young people, and more and more of the younger generation are taking up instruments and playing jazz. Centers like *Oto Space, Jazz Re:Freshed* and many more across London encourage young players. One musician told me recently, "I believe young people want to see young people play" and he was right—they do and the more young people play live music, the more will come to see them perform.

Emma Acton comments,

> *The owner of 606 Club, Steve Rubie does a great job of booking young talented musicians as well as those who are established including saxophonist Helena Kay, who was winner of the Peter Whittington Jazz Award in 2017 as well as Alexandra Ridout who won Young Jazz Musician of the Year in 2016. Steve also allows all music students to be treated as members so they are able to come into the members' bar free of charge, thus making jazz and other genres more accessible to a younger demographic.*

The members' bar mentioned above is a space where members can go and watch the music for free. For young musicians, this is very much an opportunity to see a range of different musicians and not have to pay the dining prices. Emma mentioned some of the awards which are given to young musicians—encouraging them and sustaining them in the short term while they establish themselves on the jazz circuit as professionals. There are also organizations mentioned before like *Tomorrow's Warriors*—a program using producers who work internationally and nationally with some of the most exciting, most diverse new, emerging and established jazz artists in the UK, with a special focus on those of African ethnicity and women. *Tomorrow's Warriors* has a *Young Artist Development Program,* headed by award-winning Artistic Director, Gary Crosby OBE. Sessions are completely free and run every weekend during the school term with different activities for different age groups. There are women's workshops run by the *London Jazz Festival* and female-focused shows.

There is a huge talent pool of young musicians, including many female performers from which the jazz world will draw for its future—and they are of the highest quality, which is important. It is an exciting time and truly feels as if we are on the doorstep of a new era of jazz music if only jazz could take just a little bit of change,

Jenny Green assures us,

> *It's exciting I can definitely see more of an interest in the jazz with the young. There's some great music coming out of the fusion. The trad Jazz scene still seems to be hanging in there too particularly some great Dixie New Orleans style bands.*

Changing markets

The women in this book are, for the most part, working musicians so no-one is better qualified to comment on the changing market for jazz music. There are still record labels in existence, many in fact whose range includes jazz music and vinyl has made a come-back; but most musicians accept things have changed and are continuing to do so.

Terri Lyne Carrington reminds us,

> *Sales of recorded music is kind of in the past. Streaming is what the future holds. Everyone has to adjust to a new model, which makes it*

interesting as a lot of musicians are out there performing because a lot of your income depends on live performing—this makes them stronger and stronger as it is more competitive so it's a new time period.

There is no doubt women are gaining attention and focus for their talent and musical strength. *Clash Magazine* published a positive article[2] in 2017 which highlights the challenges to age-old attitudes and the rise of women star performers in jazz. It includes women who are sidestepping the established hierarchy, "creating new structures for themselves with their own collectives, spaces and platforms" and includes broadcasters like Tina Edwards, a long-standing supporter of women in jazz music.

And for the future?

Alicia Renee *aka* Blue Eyes comments,

> *With the Montreux Jazz Festival, North Sea Jazz Festival and so many more still going strong I feel the future is definitely a positive one.*

Young women can now see their peers play. They have role models and stellar acts like Laura Jurd, Yolanda Brown, Kosi, Esperanza Spalding, Cécile McLorin Salvant, Melody Gardot, Mary Halvorson, Lauren Kinsella, Ellen Andrea Wang, Isabel Sörling and Linda Oh to mention just a very few. They can also see more established women including Cath Roberts, Estelle Kokot, Kitty La Roar, Norma Winston—and these do not even include the thirty plus featured in this book.

Jo Harrop says,

> *There are loads of young people going to jazz gigs. Many of them are musicians themselves and some just really love the music. It's a very positive thing that people still love live music and appreciate jazz especially.*

---

2 https:www.clashmusic.com/features/meet-the-women-pushing-uk-jazz-forward

Patti Boulaye adds,

> *Recently there has been a revival (in jazz) with the help of Pizza Express Jazz venues (and others) but" she adds a salutary note, "we live in the era of great advancement in technology which is disrupting jazz and other industries.*

It feels like the day is coming when gender in jazz will no longer be 'a thing'. The genie that is jazz has answered the call by many to change—it does things slowly and there are still a few areas where jazz needs to fully wake up and realize the detrimental effect misogynistic attitudes have on the industry as a whole; and that in general, any kind of sexism—or any *ism*—is a dying, anachronistic notion. People who refuse to adapt to change get left behind. Unless they embrace equality in every aspect, they will find they are travelling in others' dust—and some of it created by daintier feet than their own.

The dialogue about sexism in jazz continues and it will until the issue is resolved. There will be self-evaluation and challenging of violators—some of who will be surprised I have no doubt—because their behaviour is entrenched and outdated—but it will happen. There is a sense of awareness and also a desire almost to rescue jazz before it becomes a victim of its own, unspoken creation and loses touch with reality. That people want to rescue it and are actively changing things speak highly of how jazz is loved and respected as a musical genre. Women want it to be cherished and a place of equality. That love, that passion is what will ultimately save jazz; and the energy with which people are working to change things, is gaining increased momentum. This book, essays and other books no doubt to come, all will document the changes which are happening. However, nothing will document the change better than the coming day when sexism in jazz will be a lesson learned and completely and totally in the past. Women at the top today should have enjoyed more role models; they should have had more encouragement and mentors; but they haven't. They've had to struggle and their success has come at a cost. Women entering the jazz industry today, it is hoped, will not perpetuate the societal traps laid before them, but break them open, educate others and never, ever accept there is nothing they can do to change things.

We evolve, we change as a society and thank goodness, jazz does too. It may be difficult at times. Men need to ask themselves uncomfortable questions like 'Am I contributing to misogynist behaviour and can I change this? Do I make women prove themselves more? Do I make them feel uncomfortable?' And women must ask themselves 'What can I do to change preconceived expectations and mind-sets?' And we all need to ask ourselves, 'Do I act in a way which hurts, belittles or destroys the self-esteem of anyone else? Am I fostering creativity, talent and evolution whatever a person's race, background or gender identification?' We must ask ourselves these questions, uncomfortable as they are and then deal with the answers. We have to forgive, start anew and come afresh to jazz with the table set for everyone, no privileges, no extra portions, just complete equality. We should not blame a person for their ill-educated attitude, but see how they can be educated, understand and learn that they are only diminishing the wealth of talent they have available.

If we seek that time when we can honestly answer the questions and feel we are treating every person with total equity, then we shall have come to the place where real and unstoppable creativity will occur. Jazz will not know what has hit it and the talent on show will be exceptional—it will have included and been selected from everyone. We should expect the very best of everyone. We all need to be part of the evolution.

Seeing women performing jazz music is becoming normalized. Women are no longer tokens, novelties or mere decorations. They are increasingly seen as par for the course, equal to men, just as much a part of the jazz scene. Here jazz, in some areas at least, is taking the chance offered it to become the genre to which others point for an example of inclusive, non-issued industry, where race, background or gender are irrelevant and the only detail in question is how well you play your notes. It may still be unusual to see a female producer, manager or leader, but they are increasing in number, slowly but surely; and the future vision is one which includes men and women on equal footing in more fields.

The Women in the Book

Meet the women who discuss their journeys and without whom this book would never have come about.

Emma Acton is Marketing Manager at the world famous *606 Club* in Chelsea, London. She is also a photographer, specialising in events and music photography.

Arema Arega is a Cuban musician living in Spain. She is an artist, multi-instrumentalist and vocalist. Her music has been used for short films and she has been featured on radio shows as a rising star.

Gretchen Bennett is HR Director for a technology company in New York City. She is also the wife of Daniel Bennett— of the *Daniel Bennett Group* (DBG). The DBG tour across America and have had several widely acclaimed album releases.

Beverley Bierne is a vocalist who has sung with rock bands and in musical theatre. Her critically acclaimed album *Jazz Just Wants to Have Fun* produced by Jason Miles received many great reviews. Beverley also runs a regular jazz festival—the *Ilkley Jazz Festival*—with her husband Mark.

Grace Black is radio host for K107fm community radio station and also a jazz singer. On her radio shows, up and coming artists are well-represented and she has an ear for great jazz music.

Amanda Bloom is a promoter at *Crossover* media. She is a graduate of the Peabody Institute of Music at John Hopkins University with a degree in jazz vocal performance and has worked as musician herself.

Jane Ira Bloom is a renowned saxophonist with over 40 years experience playing and recording to a world-wide audience. She is a pioneer in the use of live electronics and movement in jazz. Since the 1970s she has led her own groups and played festivals including *Kansas City's Women's Jazz Festival.* She won a 2018 *Grammy Award* for *Best Surround Sound Album* for her trio album "Early Americans." She has won the *Jazz Journalists Award* for soprano sax of the year ten times as well as the *Downbeat International Critics Poll* for soprano saxophone, the *Mary Lou Williams Women in Jazz Award* for lifetime service to jazz, the *Charlie Parker Fellowship* for Jazz Innovation and the *International Women in Jazz, Jazz Masters Award.* She is the first musician ever commissioned by the *NASA Art Program* and was honoured

to have an asteroid named in her honour by the *International Astronomical Union* (asteroid 6083janeirabloom). She's garnered numerous awards for her creativity including a *Guggenheim Fellowship* in music composition and a residency at the *Baryshnikov Arts Center.* The *Bloom Festival*—a new jazz festival in Brooklyn, NY featuring cutting edge female artists was named in her honour. She has played with many jazz greats and toured with many combos and groups.

Patti Boulaye OBE is a British-Nigerian singer, actress and artist. She won the TV series New Faces in 1978 and has had her own TV series in Nigeria and appeared many times on UK television. Her musical roles include Yum Yum, Carmen Jones, and she wrote and produced her own West End show, *Sun Dance.* She supports numerous charities which make a real difference in Africa and has toured and released several singles.

Sarah Gail Brand is a trombone player, collaborating with many UK jazz artists on and off the key musicians on the UK improvising scene. She was described by *The Wire* magazine as the most exciting trombone player for years. Her collaborators include Mark Sanders, John Edwards, Martin Hathaway, Billy Jenkins, Elton Dean, Evan Parker, Phil Minton, Lol Coxhill, Alexander Hawkins, Maggie Nicols, Rachel Musson, Wadada Leo Smith, Jason Yarde, Steve Beresford and countless others. Sarah plays regularly with many different combos and also does solo performances. She has composed scores and presented radio shows. She is also an educator and is a professor of Improvisation at the *Guildhall School of Music and Drama*, London, and a qualified Music Therapist.

Jane Bunnett is a five-time *Juno Award* winner and has turned her bands and recordings into showcases for the finest musical talent from Canada, the US, and Cuba. She has been nominated for three *Grammy Awards*, received *The Order of Canada, The Queen's Diamond Jubilee Medal,* and, most recently, *The Premier's Award for Excellence*. Her major work today is with Cuban female musicians, with a project to encourage and mentor them. The project band, *Maqueque* has become one of the top groups on the North American jazz scene and played major jazz festivals like *Newport* and *Monterey*, featured on *NPR*'s program *Jazz Night in America*, were nominated for a *Grammy Award* for their newest release, *Oddara*, and, most recently, were voted as one the top ten jazz groups by the prestigious *Downbeat* magazine's critics poll. Bunnett is

internationally acclaimed and known for her creative integrity, improvisational daring, and courageous artistry. She has toured the world bringing her own special sound to numerous jazz festivals, displaying her versatility as a flutist, saxophone player, and pianist. Two documentaries have been made about Bunnett's work: *Spirits of Havana* by the National Film Board was presented at numerous film festivals internationally, on television (*CBC, PBS*), and in Europe. As an educator, spokesperson, and social activist, Jane Bunnett remains unafraid to explore uncharted territory in her quest for excellence.

Terri Lyne Carrington is a three-time *Grammy award* winning drummer, composer and multi-genre producer. She currently holds the position of *Zildjian Chair* in Performance at Berklee jazz Institute, Berklee College of music and is the founder of the *Institute of Jazz and Gender Justice*.

Trish Clowes is a saxophonist, described in *The Guardian* as "one of the most agile and original jugglers of improv and adventurous composition to have appeared in the UK in recent times". She is a *BASCA British Composer Award* winner and former *BBC3 Radio 3 New Generation Artist*. Her albums have received critical acclaim.

Kim Cypher is a saxophonist, bandleader and vocalist. She has played with prestigious musicians and at major events, including a private event performing for the UK's Prime Minister. She tours regularly and is one of the UKs most popular players.

Mimi Fox is an internationally renowned guitarist, composer and recording artist and has been named a winner in six consecutive *Downbeat* critic's polls. Her recordings received universal praise and she is recognized as one of the world's leading guitar players.

Debbie Gifford is a singer whose voices blends opera and jazz. She has been nominated for *Jazz Musician of The Year, Band of The Year,* and *Vocalist of The Year* in the *Annual Free Times Music Awards* and is the only female to have performed with the *Birdland Big Band*. Press releases are many and include: 'Gifford's voice is both

smooth and engulfing, wrapping itself around every note and mesmerising the listener with subtle charm (TGIF).

Jenny Green is radio host on Meridian radio, regularly hosting the popular *Jen and Sooz Jazz Mix Up Show* which highlights rising stars in jazz. She is also a singer in demand, either as a solo artist or with her top-class musicians.

Florence Halfon is a jazz A&R catalogue freelancer who works for *Warner Jazz*, researching catalogue and putting together reissues. Recent projects include the *John Coltrane Atlantic Years* mono vinyl box set, the *Ornette Coleman Atlantic* vinyl box set, the *Stan Getz Split Kick and Lee Morgan Roulette Sides 10'* reissues. She is also a jazz singer and songwriter using the name Florence Joelle. She has three albums released and is a regular performer across London and beyond.

Jo Harrop is a popular vocalist, regularly playing at major venues. She has appeared at the Royal Albert Hall and the London Jazz Festival. Her press reviews include, from *Blues and Soul Magazine* "No worries here, this girl was born to sing Jazz, Jo has all the emotional warmth and sensibility to melt the chilliest of hearts"; and from *Bebop Spoken*

Here, "A singing sensation. Her voice is amazing, think Islay whiskey, dark porter or tannin-rich red wine—deep, the lissome lady is a class act.

Barb Jungr is one of the UK and Europe's most popular vocalists. Ever effervescent, stylish and a born performer she has collaborated with many other artists as well as doing solo projects. Probably best summed up in the recent press by Glam Adelaide who said, "It's as if Edith Piaf and Nick Cave had a lovechild who was adopted by Carmen McCrae"; and *Wall Street Journal*, who said Barb,"… brings the same creativity for reinterpretation and re-examination that Ella Fitzgerald brought to Cole Porter." She has revisited songbooks of Dylan, Simone, Cohen

and many others and has won the *Broadway World Award* for her 'hard Rain' album; *Time Out New York Cabaret Nightlife Award* for *Outstanding Vocalist* and the *Backstage Award* for *Best International Artist*. Barb continues to surprise and delight audiences across the globe.

Joelle Khoury is a Lebanese-American pianist and a jazz and contemporary classical music composer. She has been participated in *Extra-muros* residencies in France, Czech Republic, Switzerland and the United-States (2013) as a MacDowell Colony fellow, where she worked on her multimedia performance *Palais*

de Femmes. In 1995, she founded *In-Version*, a jazz quintet performing original compositions which combine a contemporary bebop style with complex counterpoint lines, supporting the simplest melodies.

Wendy Kirkland is a pianist and band leader. Her current projects include *Piano Divas*, a tribute to the female pianist singers of jazz; and Hammond organ jazz outfit *Organik Force*. Press reviews include, from *JazzMann*, "One of the great unsung heroines of British jazz. The lucid warmth of her singing is accompanied by her highly accomplished piano playing..." and from *The Observer*, "Proper jazz piano, excellent band. A very classy debut."

Georgia Mancio is an award-winning Anglo-Italian vocalist specializing in jazz and Latin Music. She has worked with many of jazz and pop's luminaries and released albums on her own label, *Roomspin Records*. Georgia's consequent career in jazz music has been exceptional with seven albums released so far. She has also instigated events which support female artists and music like community-based *Live at ReVoice* and work for the BBC.

Claire Martin is ranked among the best jazz vocalists in the world. She has been awarded *Best Vocalist, British Jazz Awards* and best *New Recording, British jazz Awards* and an O.B.E. She has worked with the *Halle Orchestra, the BBC Big Band, the BBC Concert Orchestra* and many other big orchestras and bands. She has toured the world and released many CDs.

Indira May is a vocalist who has collaborated with many artists and is a rising star in the UK music scene. She has played festivals and prestigious venues in the UK and her combination of soul, jazz and funk is gaining her a fast-growing following.

Tina May is one of Europe's premiere jazz vocalists, She has worked with, among others, the *BBC Big Band, the Stan Tracy Big Band*, and she has worked with many stellar musicians. She has won many awards and played festivals and major concerts all over the UK and Europe.

Faye Patton is a guitarist, vocalist, pianist and composer and has played at across the UK, mainly around London as well as festival such as the Isle of Wight Festival. She also produces and works as a session player. Press reviews include one form the *Isle of Wight festival*: 'Her voice is truly something else... beyond compare'; and from *Jazzwise,* 'A singer-songwriter with a stylized vocal reminiscent of Tori Amos, with a more Ray Charles-influenced R&B slant.'

Carmela Rappazzo is a New Orleans based vocalist, composer and band leader. She moved to New Orleans from New York where she had enjoyed a lot of success and has released albums on which her unique vocal skills are highlighted. She played at the *London Jazz Platform* event in 2017.

Anthea Redmond is co-founder/owner and host for *Jazz Bites Radio* and trustee of the *Jazz Repository*—a massive collection left to the station by a private individual. The station encourages new jazz artists and runs 3 channels to a world-wide audience. Series such as *Women in Jazz* and *The Freer Side of Jazz* have proved very successful and the station regularly showcases and supports new jazz artists.

Alicia Renee *aka* **Blue Eyes** is an international songstress who brings a mix of jazz/funk/modern and blues to her singing. She has performed in New Orleans and also in London and has performed at the *Montreux Jazz Festival* (Switzerland), *The Jazz Café*, *London La Scene* (Paris) and recorded vocals for *Bud Light, Sprite, & KFC Commercials* as well as working with artists such as Dwele, The Last Poets, Jessica Care Moore, Buddha Monk (WuTang Clan), Killah Priest (Wu

Tang Clan), Delfeayo Marsalis, Ellis Marsalis, and others.

Emily Saunders is a jazz vocalist, composer, producer and broadcaster whose albums sell world-wide. Emily has gone from strength to strength and a major success is the JannConnects.com where people can showcase music, make connections, connect with labels, venues, gigs and find lots of information in one place.

Gail Tasker is PR officer for Gearbox records—a label specializing in vinyl and jazz. She manages campaigns for many prestigious artists.

Ellie Thompson is a Press Officer for *Prescription PR* and has worked there for 2 years. She handles PR for major artists and organizes press projects for them.

Camille Thurman is a saxophonist, vocalist, educator and composer. She has been acclaimed by *Downbeat Magazine* as a "rising star" and by *All About Jazz* as a "first class saxophonist that blows the proverbial roof of the place". She has worked with Wynton Marsalis & the *Jazz at Lincoln Center Orchestra*, Jack DeJohnette, Harry Connick Jr, Diana Krall, Pattie LaBelle, Gladys Knight, Chaka Khan, Louis Hayes, Alicia Keys and many others. She has performed at many venues and festivals including the *Kennedy Center, Dizzy's Club Coca-Cola,* the *Charlie Parker Jazz Festival, The Library of Congress,* the *Sydney International Women in Jazz Festival,* the *Tomsk International*

Jazz Festival, the *International Fano Jazz Festival* and has performed in China, Africa, South America, Europe and Central America. She received the *Martin E. Segal—Lincoln Center Award* for *Outstanding Young Artist* and was a runner up in the 2013 *Sarah Vaughan International Vocal Competition.* She was featured in a ground-breaking *New York Times* article recognizing women jazz musicians. She was a two-time award-winning recipient of the *ASCAP Herb Alpert Young Jazz Composers Award* and a winner of the *Fulbright Scholars Cultural Ambassador Grant* to Nicaragua and Paraguay among many other accolades.

Ruby Turner is one of the UK's favourite singers—known for her regular appearance with Jools Holland and she has worked for the BBC, appeared at many prestigious events including outside Buckingham Palace for the *Queen's Diamond Jubilee.* She is an M.B.E. and has worked with artists including UB40, Bryan Ferry, Mick Jagger, Steve Winwood to name but a very few.

Photograph Credits

Emma Acton by *Lily Dior*
Arema Arega by *Daniel Francis-Berenson*
Gretchen Bennett by *Unknown*
Beverley Bierne by *Goat Noise Photography*
Grace Black by *John Black*
Amanda Bloom by *Britt Olsen Ecker*
Jane Ira Bloom by *Ken Hunt*
Patti Boulaye by *The Flyer Guys*
Sarah Brand by *Agata Urbaniak*
Jane Bunnett by *Tom Erlich*
Terri Lyne Carrington by *Tracy Love*
Trish Clowes by *Danni Price*
Kim Cypher by *Ron Milsom*
Mimi Fox by *Elizabeth Martin*
Debbie Gifford by *Alexa Art*
Jenny Green by *Alicia Light*
Florence Halfon by *George Talbot*
Jo Harrop by *Francesca Brecciaroli*
Barb Jungr by *Steve Ullathorne*
Joelle Khoury by *Lowla Khoury*
Wendy Kirkland by *Roman Robroek*
Georgia Mancio by *Lara Leigh*
Claire Martin by *David Sinclair*
Indira May by *Penny Nakin*
Tina May by *James Cole-Riva*
Faye Patton by *Benjamin John*
Carmela Rappazzo by *Ryan Dean Bedingfield*
Anthea Redmond by *Jacques Redmond*
Alicia Renee *aka* Blue Eyes by *Michael McAndrew*
Emily Saunders by *Amanda Searle*
Gail Tasker by *Caspar Sutton-Jones*
Ellie Thompson by *Olivia Reynolds*
Camille Thurman by *Gulnara Khamatova*
Ruby Turner by *Caroline Harriott*

Acknowledgements

There are so many people I would like to thank without whom this book would never have been more than an idea. To those musicians who encouraged me way back when I first mooted the idea, to those who said it was not impossible, to those who said it was important that women have a voice and important I write this. Also to some in particular, namely Paul Jolly who read the first drafts—and there were many- and gave feedback based on his considerable experience in the jazz business, David Sinclair and his son Malcolm, who gifted some of his father's precious photographs and Gerard Rouy who also gave some really special photographs. To the women who gave their opinions, responded to my questions and even the ones who said 'about time'! And to 8th House for having the confidence in commissioning this book. And to the many people in the jazz industry who offer unwavering support—too many to mention, but you definitely know who you are. Thank you.

Index

ABOUT THE AUTHOR

Sammy Stein is an author, reviewer, columnist and radio show writer. She has written several books and articles on music and has had works published in *All About Jazz, Something Else Reviews, Free Jazz Collective* and *Kind of Jazz*. Her magazine contributions include *Essentials, Record Collector, The Irish Post, Pianist Magazine* and many more. Sammy has also written for several radio shows including the very successful series on *Jazz Bites Radio (US) ' Ladies in Jazz'* and the *'Single Entities'* series. She has covered gigs for the BBC and several magazines.

Sammy also devised and curated the *London Jazz Platform*—a new event for London showcasing UK and European talent as well as acts from the US in an all day rolling event. Today, she curates the *Jazz Repository*, a private collection of 58,000 jazz recordings.

Women in Jazz, her fifth book follows the successful 'All That's Jazz' published in 2017.

Also available from Sammy Stein
at
www.8thHousePublishing.com

Women in Jazz: In Their Own Words

&

WOMEN IN JAZZ - *Special Edition*

-an oversized, hardcover volume containing both books:

"Women in Jazz - The Women, The Legends & Their Fight"

&

"Women in Jazz - In Their Own Words"

Milton Keynes UK
Ingram Content Group UK Ltd.
UKHW042310091224
452185UK00001B/40

9 781926 716558